LEARN LIBRARY CATALOGUING

Dr. Anil Kumar Dhiman

and

Smt. Yashoda Rani

Ess Ess Publications

4837/24, Ansari Road, Darya Ganj,
New Delhi-110002
✆ : 23260807
Fax : 23274173
E-mail: info@essessreference.com
url:http://www.essessreference.com

First Published 2005

ISBN : 81-7000-450-0

Price : Rs. 375/-

Published by :

Ess Ess Publications

4837/24, Ansari Road, Darya Ganj,
New Delhi - 110 002
Phone : 23260807
Fax : 23274173
E-mail: info@essessreference.com
url:http://www.essessreference.com

Printed at :

Printline, New Delhi

Contents

Learning Library Science Series

Each book in this series has been written to provide in-depth knowledge of the basics of Library and Information Science and is in accordance with the B.Lib.Sc. syllabus of major Indian universities imparting the said course. To make this work series more comprehensible for the students, the books under this series have been written in Question-Answer format and the language used is very simple, easy and understandable. This series has been divided into six parts, each of which is dedicated to one basic aspect of library and information science.

The present series consists of six books in all, its first part deals with Learn Library and Society, second is Learn Library Management, third is Learn Library Classification (Theory), fourth being Learn Library Classification (Theory), fifth, Learn Reference Services, Information Services and Their Sources and the last and sixth book is Learn Computer Basics and its Application in Libraries. This gives a comprehensive and complete coverage to almost all the syllabi of most of the Indian universities imparting Bachelors' Degree in Library and Information Science (B.Lib.Sc.).

Although this book has primarily been written, keeping in mind the students making an attempt at the above mentioned Degree course, but it is hoped that this book shall find its place with anyone who is interested to know and learn more about the basics of library and information science. Not only the students, but the teachers of library and information science can derive equal benefit from this series. The books are equally suited to librarianship, library science students and library staff seeking to upgrade their skills.

Authors

Acknowledgements

It is indeed difficult to write one book and writing such a series of books is naturally much more difficult but this series could finally see the light of the day, but this could never have been possible without those innumerous books which have been consulted at every step and we are grateful to the authors of all those books, naming all of whom would not be humanly possible. We are thankful to Mrs. Sheel Sethi and Mr. Sumit Sethi, the owners of Ess Ess Publications for giving us an opportunity to present this voluminous work to the readers. We would also like to record our thanks to our friend, Mr. Sushil Kumar of IIT, Roorkee for his kind help. We feel indebted to Sh. Ram Lal Dhiman, Smt. Kamla Devi and Ms. Alka Rani who helped us at various steps. Last but not the least, we are thankful to our son Aman who could not get much of our attention while we were working on this work.

Anil. K. Dhiman
Yashoda Rani

1

Library Catalogue: Its Need and Purpose

Q. : "The objective of Library Catalogue is to fulfil various approaches of readers. "Explain.

or

"Library Catalogue is a key to the sources of the library. Discuss and also state how the library catalogue helps readers in locating reading materials?

or

Define Library Catalogue. Discuss its objectives as stated by Charles A. Cutter and S. R. Ranganathan.

or

What is Library Catalogue? Discuss its needs.

or

Discuss the need and functions of a Library Catalogue. Describe how it differs from a bibliography and publisher's catalogue?

Ans. The word 'Catalogue' comes from the Greek phrase, Katalogues. Kata means "according to" or "by". Logos has different meanings; sometimes it means simply "words", sometimes "order" and at other times "reason". Thus, a catalogue may be explained as a work in which the contents are arranged in a "reasonable" way-in a particular "order" or according to a set "plan". A "catalogue" originally means a mere list of or inventory, but broadly speaking, library catalogue means a list of books and other documents of a particular library or libraries of a particular locality arranged in a recognized order with definite plan for location and identification of materials in the library. It is variously defined by different authors as -

Charles Ammi Cutter has defined library catalogue in his book 'Rules for a Dictionary Catalogue', "as a list of books which is arranged on some definite plan. As distinguished from a bibliography, it is a list of books in some library or collection."

James Duff. Brown has also given a similar definition in his book 'Manual of Library Economy', "Catalogue is an explanatory, logically arranged inventory and key to the books and their contents and it is confined to the books in a particular library."

According to *Margaret S. Taylor*, a catalogue is a list of books like bibliography but its scope is limited to a particular collections". *S. Akers* and *Margaret Mann* describe a catalogue as a record of the material in a library". According to *S. R. Ranganathan*, a catalogue is "a methodically arranged record of information about its bibliographical resources".

H. Sharp has defined a catalogue as "the recording of information regarding manuscripts, books, pamphlets, musical composition, illus, prints, maps, slides".

According to terminology group at the International Conference on Cataloguing Principles (ICCP) held at Paris in 1961, a catalogue is "a comprehensive list of collection or collection of books, documents or similar materials".

Harrod's librarians' glossary and reference book 6th edition, has defined catalogue as 'a list of books, maps, or other items, arranged in definite order. It records, describes and indexes (usually completely) the resources of a collection, a library or a group of libraries. Each entry bears details of class number or call number to enable the item to be found on the shelves of the library, as well as sufficient details, such as author, title, editorship, place of publication, publisher, date of publication, edition, pages, illustrations to identify and describe a book. To be distinguished from (1) a list, which may or may not be in any particular order and may be incomplete, and (2) a bibliography, which may not be confined to any one collection of books or to a particular group of libraries'.

It is clear from above definitions that the catalogue is an absolute and arranged list of the reading material in the collection of a library. Complete bibliographical information of the reading material is entered in the catalogue. It also gives the information about the location of each book and other reading material in the shelves by which these can be found without wasting time.

Objective of Library Catalogue

The objective of the catalogue is to serve the need of the reader by giving him a comprehensive view of either the entire collection of books or of a section of it for the purpose either selecting one which will best serve the purpose of getting a particular book that he requires.

Charles Ammi Cutter has described, in 1876, the objectives of the library catalogue in very simple and clear words in his book "Rules for Dictionary Catalogue'. A catalogue is made:

(a) To enable a person to obtain the desired book provided he knows (i) the Author's name, (ii) the Title, or (iii) the Subject of the book.

(b) To provide following information about the books available in the library:

  (i) Books written by a particular author.

  (ii) Books related to a particular subject.

  (iii) Books available on a specific subject.

(c) To assist in selection of books (i) as to its edition (bibliographically), or (ii) as to its character (literary or topical).

The above statement of Cutter clearly groups the main objectives of catalogue as to locate and identify a book of which either the full and uniform name of the author (or his most commonly used name), exact title, publisher's name, data of publication, volumes, illustrations, size, series note, contents, notes etc. besides, the call number by which the material is to be requisitioned.

Secondly, a library catalogue helps in the expeditious location and retrieval of books and other documents. The other instrument to pursue the same end is the classification system which regulates the orderly arrangements of books on the shelves. The catalogue supplements this work and provides by means of multiple sequence.

Thirdly, a library catalogue helps in bringing together books by the author or translator and on the same subject which exist in the library. Any user can know at a glance all the works of a given author and on a given subject. It also provides information about editions, translation etc, of particular work if they exist in the library.

According to *Dr. S. R. Ranganathan,* a catalogue should be formed in such a manner that it fulfils following objectives -

(a) Every reader is able to obtain the desired book,

(b) Each book reaches the appropriate reader,

(c) Time of the reader is not wasted and

(d) Time of the employees in not wasted.

Above rules are based on the five laws of library science and these are general laws, unlike the specific rules given by *C. A. Cutter.*

According to *I. G. Mudge,* the purpose of catalogue is to form such a tool which gives correct information on four different subject points to the readers -

(a) Is any specific book available in the library for which the reader has correct information of such heading under which a modern catalogue would enter it?

(b) Complete description of the bibliographical facts about a book that is needed by a common reader and not by serious readers.

(c) Complete list of the books, booklets or reading material written or published in any other form by a particular author.

(d) Complete list of written or published literature on specific subjects available in the library.

The purpose of the catalogue can be expressed on the basis of above descriptions in the following manner:

(a) To provide information to the readers about the complete reading material or a part of it, available in the library.

(b) To give the information under various headings to the users whether the desired book or reading material is available in the library or not and its exact location, if it is available.

(c) To give subject-wise information about the status of reading material available in the library.

In short, a library, catalogue is an instrument equipped to deal with the several ways of enquiry, and of identification and retrieval of the books.

Need of Cataloguing

The importance of a library in the modern age cannot be evaluated by its large building or by the level of reading material available in it or by the qualifications of its Librarian, but it can be judged by the utility of the reading material collected in the library. Classification and cataloguing of the reading material is essential to make it useful. Classification is used for arranging the books in the shelves but the use of reading material arranged in the shelves is almost impossible in absence of the catalogue.

Cataloguing is an important and very useful tool for any library. It is for this reason that experts have called catalogue the 'Key'. This is quite appropriate for catalogue since cataloguing is the only tool by which the users can get information about the reading material collected in the library and about its arrangement in the shelves. It is doubtful if any library can function properly without the catalogue. Without the catalogue, a library would be like a dark city without light and directions in which it is almost impossible to reach the desired book. Too much precious time of the readers and the employees of the library would be wasted in finding the desired book without a catalogue in the library.

Dr. S. R. Ranganathan, had considered catalogue as an essential and important tool for success of the laws of the library science. It is necessary for providing information about the arrangement of reading material in the shelves of the library. It is the catalogue that assists every reader in finding the desired book. Moreover, the employees of the library also find the books by using the library catalogue without wasting any time. In this manner, the services of the library can be properly utilized only by its catalogue. A well organized, accurate, elaborate and complete catalogue adds to the prestige and utility of a library. On the other hand, an inaccurate and incomplete catalogue will not only spoil the image of the library but the employees of the library will also face a lot of difficulties. The staff providing reference service to the readers will also misguide the readers by using an incomplete and inaccurate catalogue. Berides, the employees involved in the work of book selection and in the process of preparing purchase orders will remain in the dark and cause much loss to the library. As a result of poor cataloguing, the use of the library will reduce day by day and the readers will discontinue to use the library.

Functions of Library Catalogue

The functions of a library catalogue may be grouped in two categories.

– Functions in reader's service.

- Functions in library operations.

The first function incorporates reference service, guidance to the reader about a particular book of a particular author, and on a particular subject. The second function includes the assistance in book selection, guidance to library staff.

J. H. Shera and *M. S. Egan* have mentioned two very important functions of catalogue -

1. To properly determine without wasting time whether some book whose title and author's name is known, is available in the library or not and if it is available then the location where it can be found?
2. Which books and other reading material are available in the library on a particular subject; the location in which these can be found.

Margaret Mann has mentioned the following functions of a library catalogue -

1. To present the record of each book available in the library to the readers on the basis of the author's name, title, translator, editor, series or any other name of some person or entry which can possibly be used by the reader to obtain a book. The detail of description provided in it depends upon the requirements of the library.
2. To arrange the entries of the authors' names in such a manner that all the books of a particular author can be received from one place under a single name. The method used for it should be such that it becomes possible for the reader to obtain a particular book or to get the knowledge of the works of some particular author that is available in the library.
3. To present the entry of literary work or its part under the specific subject of the work.
4. To present the subject entries in a way by which similar subjects are brought together and related subjects are coordinated.
5. To present the title entries when needed.
6. To provide the directions when required.
7. To present the descriptive title, printing description, number of pages etc. and the necessary comments for every work.

8. To mention the call number by which location of the books is known.

International Conference on Cataloguing Principles (Paris) (1961) enumerated the following functions for a author-title catalogue.

1. Whether the library contains a particular book specified by
   (a) its author and title or
   (b) if author is not named in the book, its title alone; or
   (c) in the absence of author and title, a suitable substitute for the title and;
2. Which works by a particular author and which edition of a particular work are in the library.

According to *Dr. S. R. Ranganathan,* "Function of catalogue is to help in using the material of the library according to the laws of library science."

Thus, function of the catalogue is to serve the underlying concepts and rules of the library science and to achieve their objectives. These underlying concepts and laws of library science are - books are for use, every reader must be provided the desired book, every book should reach the appropriate reader, saving time of the readers and employees, library is a growing institution.

Library Catalogue *versus* bibliography and the Publisher's Catalogue

Though, Bibliography and Catalogue are generally used as synonyms but there are fundamental differences among them. Both Bibliographical Catalogue and Library Catalogue are the catalogues of books in the library. The basic difference in these two is that the library catalogue gives the information of the reading material available in the library on a particular subject, which books written by a particular author are available in the library and also if a particular book is available in the library or not. On the other hand, bibliographical catalogue gives the information of which books on a particular subject have been published.

Whereas, the publisher's catalogue is a list of publications published by a publisher. The difference between. Library catalogue, Bibliography, and the Publisher's catalogue can be understand as follows:

	Library Catalogue	*Bibliography*	*Publisher's Catalogue*
Purpose	Serves inventory and retrieval functions. Its purpose is to satisfy the laws of library science.	Serves inventory functions. Purpose depends upon kind of bibliography.	Serves inventory functions. It is a trade bibliography, whose basic purpose is to help in the selling of items included.
Scope	Contains information about documents available in a particular library and in some cases about a number of libraries. Ordinarily, it is not restricted with regard subject, material, language, geographical area of coverage, place of publication and time.	Cannot claim to be universal. Usually, it is limited with regard to subject, material, language, geographical area of coverage, place of publication and time. But is not usually to limited to a particular library.	Is limited to documents published by a publisher or publishers.
Users	Serves a large number of users, including scholars and librarians.	Serves mainly scholars and libraries.	Serves scholars and librarians.
Physical form	Is usually to be found on cards.	Usually occurs in the form of book (printed or mimeographed).	Occurs in the form of book (printed or mimeographed).
Code	Is based on a standard code.	Usually does not follow a standard code except when it is prepared by a librarian. There is much variation in practices.	Usually does not follow a standard code. There is much variation in practices.

	Library Catalogue	Bibliography	Publisher's Catalogue
Entries	All possible entries provide reasonable number of approaches.	All possible entries provide reasonable number of approaches.	Usually fewer entries are given.
Amount of information	The amount of information varies. However, information about price, binding, channel of availability are not provided. Annotation is provided rarely.	May contain more information. Often, an annotation is provided to help users to decide whether the given document would be useful or not.	Usually contains the least information. Quite often information given is incomplete.
Preparation of entries	Cataloguers prepare entries from the documents themselves. In the preparation of entries, cataloguers, accept statements given in the documents being catalogued at face value. For example, information about authorship, edition, year of publication, etc.	A bibliographer takes into consideration internal and external evidence but takes his decision on the basis of his own critical appraisal. Thus, if the publisher calls a work a new edition, then he is likely to verify the claim.	Is prepared from the documents themselves.
Arrangement	Is either dictionary-wise or a classified including alphabetical part one.	Arrangement varies, though classified arrangement is used quite often.	Arrangement varies. It usually follows an alphabetical arrangement.

	Library Catalogue	*Bibliography*	***Publisher's Catalogue***
Efficiency	Is attempted to be made simple, logical and easy to use. An ordinary user would be more or less satisfied with what is listed in the catalogue; is also able to meet the requirements of scholars to a limited extent.	A good bibliography is a work of scholarship, prepared by a scholar. Thus, a bibliographer tries to do a better job, though a bibliography is meant to serve comparatively few readers.	Is in no way a work of scholarship. It serves the purpose of a publisher adequately.

Q. : Explain briefly complementary nature of classification and cataloguing.

Ans. Cataloguing and classification are two interrelated processes that are performed in a library. The basic purpose of these two operations is to aid the readers of the library in locating and selecting appropriate library reading materials required for their study and research, in case such materials are present in the library. To a large extent, these two processes are complementary and supplementary to each other.

Classification decides the subject of the book and hence books are arranged according to class numbers on the shelves of the library. As books are physical entities, these can be placed only at one location on the shelves of the library. When books deal with only one subject (e.g., An Introduction to Mathematics or Biology etc.) then this scheme is useful to the readers. But when a book/document deals with two or more main subjects or subdivisions of a main subject, we cannot keep the book, being a physical entity, at two places/locations on the library shelves.

Now-a-days, Multifocal reading material or books covering more than one subject are published in large quantities. Complete description of such reading material in the library is presented to the reader by the library catalogue only. The books are arranged in the shelves according to microscopic classification of specific subject. As a result, only a single approach of the readers can be satisfied as far as the subject of the reading material is concerned. This becomes very difficult in case of multi-subject or multifocal books and reading material. For example:

"Introduction to Physics and Chemistry"

A book bearing above title is obviously related to two different areas of science i.e. physics and chemistry, but it can be placed under only one of these two specific subjects by using any system of classification. On the other hand, this book can be useful for the readers of chemistry and also for the readers of physics. Hence, such books can be placed under both subjects, separately, in the library catalogue. Similar is the case for books of anthologies and readings where contributions are made by various authors. In these situations, author analytical entries are prepared in order to bring to the notice of readers the authors of different contributions.

A library catalogue can also be used as a reference tool for answering many questions of users of documents. In fact, the library catalogue is used on most occasions as the starting tool for answering enquiries related to information on documents.

For example readers 'queries on books written by a particular author, books on a subject or full name and year of birth of an author, real name of a pseudonym or a full name of an Institution, etc. can be answered with the help of a library catalogue.

A library catalogue usually contains other valuable information on documents, besides bibliographical data for accessing and locating documents. The Notes Section, Collation (which includes illustrations and related data), etc., provide useful starting points for a search for documents on subjects.

Thus, we find that cataloguing and classification are supplementary and complementary to each other. Both these activities jointly bring to the notice of the readers the whole contents of the documents possessed by the library. So, Library Cataloguing and Classification are complementary of each other and where classification ends, the purpose or the works of catalogue starts.

Q. : Discuss briefly the relevance of the Library Catalogue in relation to the Five Laws of Library Science.

or

Discuss the implications of the Five Laws of Library Science for Library Catalogues.

Ans. The Five Laws of Library Science are a set of basic guiding principles for designing and operating a library or a library system. In fact, each one of the activities of a library may be deduced from these Five Laws. For the preparation and production of a library catalogue, a number of useful guidelines are implied in these Five Laws.

The First Law 'Books are for use' indicates the necessity of organizing the collections of a library for maximum use, by providing a number of physical facilities and introducing readers' services. One such facility is the provision of library catalogue, which throws open to the users the entire collections of a library.

Physical form of the library catalogue should be such that it is flexible, can be kept up-to-date by adding entries for new document added to the library from time to time. Similarly, information about the document in the entry should be adequate to identify a document. The annotation and various notes are given to help the readers to make a choice among documents possessed by the library. Obviously without this essential and indispensable tool, users would find it difficult to use the collection. Therefore, a library catalogue is a must.

The Second and Third Laws 'Every reader his book'; 'Every book its reader' imply the way a library catalogue should provide access to the collections of a library, to meet the requirements of users as children, specialist users, physically handicapped persons. Special kinds of analytical entries of documents are to be prepared to reveal the basic contents of documents. For instance, an excellent chapter on information storage and retrieval, forming part of Handbook in Special Librarianship is likely to be missed by a student of library science, if there are no analytical entries for the document.

The Fourth Law 'Save the time of the reader' places great emphasis on time. A catalogue should not only be simple in its design and construction but also should save the time of a reader. Every approach to a document, that is author, title, subject, series, etc. must be provided in a catalogue. Cross-reference entries, (i.e., see and see also entries) should be provided for change of names of persons, countries, subjects and institutions. Similarly guidance in the use of library catalogue should be provided by organizing orientation courses for newcomers in the library.

The Fifth Law 'A library is a growing organism' enjoins a library to view the catalogue in its widest perspective, keeping in view changes and growth in the nature and variety of publications, other forms of documents, needs of users, and such other environmental factors. The advent of the computer and communication technologies has introduced far-reaching changes both the physical forms of library catalogues and in their internal structure.

Terminals of computers are located at distant parts of the library. Only one main entry is adequate to access the documents and added entries are replaced by access points. Library networks also provide access to resources of other libraries. Change is inevitable and a library should always remain alive to changes.

Thus, catalogue of the library serve the underlying concepts as stated by Dr. Ranganathan in his five Laws of Library Science.

Q. : White a short note on Shelf-list stating its usefulness in the library.

Ans. The shelf list is an important library tool which has varied in scope and purpose over the years. In the earliest day of museums and libraries a catalogue was developed which served as an inventory of an institution's treasures. These first catalogues were in essence shelf lists because there were no alternative access points. Somewhat, later, location symbols were added. This was especially true in monastic libraries because they often had some books or manuscripts stored in cloisters and others in chapels. Eventually, a separate shelf list record evolved for inventory purposes. This enable a library's catalogue to expand in other directions and offer alternative access points to the resources of the library's collection. Indeed, catalogues were often initially thought of as indexes to the shelf list.

A shelf list is an essential tool for nearly all library. It is a file consisting of one entry for each bibliographic item (print or non-print) cataloged for a particular collection. This file is usually maintained in the order in which the materials are found on the shelves. Ordinarily this is according to call number within a classification scheme; however, it could also be arranged in some other sequence such as accession number order or alphabetical order, particularly in a very small library. In other words, it is a catalogue of books in the order in which they stand on the shelves. However, keeping in view the local needs of the library, the shelf order of the books can be changed.

Exceptions to the Shelf Order

The shelf lists are usually arranged according to call number within a classification scheme in order in which the books stand usually on the shelves. However keeping in view the local needs of the library, shelf order can be changed.

(i) One exception to shelf order sequence is the library in which different sizes or types of material are shelved separately but the shelf list is still maintained in a single sequence by classification.

(ii) Second example is found in large library systems where there are many branches or departmental libraries. In these instances the Central Library-Shelf list also serves as a union list.

Amount of Information

There is no fixed set of data in a shelf list record. The information included varies from library to library and by time period. In earlier era, it was thought to be a time-saver to limit a shelf list record to very brief cataloging information. Recently, use of all the data found on a complete catalogue card has been favored. Any shelflist card should include a notation of all copies of all volumes or pieces of a title. Sometimes this will be on the face of the card and sometimes on the back. When necessary, additional cards are prepared and attached to the first. The price is often included because it is useful information if an item must be recorded or if a borrower must be charged for lost or damaged material. The source of the acquisition is usually not included, but either the date or an accession number incorporating a date is normally present.

Shelf List - Format

There are following formats :

1. Card Form : After its development in manuscript or book catalogue form, the shelf list in card format became widespread during the 19th century. It has proved to be a flexible tool and one that is relatively easy to store and maintain. However, despite its essential simplicity and utility, it has obvious limitations.

2. Machine-readable Form : However, as technological hindrances persuade libraries, the shelflist record is frequently being converted to machine readable form. An early example of this is the conversion of the widener library shelflist at Harward University.

Machine-readable shelflist provide possibilities for a variety of products and services not available from a shelflist in card format. Various projects which take advantage of machine-readable shelflists include, new acquisitions lists issued at regular frequencies in call number sequence; lists of the collection as an aid to bibliographers in weeding or selection; statistics on the growth of the collection.

Usefulness of Shelf List

1. Serves as an Inventory of Documents : Shelf lists serves many purposes. The most common use is to act control record of those items officially added to the collection. As such, it is essential when the collection it represents is being inventoried. It can serve as base for damage, claims and/or rebuilding the collection in the event that there has been a disaster. A shelflist also provides a basis for the establishment of a collection's value. In some cases the shelflist itself may be insured.

2. Serve the purpose of a Classified Catalogue : As the shelflist ordinarily groups materials by classification number, it facilitates accurate classification and can serve as a substitute for a classified catalogue.

3. Serves as a Guide to Material Selection : Many other uses of the shelflist result from its classed arrangement. One is its service as a guide to materials selection, because it facilitates the determination of the extent of the collection in any specified subject area.

4. Tool for Comparative Evaluation : Measurement of shelflist can be a method of comparative evaluation of the collections of similar libraries, particularly research libraries.

5. Serves the Need of Subject Bibliographies : The subject access can be made available by photocopying or typing from a card file, or by printing subject catalogue or lists in call number sequence from a machine readable file.

6. Tool for Weeding out Library Collections : Due to paucity of space, each library has to weed out the books which have become obsolete due to physical condition or due to new editions of a particular title. In all, such cases shelf list act as a helpful tool for providing the information of old editions of books and the easily removal of record after the books are weeded out.

7. Tool for Stock Verification : Shelf list is a comprehensive inventory of books arranged in the order in which books stand on the shelves, hence it is very significant tool for stock verification of books.

8. Serves as a Supplement List for Recent Arrivals : Shelf list is classified record of books in a library. This also facilitates the subject approach of the readers. A reproduction of portion of the shelf list from time to time can be used as list of recent arrivals in the library in a particular time period.

9. Facilitate Co-operative purchasing among Libraries : The ability to reproduce shelf list record and make it available at dispersed locations also facilitates co-operative purchasing among libraries and leads to better utilization of resources.

Concluding, it can be said that the shelf list will remain an important part of library card in the forseeable future. It will doubtless be modified by and take advantage of new machine-based technologies. In any case, it is and will remain a necessary tool for inventory, evaluation, call number assignment and dissemination of subject grouped holding information about any collection, it is whether print collection or non-print materials.

Q. : Write an essay on evolution of catalogue.

or

Write briefly on some modern cataloguing rules or codes.

Ans. Cataloguing is one of the oldest library crafts and these were first prepared to serve as inventory lists. The complete history of evolution or development of catalogues or cataloguing codes can be studied under following heads -

(1) Early Stage (250 B.C. - 800 A.D.)

Some such methods though primitive, existed almost until the time the manuscripts came to end and ceased to be the primary vehicles of communication. The discovery of Assyro-Babylonian clay tablets, the wall inscriptions at Edfu and the extant remnants of the papyrus rolls of the Egyptian, Greek and Roman civilizations testify this fact. The catalogues and the materials they listed, both were in primal forms as, clay tablets, inscriptions and papyrus rolls. From the archaeological finds of the Assyro-Babylonian clay tablets (1668-626 B.C.), the antiquity of the library catalogue can be easily placed around 2000 B.C. These tablets were similar to press guides with bibliographic data, such as title (occasionally, with opening words), number of tablets constituting a work, number of lines on a tablet, distinct subdivisions and location marks inscribed on them. They served as simple location devices. However, all such primal forms were not verily catalogues.

This system with no change continued to exist well into the first seven centuries of the Christian era. The fall of the Roman empire in the 6th century brought, about a deliberate destruction and dispersal of the hitherto great collections of the private, public and temple libraries. The emergence of Christianity as the state religion in the 3rd century having already dealt a severe blow, the temple libraries began to disintegrate. Their place was now taken by the monastic libraries. As the major instruments of education in the middle ages (300 AD - 1100 AD) monasteries served the cause by collecting, producing and preserving the books useful in the learning by the clerics. The famous work, institutions of Cassiodorus (6th Century) was intended to serve as a scholarly model with an annotated guide to what was valuable reading of the times. The need of catalogue was not felt. Efforts were made later in compiling inventories. A list of books given by Gregory the Great in the 8th century AD to the church of St. Clements (Rome) was the earliest of the monastic library catalogues. It was a marble tablet with an introduction or prayer and a few biblical works inscribed on it. The catalogue of the monastic library of York composed by Alcuin in verse which could be either a list of famous authors or a bibliography was the next. Another example is De Trinitate of St. Augustine, which too was simple list of works transcribed on the flyleaf of a work.

(2) Age of Inventory (1200 A.D. - 1500 A.D.)

Such simple lists were attempted in good numbers in the succeeding periods (900 A.D. - 1100 A.D.). Louis Pious (814-840 A.D.) issued a decree requiring the monasteries and cathedrals to list all the books in their possession. So the catalogues of the monasteries and cathedrals were compiled to serve the need for inventories of the material in possession. Books were arranged not by author but by the importance of the work in the order of Bible, other religious and secular works. Contents were not indicated in the case of collections as works of the same author and works of various authors on the same subject bound together, was in the practice. The old traditions of the pre-Christian era continued.

(3) Age of Finding List (1600 A.D. - 1800 A.D.)

Although the inventory idea persisted, many catalogues of the 16th century such as, the catalogue of St. Martin's Priory of Dover, the Syon Catalogue, the Catalogue of the Bretton Monastery, etc. contained many additional details such as content notes, names of editors, translators, etc. in the entry and provided with author and other indexes. The 16th century proved a further productive period influenced by great bibliographers like Gesner, Treflerus, Maunsell, to mention a few. Of particular significance was the contribution made by Andrew Maunsell, a bookseller and a bibliographer in his own right, who published a bibliography of books in English. He adopted dictionary arrangement making entries under the surnames of authors with added entries provided under editors, subject words, etc. in a limited way. Through his procedure, the concept of main entry to be distinguished from the added entries as the one made under author with full bibliographic description emerged. The idea of uniform heading also owes to him. He entered the Bible and books of the Bible under the uniform heading of Bible.

By the close of the century, although the vestiges of the inventory catalogue still existed, the need for uniformity and systematic approach to catalogue was recognized. Full description became evident. Author entry gained importance as the primary entry providing the basic approach. Added entries were sought for additional approaches.

Printed catalogue became the fashion. Efforts at standardization received new inspiration from men like Naude, Dury, Brillet and others.

The Bodleian catalogues produced during the century marked a milestone and greatly influenced the succeeding studies of cataloguing practice. Initially intended as shelf guides on single printed pages with supplements to follow, a catalogue of printed books and manuscripts of the Bodleian library was printed in 1605. Thomas Bodley and Thomas James were the principal men behind it. The last of the Bodleian catalogue issued under the guidance of Thomas Hyde in 1674, marked further improvement. It continued the alphabetical order and other procedures as in the earlier catalogues but provided better assemblage of literary units. The preface contained rules which remained authoritative until the middle of the 19th century.

The next century i.e., 18th century was rather a period of stabilization than innovation or solution. Libraries, more importantly the university and private collections grew in size without definite improvements in organization. The spread of ideas was slow. Only the printed catalogues did serve the purpose but in a limited way, as examples. But most of them were influenced by the early bibliographers who were immature and were not concerned with logic or theory.

(4) Modern Catalogues (1900 A.D. on wards)

The 19th century was an age of great many codes. Catalogue was considered a finding list with the Bodleian concept of literary unit occasionally given expression in compilations. There ensued a spate of debates on the relative merits of author, dictionary, and classed alphabetic-classed catalogues. Author (under surname) and title (for anonymous work) entries constituted the author catalogue. From this author catalogue did develop the dictionary catalogue. It consisted of duplicate entries under authors, titles, subjects and forms. For example, the catalogue of the printed books of the Society of Antiquaries of London (1816), supposed as the first true dictionary catalogue, employed duplicate entry approach in one single alphabetical file. Classed catalogue was limited to subject arrangement in systematic order by grouping related subjects together or in proximity. As the purpose of the catalogue became better clarified, the classed catalogue gained importance. The alphabetic-classed catalogue too became popular during the middle of the century. It was rather an amalgam of dictionary and classed catalogue.

The first half of the century was, thus, characterized by a variety of combinations of arrangements and indexes, broadly divisible into two categories. The first category constituted lists arranged in subject or classed order, i.e., broad subjects or classes in shelf list order with works sub-arranged according to accession and chronologically by imprint date, title or author. The second category consisted of alphabetically arranged indexes to classified file which was not a systematic one.

In 1850, Charles C. Jewett's code for the catalogue of the Smithsonian Institution was accepted. His code, consisting of 39 rules, was published in 1852 under the title *Smithsonian report on the construction of catalogues of libraries ... and their publication by means of separate stereotyped titles, with rules and examples.* This code may be considered a landmark in the history of cataloguing. Jewett acknowledged his debt to Panizzi. He extended the principle of corporate authorship further than Panizzi, entering all corporate bodies directly under their names.

In 1876, Charles Ammi Cutter published his *Rules for a printed dictionary catalogue.* It was issued in 1876 as the second part of the Bureau of Education's special report on *Public libraries in the United States of America.* A second enlarged edition came out in 1889, a third one appeared with additions, corrections, and an alphabetical index in 1891, and the fourth edition was issued in rewritten form in 1904.

It was the first American code to receive recognition. This code goes beyond the practices of a single library and is the first complete code for preparation of a catalogue. It is also the only code, which attempts to provide rules in a systematic and exhaustive manner, based on principles for the preparation of all the entries required for a dictionary catalogue. Rule for author, title, subject, and form-entry as well as for description, and on filing of entries are included and the reason for each rule is stated.

Cutter was the first person to recognize and recommend the use of a corporate body as an author in a well defined manner. Rules for treatment of corporate authorship are detailed enough and excellent comments and explanations are to be found attached to these rules. He frequently provides alternative rules depending upon the size of the library, physical form of the catalogue and the type of library. Thus he suggests, short, medium, and full cataloguing. He also emphasized the "convenience of the public," especially in those cases where no rule can be laid down.

Cutter supported Jewett in most of the rules, especially on those principles in which Jewett differed from Panizzi. He entered pseudonymous works under the real name. He, like Jewett, did not use form heading for headings of the main entry (unlike Panizzi). He, like Jewett, also entered anonymous works under the first word of the title excepting anonymous biographies. He had no use of form heading for main entry but used these as subject headings.

According to Cutter, catalogues should not only point the way to an individualized publication but should also assemble and organize literary units. He was the first person to state that the other object of author entry is to provide for or showing what the library has under a given author.

It has been rightly said that "No writer on cataloguing can fail to owe much to Cutter who, if he fails to propose the correct solution, almost always shows that he has glimpsed it." His code has been described as a classic, with an overpowering influence on all who followed him. "It appears to have been the chief source of later codes in English language." His influence on the Anglo-American code of 1908 is clearly evident in the American alternative rules and in the treatment of corporate authorship.

Between 1841 and 1900, a large number of catalogue codes were brought out. In addition to British Museum rules, there were Bodleian and Cambridge codes. In the USA, codes were brought out by Linderfelt, Dewey and the Library of Congress. In Germany, Dziatizko's Instruction and Prussian Instruktionen, came out. Codes also appeared in Belgium, Scandinavian countries, France, Italy, etc.

The supplementary alphabetical subject indexes created the need for standard lists of subject headings as aids. Since the practice or picking up subject words from the title lacked uniformity and made syndetic structure difficult, adoption of a better system specially needed for construction of dictionary catalogue was felt. This initiated efforts towards development of standard lists of subject heading. The ALA published such a list entitled, List of Subject Headings for use in the Dictionary Catalogue in 1895. It was considered as a standard list suitable for all types of libraries and found wide acceptance. The third and final edition was brought in 1911 when the Library of Congress List of Subject Headings (issued in 3 parts between 1909 and 1913) replaced it. Besides these two, three other publications viz., Poole's Index to Periodicals Literature, the ALA Index (an index for collections and composite works), and the Catalogue of the ALA Library (intended to serve as selection tool, cataloguing guide and printed catalogue), all published in 1893. However, the idea of specific subject entry was still in the process of making with insistence on the use of standard terms in titles to indicate the subjects. The introduction of printed catalogue card service in 1901 by the Library of Congress was yet another development.

Some of the important codes are briefly discussed as under -

1. AA Code : A draft code was printed by the Library of Congress in 1901, entitled *ALA Rules - Advance Edition.* At this stage M. Dewey suggested that the ALA and the Library Association (Great Britain) should jointly produce an Anglo-American code. It was further suggested by John Minto "that code should be printed in two editions (English and American) but that the editions should as far as possible be identical in arrangement and wording." Thus, the Anglo-American code in two editions was published simultaneously in two countries in 1908. This code was the result of the combined efforts of Committees of the Library Association (Great Britain) and American Library Association "with a view to establishing unity of practice throughout the English speaking race". The code laid emphasis to meet the requirements of "larger libraries of a scholarly character".

The two committees differed only over eight rules. The two major differences were: (i) British edition entered noblemen under the name and American edition entered under the noble title; (ii) British edition entered periodicals under the first title and American under the latest title.

This code had a great influence and it was a part of the attempt to establish the practices of the Library of Congress throughout the United States.

2. Vatican Code : In 1927, the Vatican Library compiled a new catalogue code *Rules for the catalog of printed books* (published in Italian, in 1931) for its collection, commonly called the Vatican code. The Carnegie Endowment for International Peace donated funds to help it to compile the code, which is for a dictionary catalogue, based on Cutter's *Rules for a dictionary catalog.* Leading Americans like J.C.M. Hanson and W.W. Bishop were greatly responsible for bringing out the code.

3. ALA Code : By the second decade of twentieth century, the AA code (1908) was under severe criticism and the need for revision was repeatedly mooted. In the thirties, committees of the American Library Association and the Library Association (Great Britain) started the work of revision. At the outbreak of the Second World War, the Library Association dropped out but American Library Association continued and produced a draft code in two parts in 1941 (Part I Entry and headings; Part II Description of book). Because of criticism, part II was deferred and revision of Part I later came out in 1949 under the title *ALA cataloging rules for author and title entries.* In the fall of 1949, the Library of Congress brought out its *Rules for descriptive cataloging* and was accepted as a substitute for part II of the preliminary edition.

These rules are primarily limited to choice of entry and form of heading for author and title entries. The subject headings are merely mentioned in a few cases.

This code tried to codify experience rather than adopt principles of cataloguing. Many of the rules are inconsistent. A few of the rules form exceptions to the basic rules. There are not only exceptions but exceptions to exceptions are also to be found. In certain rules, the wording is faulty. The code makes artificial distinction between a society and an institution, making the application of these rules difficult.

As compared with the Anglo-American code, the rules are more detailed. More examples and more types of literature have been covered. In fact, this code was greatly criticized for over-elaboration.

In spite of being a committee product, "ALA is a remarkable achievement." It was adopted by a large number of libraries not only in the United States of America but in various other countries, especially the English-speaking world.

4. Classified Catalogue Code : Ranganathan (Shiyali Ramamrita) (1892-1972). *Classified Catalogue Code with Additional Rules for Dictionary Catalogue Code.* Ed 5. Assisted by A Neelameghan.

The code (CCC) is the first and the only code designed in India. The first edition of CCC appeared in 1934 and was continued through five editions, the last (i.e., the 5th edition) coming in 1964. Each later edition was an improvement on the earlier one, the revision, addition or improvement made on the basis of practical application and critical examination supported by teaching and reasoning. This empirical, analytical and critical approach shaped the code progressively.

Its second edition (1945) demonstrated the symbiotic relationship between classification and cataloging and evolved chain procedure for subject cataloguing/indexing. Rules for style of writing and alphabetisation correlating the two through Gestalt theory of alphabetisation were other added features of this edition. Ranganathan's comparative study of classified and dictionary catalogues and evaluation of Cutter's rules helped him to publish his Dictionary Catalogue Code in 1945.

The third edition (1951) added rules for compiling union catalogue of periodical publications, abstracting periodical and incorporating as well, a glossary of English Sanskrit terms to be helpful for developing cognate terminology in other Indian languages.

The fourth edition (1955) implemented the layout for a catalogue code (in the light of Heading and Canons), added supplementary rules for national bibliography, rearranged the rules for determination of authorship, choice of heading and rendering the heading. It also incorporated further additional rules for style of writing effecting corresponding changes in the rules for alphabetisation. This edition, as a result of his comparative study of five codes (Heading and Canons published in 1955) made necessary further corrections and alterations which eliminated the need for a separate dictionary catalogue code.

While the codes for alphabetical, author and dictionary catalogues are quite large in number, the codes oriented to classified catalogue are few in number, Ranganathan's Classified Catalogue code (CCC) is one prominent code of these few. After Cutter's rules and

Vatican code, the CCC is the only other code which is complete to cover all the cataloguing procedures and to provide rule for entry, description, subject cataloguing/indexing and filing.

Before Ranganathan, there were no catalogue codes ever produced in India. Neither was there an established bibliographic/ cataloguing tradition. It was mostly an intuitive effort but applying scientific method to ensure precision and correctness. This however, does not go to say that the code was entirely a product of prestine mind. Ranganathan, educated in England had the benefit of exposure to western thought and practice, which definitely provided the needed background to work out independently. There are, therefore, many influences. Yet the code is distinctively Ranganathan's own. What is his own adds to the merit, and what is not to its weakness.

Structurally, it is a well laid code. The code can be divided into three units. The first 9 parts/chapters (A to H and J) form the approach. Many basic issues, more importantly, canons and normative principles; parts and physical forms of catalogue, centralized cataloguing; recording, style, language and script, arrangement of entries; conflict of authorship and resolution (determination of authorship); name of person, (i.e., structure, element, etc.,) are dealt with. The next 11 chapters (K to N, P to V) constitute the substantial part, i.e., rules for rendering names (persons, corporate bodies, geographical entities); preparation of class index entries; main and book index entries for different categories of books and periodicals; additional rules for compilation of union catalogues of books and periodical publications; National bibliography; indexing periodical; abstracting periodical; and cataloguing of incunabula and non-book materials. The last part (W) constitutes end matter (glossary of terms, bibliographic references and index).

The rules are marked for their simplicity, clarity and brevity. The code draws a distinction between a library catalogue and a bibliography. Elaborate description is a necessity in bibliography and not in a library catalogue. Therefore, CCC does not prescribe recording of print, collation, many details in notes, statement of responsibility in the title section, etc. The rules for determining authorship are based on a set of problems explained as conflicts of authorship. The rules relating to rendering of names/heading for persons, corporate bodies and geographic entities are based on language, nationality and cultural preferences which are postulated through principles.

The empirical approach and application normative principles in drafting and arranging the rules have made CCC a model code. The fact that it does not cover the entire range of various forms of material makes it a less comprehensive code. No code can be perfect in all details and CCC is no exception.

5. AACR : In 1961, IFLA (International Federation of Library Associations and Institutions) held an International Conference on Cataloguing Principles at Paris. A set of rules was submitted and voted. This was an important attempt to evolve an international catalogue code. The Paris principles had a profound effect on cataloguing practices throughout the world. Many of the catalogue codes produced after 1961 do reflect such an effect. It is also true that these principles have not been fully accepted by different countries. ICCP did succeed in getting international agreement regarding rules for headings.

Besides, from the beginning, the ALA code published in 1949 was regarded unsatisfactory. Therefore, in 1951 the ALA requested Seymour Lubetzky to "prepare a general analysis of the 1949 code". The *Report* was published in 1953. Lubetzky strongly criticized the code and ALA accepted the Report. Work was begun on a new code, not a mere revision of the code of 1949. The new code was published in 1967 in two editions - the North American edition and the British edition. The code was prepared by the American Library Association, the Library of Congress, the Library Association, and the Canadian Library Association. The North American text and British text are very much different in physical appearance but the rules in the two texts are essentially based on the same principles and practices but with a few alternative rules for choice and rendering of headings. This paved the way for preparation of AACR rules.

AACR-1 (1967) : *Anglo-American cataloging rules/*prepared by the American Library Association, the Library of Congress, the Library Association, and the Canadian Library Association. - North American Text.- Chicago: American library Association, 1967- Reprinted in 1970 with supplement of additions and changes. - British text published: London Library Association, 1967.

The International Conference on Cataloguing Principles convened in Paris in October 1961, adopted and accepted a statement of principles in whole or part by delegations from 53 countries and 12 international organizations. The Report of the International Conference was issued in 1963. It drew upon Lubetzky's 1960 code and restated the objectives of both Lubetzky and Cutter. The statement of principles rested on the objectives and were expressed in specific terms. The importance of this report lies in its endorsement of corporate entry and establishment of natural rather than grammatical order of arrangement of title, thus, removing the major differences between the Anglo-American and Germanic traditions of cataloguing. Following the International Conference on Cataloguing Principles many other national catalogue codes were revised or developed, eg., the German Code (Regeln fur die alphebetische katalogisierung, the Swedish code, the Danish code, etc.) leveling the differences between national practices.

The new code (known as AACR 1) appeared in 1967 and was received by the profession with a mixed reaction. The rules in the code were organized in 2 parts, part 1 dealing with entry and heading consisting of four chapters, and part 2 covering description presented in 10 chapters.

The code applied reevaluation of the existing practices. It was seen as a better code in terms of its more logical grouping of the rules with emphasis on conditions of authorship rather than on classes of authors (married women, princes of blood, etc) and kinds of publications (anna, dictionaries, encyclopaedias, etc). It corresponded, more than the earlier codes to the patterns of intelligent users instead of blindly ruling of preparation of entries, which may be precise, consistent and technically correct. It gave preference to the form of name preferred or used by the author than his real/official name. Title page of the item catalogued was prescribed as the source of information for cataloguing against the old practice of deriving details from outside sources. Similarly, in the case of change of names of corporate bodies, entry was required under the changed/new name. The code, further emphasized the function of assembling bibliographic units by providing uniform title entry more widely. But some of the vestiges of old practices remained. For example, the authorial status to editors and compilers, entry under place names for certain corporate bodies continued. On this and certain other points since the American and British Committees could not reach agreement, the code was published in two slightly differing texts like the 1908 code.

When work on AACR 1 began, books and periodicals were the basic and popular materials. Card catalogue was the norm. But when the code appeared in 1967 the situation changed vastly. As a result of technology, a variety of new media (non-book materials) found their way into libraries. Computer manipulation of data made possible other forms of catalogue. The need to integrate the descriptive records (catalogue entries) of different forms of material (book and non-book items) necessitated studies to find analogies between their characteristics). IFLA brought out a document entitled International Standard Bibliographic Description (for single and multi-volume monographic publications) in 1971. This was later improved/revised and published in 1974 as ISBD (M): International Standard Bibliographic Description for Monographic Publications. Along with it another standard for serials, viz., ISBD(S) International Standard Bibliographic Description for Serials was also published. The AACR I incorporated Standard Bibliographic Description for Serials was also published. The AACR incorporated these documents and revised chapter 6 (separately published monographs) in 1974 followed by chapter 12 (for audio-visual media and special instructional materials) in 1975 and chapter 14 (for sound recordings) in 1976. IFLA's International standards for other kinds of material including a general one followed in succession.

This piecemeal revision was found unsatisfactory. It needed development of overall principles and integration of descriptive rules for various media. The expanded cooperation between the cataloguing agencies in, Great Britain, America and other countries as well as the increase in the use of UKMARC and LCMARC brought about agreement for a single unified text of code, the ambiguities and differences resolved.

AACR-2 (1978) : *Anglo-American cataloging rules/*Prepared by the American Library Association, the British Library, the Canadian Committee on Cataloguing, the Library Association, the Library of Congress; edited by Michael Gorman and Paul W. Winkler, 2nd ed. - London: Library Association; Chicago : American Library Association, 1978.

This second edition proved superior revealing basic principles that provided the edifice of the code. It followed "the sequence of cataloguers' operations in most present-day libraries and bibliographic agencies," i.e., first examining the item and describing it and then determining the access points. The code therefore, presented the descriptive rules in part 1 followed by rules for determining and establishing headings/access points in part 2. Part 1 begins with a general chapter which can be applied to all materials in general followed by chapters on specific media which are elaborations of the provisions of the general chapter. These rules were also based on ISBDs (the general and specific ones). In the description, the code permitted alternative rules and options to suit the needs of the libraries and cataloguing agencies. In the rules for access points, it worked out many terminological improvements to remove conceptual irritants, eg., statement of responsibility in place of statement of authorship, corporate entry, instead of corporate author, etc. It standardized punctuation to conform to the pattern established in ISBDs.

AACR-2, 1988 revised : *Anglo-American cataloging rules/* prepared under the direction of the Joint Steering Committee for Revision of AACR, a committee of the American Library Association, the Australian Committee on Cataloguing, the British Library, the Canadian Committee on Cataloguing the Library Association, the Library of Congress: edited by Michael Gorman and Paul W Winkle.- 2nd ed., 1988 revision.- Ottawa: Canadian Library Association; London: Library Association Publishing Limited; Chicago: American Library Association, 1988.

The implementation of AACR 2 (1978) code was begun by the Library of Congress in Jan 1981. Like the earlier edition (AACR 1), the second edition too appeared at a time when there were rapid developments taking place. More important and of greater immediate relevance was the emergence of many new forms of material which were still in shaping.

Although the code (AACR 2) resolved the problems of authorship more satisfactorily, the rules were found inadequate in dealing with new media. In course of implementation of the code, some rules presented themselves as confusing, insufficient and complicated. This gave rise to differences in interpretation. Therefore, attempts were made to clarify, expand or alter rules in necessary cases. The Library of Congress notified the interpretations and modifications in its *Cataloguing Service Bulletin.*

Three sets of revisions of AACR 2 comprising of Geographical corrections, Textual amendments, and altered and additional rules were issued in 1982, 1984 and 1986. These were followed also by a draft revision of chapter 9 for computer files. The code too came into wider use and found translations in many languages (e.g., Arabic, Bahasa Malaysia, Chinese, Danish, Finnish, French, Italian, Japanese, Norwegian, Portuguese, Spanish, Swedish, Turkish, Urdu and possibly others. In view of the changes and additions that were brought out and the growing popularity and use of the code, it was decided to revise it. The revised code, it was further decided, to be named as AACR 2, 1988 revision and not as 3rd edition. The revision sought to incorporate the additions and modifications already made as well as further revisions contemplated, viz., description of material for the blind (tactile), rethinking of the concept of separate bibliographical identities, rewording and addition of new examples.

The revision, therefore, did not result either in the change of basic concepts, principles or structure. While the prominent changes applied to computer files, other changes related to the material for the blind, sound recordings, music, etc. in order to achieve greater conformity in establishing headings, a few rules were changed. These changes include redetermining of title proper, redesignation of GMD in a few instances, addition of distinctions in the rules for choice of pseudonyms, deletion of option to qualify place names by adding larger areas/jurisdictions, addition of geographical identifiers to identical corporate bodies, redefining the type 3 subordinate corporate body, recasting of uniform titles, entry additionally under corporate name (other than publisher, distributor, etc.) in the case of some cartographic material, etc.

The rules are presented in two parts. Part one consists of descriptive rules in 13 chapters. Chapter 1 has the general rules which provide the general frame within which descriptive rules for specific classes of material follow. Chapter 13 also contains general rules for analysis of specific types. These are as follows:

Part 1. Description: Chapters 1. General rules of description, 2. Books, Pamphlets and Monographs, 3. Cartographic Materials, 4. Manuscripts (including manuscript collections). 5. Music (Published music), 6. Sound Recordings, 7. Motion Pictures and Video Recordings, 8. Cartographic Materials, 9. Computer files, 10. Three-dimensional Artifacts and Realia, 11. Microforms, 12. Serials, and 13. Analysis.

Part 2. Headings, uniform titles and references : Chapters 21. Choice of Access Points, 22. Headings for Persons, 23. Geographic

Names, 24. Headings for Corporate Bodies, 25. Uniform Titles, and 26. References

The third part constitutes the end matter. It consists of Appendixes, A. capitalization B. Abbreviations. C. Numerals, and D. Glossary, and an Index.

Each part has one introductory chapter. The rules in the 12 chapters of part 1 (Description) have mnemonic numbering to facilitate to and form reference to rules applying to appropriate areas. The descriptive rules are presented first, obviously because cataloguing begins with description, then follow the tasks of determination and establishment of headings. So, rules for access points, choice of forms of headings are given in the second part. The gap between Chapters 13 and 21 is left to incorporate descriptive rules for new classes of materials that may come (in which case Chapter 13 may be renumbered). In both parts the rules follow the order of general to specific. The code has provision for optional rules and alternative rules to accommodate the varying requirements of libraries.

The preface states that "cataloging rules cannot be static, they must be allowed to respond to changing needs". What is meant by this is that revision does not stop at any time. It goes on. Further revisions become necessary. So, for the present, AACR 2. 1988 revision is the latest in the Anglo-American family of codes. All the earlier ones stand superseded.

Concluding, it can be said that up to the middle of the 19th century, most catalogues were based on rules prepared by cataloguers of libraries to suit individual libraries. These rules were evolved through tradition and were not based on any explicitly stated normative principles.

Later, need for standardization of cataloguing rules began to be felt. Thus, rules began to be formulated in a systematic manner so that the same set of rules in the form of a catalogue could be used by a number of libraries. The result was the formulation of a large number of catalogue codes.

During the last few decades, need was felt to prepare a universal cataloguing code to achieve worldwide standardization of catalogues. This led to the holding of the International Conference on Cataloguing Principles in Paris in 1961, where an attempt was made to achieve agreement on principles of cataloguing. *Anglo-American Cataloguing Rules* are based more or less on the principles accepted at the conference. Since 1945, *Classified Catalogue code* (2nd ed.) has been based on normative principles stated in an explicit manner. Thus, Catalogue codes are beginning to be based on normative principles stated explicitly, and cataloguing has certainly matured to adopt scientific methods.

2
Forms of Library Catalogue

Q. : Discuss the various physical forms of Library Catalogue.

or

Which physical form of Library Catalogue will you prefer in an Indian College library and why? Elucidate.

or

What do you understand by non-conventional or modern forms of Library Catalogues? Discuss the various forms of these in relation to their advantages and disadvantages.

or

Enumerate different physical forms of Library Catalogues. Describe its non-conventional forms.

or

Differentiate between conventional and non-conventional forms of catalogues. Describe some of the non-conventional forms.

Ans. The external form or the physical form of a catalogue refires to the manner in which the catalogue is presented. In other words, the physical form of the catalogue is the outline and physical shape in which a catalogue is presented for use. The change in the form of documents from clay tablets in ancient times to printed forms in early nineteenth century, in addition to 20th century microforms and non-print forms has influenced the physical form of catalogue accordingly.

The physical forms of catalogue from distant past to the present, may be broadly arranged in the following categories.

1. Conventional or Traditional Form

   (i) Book or Register form

(ii) Guard Book form

(iii) Sheaf form

(iv) Card form

2. Non conventional or modern form

(i) Visible Index Catalogue

(ii) Microform Catalogues

(iii) Computer Output Microform (COM)

(iv) Machine Readable Catalogue (MARC)

(v) CD-ROM Catalogue.

(vi) On line Public Access Catalogue (OPAC)

Each of these, is discussed below :

1. Conventional or Traditional Form

The predominant types of physical forms of catalogue falling in this category are:

(i) Book or Register Form :– This is the traditional form of the catalogue. In this form, the entries of documents of a library are written by hand in a bound register or ledger, pages are set apart for different letters of the alphabets. These alphabets are arranged alphabetically. Minimum information about the document such as author, title, editions, accession number and class number is given for each book. There may be a separate register for authors or titles or subjects.

Large libraries and other libraries with sufficient funds get the catalogue printed. This catalogue is called main catalogue and all future catalogues are printed as complements of the main catalogue. On the other hand, the information about the reading material in smaller libraries is entered in one or more registers. Information about the new books received in the library in future are is also entered in the register.

Advantages : Following are the advantages of this form of catalogue:

1. It is very simple and easy to use because of its traditional and well known form and shape.
2. Since many entries are written on a single page, users can observe these entries in a single glance, which saves time of the readers.
3. As this form of catalogue is very easy to handle, the users can use it in any convenient locations.

4. This form of catalogue requires very little space in comparison to other forms because many copies of this catalogue can be placed on the top of one another in a single place.
5. If the catalogue is printed then it can also become a source of income for the library to a certain extent as the library can sell its copies to the users.
6. The users can purchase this form of printed catalogue and use it in their homes to get the information on the books in the library collection.
7. The printed catalogues of large libraries are helpful in book selection, classification, cataloguing etc. for other libraries.
8. Printed catalogues are very helpful in inter – library loans of books and co-operation between libraries.
9. Since there are many printed copies of this catalogue, a number of readers can use it at the same time.
10. This form may be helpful in centralized cataloguing.

Disadvantages : This form of catalogue suffers from following drawbacks along with its merits mentioned above.

1. The major drawback of this form is that it can not be kept updated, as the entries of new books cannot be made in it in proper place Moreover, the entries cannot be removed from it when required.
2. This form of catalogue is not flexible in the sense that new entry cannot be made between two previous entries without spoiling the appearance of the catalogue. Moreover only a small number of new entries can be made in this manner.
3. Entries of new books cannot be made in their proper place but these are made at the end or in supplementary catalogues. The entries of books withdrawn cannot be removed form it. Hence, this form of catalogue can be best used only in those libraries in which new books are not purchased and earlier books are not withdrawn.
4. Since a lot of time is taken in printing of catalogue, some books remain out of use for such period. Readers are always interested in new books and the printed catalogue cannot provide them information of latest books received in the library. In this manner, the printed form of catalogue always lags behind the present.

5. Lot of efforts is involved in preparing the printed catalogue. The printing of supplementary catalogue makes it evens more labour intensive and more expensive. It is because of this expenditure that all types of libraries cannot get the catalogues printed.
6. The catalogue becomes poor in shape and appearance over long use. The paper used for it becomes dirty, torn and bulges out after some time. Besides, the hand-written register catalogue has to be kept very carefully; else it is damaged too soon.
7. Only a limited number of readers can use the register form of catalogue. Moreover, only one person can use it at a time.

(ii) Guard-book Catalogue : – In this form of catalogue, entries are made on slips of paper and mounted in the required sequence on the blank leaves of large guard-books. The entries have to be kept as widely spaced as possible to allow for additional insertions. In case of filling up of a page the entries are cut form the particular page of the Guard-book and further dispersed over an increased number of leaves.

Advantages :

1. It retains the format of the book-catalogue, though it is much less compact.
2. It permits insertion of entries, though some additional effort has to be made for this job.
3. Updating of sequence is possible.

Disadvantages :

1. The size, number and bulk of the guard-book increases with the passage of time.
2. It is difficult of maintain strict order of entries in Guard-Book.
3. A lot of time is wasted when already mounted entries are cut and remounted on new pages of Guard-Book.
4. The constant withdrawals required by most libraries may make this form impracticable.

(iii) Sheaf Form : – This form of catalogue was introduced in 1871. In this form, each entry is recorded on separate paper slips of a uniform size generally 6”×4” size notched at the left edge and protected by board on front and back . These slips are files in a specially made loose leaf binder secured by mechanical clasp or metal fastener. Such a binder contains about 500 to 600 slips each. These binders are kept in specially constructed pigeon holes for a catalogue cabinet.

Entries can be arranged in any order. They can easily be inserted or withdrawn without affecting the arrangement of entries.

Advantages : The following are the merit or advantages of sheaf-form catalogue:

1. It includes merits of both printed form and the card form of catalogue. It is like the book form in appearance while the facility of adding and removing the entries in this form is like that of the card form of catalogue.
2. This form of catalogue can be kept updated because of the facility of adding new entries in proper place and to remove the entries for it.
3. It is more economical in comparison to the book form and the register form of catalogue because no other material except the paper slips and the paper binding are required for it.
4. This form of catalogue is very easy to carry anywhere in the library and it can be used in any convenient location in the library.
5. Very small space is required for it in the library.
6. The traditional physical form of this catalogue makes it easier to use.
7. A number of persons can use many sheaves arranged in alphabetical order or classified subject-wise at the same time and thus, save their time.
8. Many copies of this catalogue can be made without spending large amount of money by typing more slips.

Disadvantages : Its main drawbacks are:

1. Adding and removing entries from this catalogue is time consuming.
2. Much space remains unused in the large slips measuring 6”×4” of this catalogue, which is the wastage of material.
3. It gets damaged soon.
4. Its appearance becomes poor by regular use. It bulges and the corners of its slips tear off in some time.
5. It is not suitable for government cataloguing and central cataloguing.

(iv) Card Form : – This form of modern library catalogue was introduced after the French Revolution in the end of 18th century. The credit of introducing this form of catalogue goes to the French Librarians. This catalogue form is most popular and commonly used now in modern libraries all over the world because of its amazing efficiency and ability to remain updated.

In this form, cards of uniform size (5"×3" or 12.5 × 7.5 cm) are used for each entry, which are then arranged in any desired order in cabinet drawers specifically made for this purpose. A hole in the middle of the bottom edge of each card is meant for a locking rod to prevent removal of the cards. Each entry, in it, is a unit which can easily be manipulated.

Advantages : The following are the advantages of this form of catalogue:

1. The most important merit of this form is its extreme flexibility. Entries of new reading material can be easily added in it in their proper place without disturbing other entries. Similarly, the outdated entries or the entries of the withdrawn books can be removed without any difficulty. The order in which the entries are arranged can also be changed in this form of catalogue.
2. The facility to add new entries in their proper place and to remove outdated entries or entries of withdrawn books, or to change the order of the entries makes it very easy to keep this form of catalogue updated.
3. This form of catalogue is more lasting than other forms of catalogues. It does not get damaged easily even after long use by the readers. Use of good quality cards in this catalogue further increases the service life of the catalogue. The catalogue remains neat and attractive because the entries are not rubbed out or over-written in order to add or remove entries from it.
4. The splendour of the Card Index Cabinet impresses the readers. It is very convenient to look up the desired information in this form of catalogue. Many users can use this form at the same time.
5. It is very convenient to get information about the books in this form because the place for entering information on the cards is fixed.

6. It can be made more beneficial for the readers by using sufficient number of guides with it.
7. There is scope for internal and external improvement in this form of catalogue. In this manner, this catalogue can be always kept neat, attractive and updated.
8. This catalogue is less expensive in comparison to the printed form of catalogue.
9. Co–operative cataloguing can also be used in this form of catalogue by which similarity in physical form of catalogue can be maintained at international level.

Disadvantages: This form of catalogue is also not free from drawbacks. Following are its demerits.

1. It wastes more time of the readers because entry of only one book is written on each card or the didadvantages:
2. The card cabinet requires more space. It can be used only in standing position and only in the place where the cabinet is kept. so, this is inconvenient in its use for the users.
3. Many entries of each book are made in this; as a result of which, the size of the catalogue becomes unlimited.
4. Users find psychologically difficult to use this catalogue due to its unfamiliar form. Moreover, this form becomes practically difficult to use because of unlimited growth in its size.
5. It requires lot of expenditure because the cards, cabinet and other material used for it are very expensive.
6. It is time consuming and labour intensive because only a single copy of the catalogue can be prepared at a time. Hence, carbon copies etc. cannot be made for this form of catalogue.
7. A large number of guides are to be used in order to increase the utility of the catalogue. Forming these guides is costly, time consuming and requires much efforts.
8. It becomes difficult to maintain this form of catalogue when its size become too large.
9. It is quite easy to remove or damage the cards in this catalogue. Hence, there is always a fear that the users will knowingly or unknowingly take out the cards or damage these.

It is clear from above discussion that the merits of the card form of catalogue are much less than its demerits, but this form is more popular and used more in all modern libraries of the world, as it remains updated because of its flexibility.

2. Non-conventional or Modern Forms

The change in form of documents from book to non-book material such as microfilms, microfiche and more recently CD-ROM and multimedia interactive computer works and text files on Internet has influenced the traditional forms of catalogue. Physical forms of catalogue have undergone a drastic change. With the result, various non-conventional or modern and sophisticated forms of physical forms of catalogue have been developed to make the work of information retrieval exhaustive and expeditious.

The non-conventional physical forms of catalogue are described as follows:

(i) Visible Index Catalogue:— Visible index catalogue consists of strips mounted on a frame of cards held flat, hinged and with edge of each card protruding so as to make the heading visible. The cards are usually of the size 12.5 × 20 cm.; the card is inserted into a hinged kraft pocket, exposing the top portion. These pockets are held in a specially prepared steel cabinets.

Such steel cabinets are available in India under the trade name Kardex. Generally, Kardex is used in Indian libraries for maintaining records of current journals and periodicals. 'Chaindex' and 'Stripdex' are other two names under which visible Index form catalogues are commercially available. However, these are rarely used in Indian libraries. Kardex is quite popular in Indian libraries for maintaining periodical records.

Kardex is not usually recommended for maintenance of library catalogues.

(ii) Microform Catalogue :– In microform catalogue, entries are greatly reduced and printed upon a film or fiche. The microform catalogues cannot be read by naked eyes. A suitable microform reader, magnifies the reduced images on the film or fiche and projects them on to a screen, is necessary for consulting a microform catalogue.

Microfilm is housed (rolled) in a cassette containing two reels so that the film can be wound forwards or backwards within the container at the time of consultation. Microfilm readers usually allow the rotation of images through 90 degrees. Wheareas, the Microfiche is a transparent card type format which generally gives 200 frames per card. Microfiche has the advantage of a direct access to a particular frame whereas a microfilm requires a serial search through the film to locate a required entry which is a time consuming process compared to direct access method afforded by microfiche.

Advantages: Its advantages are:

1. Microform catalogues are easy to use and maintain.
2. These are compact and occupy less space in the library.
3. They are portable and accessible to users depending upon number of copies of catalogues and the machines available.
4. Multiple copies of these catalogues can be prepared easily at least cost.

Disadvantages : The main disadvantages are:

1. These can not be used without microform readers.
2. These require special care and protection from heat, light and sun.

(iii) Computer Output Microform (COM) : Computer Output Microform (COM) is a more recent method to produce a microform catalogue directly from machine-readable records.

The COM device converts the digital information contained on the computer generated magnetic tape into print displayed on microform. Thus, the recent advances in micrographics have been combined with the technology of the computer in catalogue production, resulting in the lower costs and more efficient updating.

Special readers are required for the magnified display of COM generated image and the printers, which can be used to create paper copies. Several book jobbers and vendors, around the world have developed software capable of producing COM catalogue from library supplied bibliographic data.

Advantages :

1. COM catalogue is inexpensive to reproduce and can be placed in various locations inside and outside a library.

2. There can be separate films for another entries, title entries and subject entries.
3. Several records can be viewed at a time.
4. Entries can be easily printed, if printer is available.
5. Equipment is relatively inexpensive.

Disadvantages :

1. Deleted materials remain in the file until the next update.
2. Microforms are not often very readable as compared to print.

(iv) Machine Readable Catalogue (MARC) :– In a machine-readable catalogue entries are rendered in a format which permits input and storage on magnetic tape or magnetic disc manipulation in a computer. MARC format, UNIMARC, and Common Communication Format (CCF) are standard formats. The history of MARC format goes back to the late 1960s, when the Library of Congress and other research libraries recognised that computer processing of bibliographic information had to be employed in order to solve problems such as cataloguing backlogs, and to provide better services to readers. This led to adoption of the MARC-I communication format for exchange of bibliographic data among libraries in 1967.

Librarians were not unanimous regarding type of an automated cataloguing system. The format MARC-II was a considerably improved version - 1 in the light of experiences and opinions of important libraries and a specific survey carried out for studying the requirements of the users. Access to the catalogue entries may be 'off-line' or 'on-line'. 'Off-line' means that the computer can be used only at certain times. At the available computer time, search must be made for a collection or batch of enquiries. On-line systems, however, are linked directly to the computers which can be used immediately or at any time for processing enquiries and searching.

There are three major computer produced physical forms of library catalogues which are relevant to off-line access. These are:

— *Printed form :* Entries are printed in a conventional book format and are available in multiple copies.

— *Card form :* Each entry is transferred to one or more cards of standard catalogue card and are files just as in a conventional card catalogue.

— Microform entries are transferred to microfilm or microfiche and are used with appropriate microform readers.

In these forms, they are no more than the conventional catalogue forms, the only difference being their mode of production.

In an on-line catalogue, the entries are held in computer files and can be projected on the screen or printouts obtained.

Advantages : The machine-readable catalogue performs, all the functions of a library catalogue with greater efficiency and speed than any other form. As its advantages are concerned, a computer readable catalogue :

— can be kept updated with speed and efficiency.

— can search for any bibliographical element, such as author, subject, publisher, price.

— is user friendly.

— can easily be multiplied.

Disadvantages : The only disadvantage of computerised catalogues, particularly, in India, is the acute shortage of manpower to design and operate machine-readable catalogues. Users should be tuned to the computerized systems to exploit fully the capability of a machine readable catalogue.

(v) CD-ROM Catalogue: – CD-ROM (Compact Disc Read only Memory) is latest MARC format. A CD-ROM catalogue provides excellent search facilities.

It is advantageous to transport CD-ROM Catalogues from one place to another even by post. CD-ROM with accompanying software performs some or all of the following functions :-

(a) Local-public access catalogue.

(b) Union Catalogue in support of inter-library loan.

(c) Reference database of bibliographic information.

(d) Resource data file for extraction of records to be used in retrospective conversion, card production, and on going additions to a local online database.

It is wrong to compare CD-ROM to microform. The microform search is similar to manual catalogues whereas CD-ROM offers the same facilities as online searching as it provides a better user interface. Graphics and sound can also be provided through interface. Although

CD-ROM is slow in comparison of online retrieval, it does not cause any problem in library catalogue situations.

(vi) On-line Public Access Catalogue (OPAC)

The ''Online Public Access Catalogue (OPAC)" is the newest and sophisticated catalogue format. It is pertinent to mention here that all online catalogues are Public Access Catalogues. OPAC has overshadowed all other events in the history of cataloguing during the past decade. OPAC can be accessed via a computer terminal. Such catalogues allow any person to browse the catalogue database to know whether library has got specific title of document and if library is using an integrated library software package. The inquirer may also know whether the book is available with the library or issued out. Even it is easy to know the person holding the book. Hence, reminders/ reservations can be effected. Online catalogues are also known as real time interactive retrieval systems. In other words in OPAC user is connected directly to the information source i .e., catalogue.

Advantages:

1. Online computer catalogue can be easily updated and can also provide ''See" and "See also" reference easily.
2. CRT terminals can be provided at many places.
3. New access points and search capabilities can be added at any time.

Disadvantages :

1. Systems failure hinders access to the catalogue and hence the collection.
2. Safety of cataloguing data on Hard Disc is problem.

But, whatever the form a library is going to be adopted, the following requirements should be considered while choosing the physical form of a catalogue for the library:

1. To keep the catalogue updated.
2. To keep all entries of same heading together.
3. The catalogue should fulfil the needs of the readers as well as the employees equally.
4. The catalogue should be easy and convenient to use.
5. Catalogue should be compact in shape.

6. Catalogue should be able to provide the information of the reading material quickly.

A comparative study of different physical forms of library catalogues by Hunter and Bakewell (1983) is reproduced below for quick decision.

Comparison of Physical Forms of Library Catalogue

Forms of Catalogue	*Easy to use*	*Easy to keep up-to-date*	*Easy to scan multiple copies*	*Easy to produce*	*Bulky*	*Easy to guide*	*Other factors*
Printed	Yes	No	Yes	Yes	No	Yes	
Guard book	Yes	Yes, with some effort	Yes	Feasible but important	Yes	Yes	Time consuming to compile. Withdrawals are a problem
Card	Debatable	Yes	No	No	Yes	Fairly easy	One user can monopolize a complete section
Sheaf	Yes	Yes	No, unless multiple entries to page which makes updating difficult	Not usual but it is possible	Yes	No	Binding mechanism can be awkward. Sheaf slips are filmsy
Visible Index	Yes	Yes	Yes	No	Depends on type	Yes	–
Micro form	Debatable	Yes	Yes	Yes	No	Yes	Requires a machine to read.
Machine Readable	Yes, but some training may be neccessary	Yes	No, but other search facilities compen-sate	A number of access terminals may be provided	A terminal as small as a portable	Not applic-able	typewriter

But for a small library, it is better to adopt the card form of catalogue because it not only fulfils above requirements but it has all the qualities of an ideal form of catalogue.

Q. : Discuss the various inner forms of Library Catalogue. Which one will you prefer to adopt in your library and why?

or

Make a comparison between a dictionary catalogue and a classified catalogue. Explain which of these two types would be more useful for a University library?

or

Describe briefly dictionary catalogue and compare it with a classified catalogue.

or

Describe briefly classified catalogue and compare it with a dictionary catalogue.

Ans. The cataloguing process comprises of two operations. The first is the creation of varieties of entries for documents acquired by a library. The second is the organization of these entries in a logical and helpful order for storage and retrieval. The entries of the library catalogue are formed and arranged according to these different catalogues. For this reason, these entries are also called the kind of catalogue or the internal form of the catalogue. There have been changes in the internal form of the catalogues with the change in the thinking in which customer services should be provided.

The catalogues have been divided as follows on the basis of the internal structure:

1. Alphabetical Catalogue:
   - (i) Author Catalogue
   - (ii) Name Catalogue
   - (iii) Title Catalogue
   - (iv) Subject Catalogue
   - (v) Dictionary Catalogue
2. Classified or Classed Catalogue:
   - (i) Classified Part
   - (ii) Alphabetical Part
3. Alphabetico-classed Catalogue :
   - (i) Subject Part
   - (ii) Alphabetical Index

1. Alphabetical Catalogue:

Its following types are recognized –

(i) Author Catalogue : This is the oldest and the most important form of catalogue. The author is presented in it in a very elaborate manner. It includes collaborator like the editor, translator, illustrator etc. In an author catalogue, the entries of documents are under authors' name and are arranged alphabetically. In other words the leading section of an author catalogue would be the name of an author. This catalogue provides, the information about which books of a particular author are available in the library or whether a particular book of a particular author is available in the library or not?

Libraries may have author catalogues arranged in three different ways, a) There may be an exclusive author catalogue without mixing it with any other entries such as titles, subjects, series, etc. (b) Author entries may form part and parcel of a dictionary catalogue, (c) Author entries may form part of the alphabetical index of a classified catalogue. Irrespective of the form in which an author catalogue exists, it provides an important approach to a library catalogue, as it fulfills an essential function of a catalogue.

Merits:

1. Information about all available books of an author is easily received from a single place at the same time.
2. It is very easy to determine whether a particular book of some specific author is available in the library or not.
3. In case there are many works having the same title, then these can be separated by the name of the author only.

Demerits:

1. This catalogue, provides answer to only a limited number of questions raised by the readers. Hence, it cannot satisfy other needs of the readers, such as those related to the title, series, subject etc.
2. Knowledge of the author's name is essential in order to make use of this catalogue. There are many ancient and medieval works of writing those do not contain the name of their author. In such situations, the entries are formed according to the title. Thus if the author's name is not known, it is difficult to get the information about such books.

3. The manner in which author's name is presented in the entries if unknown to most readers. The readers feel difficulty in such a situation.

4. There has been tremendous growth in the number of books and authors in modern age. Thus, it is not easy to remember the books by the name of the author. Moreover, the readers are now generally more desirous of getting the reading material of their interest on the basis of specific subject and this catalogue is completely unable to meet these demands.

5. It is necessary that the readers have correct knowledge about the author and the title in order to make use of this catalogue.

Some important examples of this catalogue are: Author catalogue published by British Museum, Catalogues published by London Library, the Catalogue of books represented by Library of Congress, and the Print Author Catalogue of the National Library of India.

(ii) Name Catalogue : A name catalogue is a variation and extension of an author catalogue. It contains entries for works of an author and also for books written on him. All entries are arranged alphabetically by the name of the author. In other words, a name catalogue is a mixed type of catalogue which combines, the author and subject entries representing the author as a subject into one alphabetical sequence. In this type of catalogue, biographies and other critical studies of an author, are arranged along with his original works. The author entries include:

— corporate authors, both as an author as well as a subject,

— name series,

— place name forming part of an author heading.

Name catalogue serves as an author catalogue and also as a subject catalogue as far as the author as a subject is concerned. Any reader interested on the works by or on an author may find this type of catalogue very useful to find specific material of his interest. For example, in this type of catalogue, one can find the works of Rabindranath Tagore as well as works on him arranged in a single alphabetical order under Tagore.

As its examples in concerned, the Catalogue of the British Museum Library (now the British Library) is near name catalogue which includes references from all names that occur in titles.

(iii) Title Catalogue : In a title catalogue, the titles of documents occupy at the leading section of entries, which are arranged in an alphabetical order. Queries of readers who remember only the exact title of the book can be answered with the help of a title catalogue. However, it is noticed that many of the readers do not spell out a title exactly the way it appears on the title page, particularly in case of non-fiction titles.

To fulfil title approach of readers, entries can be selectively provided in catalogues of public libraries for fiction and for those that are well-known by their titles.

(iv) Subject Catalogue : In an alphabetical subject catalogue, entries are made under the name of the specific subjects of documents. Irrespective of their affiliations, specific subject entries are strictly arranged in an alphabetical order. The fundamental rule of entry in an alphabetical specific subject catalogue is to enter a work under its specific subject. For example, a book on 'Roses' will be entered under 'Roses' and not under 'flowers' or 'Botany', which are broader than 'Roses.

In almost every type of library, the predominate requests for documents are by their subjects. Hence extensive provision must be made to give adequate representation to subjects of documents, with a considerable number of cross-references, directing the user to the various aspects of a subject.

(v) Dictionary Catalogue : The dictionary catalogue derives its name from the general meaning of the word 'dictionary'. A dictionary catalogue gives information about, documents available in a library with reference to their authors, titles, subjects, etc. All the entries getting arranged in a single alphabetical order. It resembles arrangement of entries as in a natural language dictionary in which all words, irrespective of their origin, parts of speech (nouns, verbs, adjectives, adverbs, etc.), usage, etc. are arranged in one single alphabetical order.

Dr. S.R. Ranganathan has written while defining this catalogue in his 'Classified Catalogue Code' that, "Catalogue in which all the entries are Word Entries."

Anglo American Cataloguing Rules has described it as, "catalogue usually on cards, in which all the entries (author, title, subject series etc.) and their related references are arranged together in one general alphabet."

This is a single volume catalogue. Hence, it is called unipart catalogue or mono-catalogue. It is a complete catalogue by which all the wants of the readers are fulfilled.

Some libraries prefer to display the dictionary catalogue in two separate parts: the first part containing author and title entries with cross references, if any, and the second part is reserved exclusively for subject entries with cross references. This is called 'divided catalogue'. This type of separation poses some problems for users, as they have to refer to both these parts located at different places, to find out the information for a document of their interest.

Merits : Following are the advantages of dictionary catalogue:

1. *Convenient and Easy to Use :* This catalogue is very simple and convenient to use for the readers since the headings of the entries in it are in natural language. This is also simple to use because all entries are arranged in the same alphabetical order, as determined by a dictionary. In the words of *H.A. Sharp*, "The ease of using it is the reason for its enduring popularity."
2. *Completeness :* This is a complete catalogue since all the entries i.e. subject, author, title, collaborator and series etc. and the related index entries are included in it. The readers can use these to satisfy their needs.
3. *Time Saving* **:** This catalogue saves the time of the readers since it quickly provides answers to the queries of the readers by providing direct answers and due to the specific headings that are included in it.
4. *Knowledge of Classification Scheme is not Necessary:* The subject headings in it are not formed according to any classification system. Moreover, all entries together with the subject entries are formed in natural language with which the readers are already very well acquainted. Hence, there is no need to have prior knowledge of classification procedure in order to make use of this catalogue.
5. *Assists in finding Related Subjects :* See' and 'see also' subject entries co-relate the main subjects, similar subjects, opposite subjects as well as the synonymous words. This proves to be very helpful to the readers in gaining information of reading material related to the specific subject of their choice. Even if

the related subject headings are in different places in the catalogue due to the alphabetical arrangement, the reader does not face any difficulty in finding them.

6. *Formation of Subject Headings for facility of Users:* The cataloguer can form the subject headings in this catalogue according to those descriptive points which are suitable to the nature of the library and useful from the readers point of view as the subject headings and subjective cataloguing remain independent in it because this catalogue is not based on the system of classification. Moreover, the cataloguer himself remains free from the influence of classification.

7. *Related Specific Subject Brought together:* This type of catalogue can sometimes also arrange such related subjects together in a logical manner, which are scattered due to the classification arrangement.

8. *Single Entry satisfies Two Queries:* Arranging all entries in a single alphabetical order not only satisfies all the needs of the readers, but it also reduces the number of entries because there is a similarity in the names of the author and subject of some books, while there is similarity in the title and subject of some others. In this manner, a single entry is able to fulfil two queries.

Demerits : This catalogue suffers from following demerits along with the merits mentioned above:

1. *Not so easy and Convenient to Use:* This catalogue is not as easy to use as it seems. It takes the form of a complex system due to the uncountable subjects and general subject directions, by which its use does not remain easy and simple.

2. *Growth in Size of Catalogue:* The size of the catalogue becomes very large due to the arrangement of all the entries in a single order and by inclusion of uncountable number of guidelines and directions.

3. *Complex Arrangement of Headings:* The work of arranging the personal names, titles, institutions and names of places under a single order is very difficult and complex. As a result of this, chances of mistakes remaining in this catalogue are always present.

4. *Incomplete Subject Direction:* Co-relation is established between

the related subjects by 'see' and 'see also' subject directions. These are always incomplete.

5. *Difficult to Receive Information on Books of Desired Subject:* Gaining information about the books of desired subject is a very difficult, laborious and time consuming work because the information of the related subjects gets scattered due to the alphabetical arrangement

6. *Subject-headings become Outdated:* The subjects that are used become old and unpopular over time. Hence, it becomes necessary to update the subject entries, which is an expensive, time consuming and labour intensive work. Sometimes, a single specific subject is known by two or more different names or words. In such cases, it becomes difficult to decide which one of these should be used for the subject heading.

7. *Language Barrier:* The alphabetical headings can be in a single language only. This poses a problem in forming the catalogue of multilingual books.

2. Classified Catalogue

A classified catalogue is a form of subject catalogue, in which the entries are arranged by the class number which representing the subject of document, according to the classification scheme chosen for a library.

According to *Dr. S.R. Ranganathan,* classified catalogue is a Catalogue in which some entries are Number Entries and some are Word Entries. This catalogue is divided in following two parts:

(i) Classified Part: The main entries and the cross reference entries are arranged in this in an order of classification according to the system of classification. Book numbers are entered in the leading section of these entries. These represent the specific subject of the books in the artificial language of classification.

While displaying the entries in a classified catalogue, merely giving the class numbers would not be very helpful to users of the catalogue. The class numbers are not intelligible to persons who have no knowledge of the classification scheme chosen for the library. Therefore, while displaying the class numbers in guide cards, for entries under them, it is absolutely necessary to give their verbal equivalents of the divisions of class numbers. These verbal equivalents provided for class numbers in a classified catalogue are known as 'Feature Headings'. These headings are the translation of the class numbers of documents into their verbal equivalents, representing the different hierarchical levels of the subject.

Feature headings are verbal extensions, as well as being the major source of indexing terms, will indicate the terms which should be used for guiding, both in the catalogue and on the shelves. In general, libraries provide quite inadequate guides to their systematic arrangement, assuming that readers can find their way through the catalogue with a minimum to help. It may be thought extreme to make a guide for every feature heading, but this is what is done by BNB, and there is no doubt that it makes the systematic arrangement a great deal easier to use. An extract of a page from BNB and a page from American Book Publishing Record to illustrate the points mentioned above.

BNB

421 - **ENGLISH LANGUAGE WRITTEN SPOKEN CODES**

421 .52 English Language Pronunciation

'Honey, John

Does accent matter?: the Pygmalion factor/John Honey. - London

Includes bibliography and index

ISBN 0-571-14509-4 (pbk): f4.95;

CIP entry (Jan.) 1 .Ti.

B88-390616

4.23- ENGLISH LANGUAGE INTONATION

Manser, Martin H.

Information in context : intonation practice for upper-intermediate and advanced learners of English/Barbara Bradford; advisory editor.

David brazil. -Cambridge University Press, 1988,- 2v. : ill, maps; 23cm.

ABPR

422 English Etymology

CANNON, Garland Hampton

Faber. 1989. - [2001] p; 20cm 1934

Historical change and English word—formation :

recent vocabulary/Garland Cannon, New York: P. Lang, 1987 p.cm. (American university studies. Series IV. English language and literature: vol 46) Includes indexes. Bibliography: p.[PE 1175.C35 1987] 1986-32206 ISBN 0-8204-0403-9 : 35.00

1. English language-word formation.

2. Linguistic change. I. Title, II. Series.

ABEL, Ernest L, 1943- 422.03 Alcohol wordlore and folklore: being a compendium of linguistic and social fact and

ISBN 0-521-31915-3 (Teacher's book) : f4.50 (pbk) : No price ISBN 0-521-31914-5 (Student's book) : f3.95 ISBN 0-521-266490-1(Cassette) : No.price I .Ti 2. Brazil, David

B88-390616

423- ENGLISH LANGUAGE DICTIONARIES

Manser Martin H.

Dictionary oponyms/ Martin H. Manser. - London : Sphere, 1988.

- 306p : ill, ports : 20cm

ISBN 0-7221-6312-6 (pbk) : f4.50 I. Ti

B08-62432

423.1- English language. Unusual words - Dictionaries Schur, Norman W. 1907 100 most challenging words/Norman W. Schur. - New York : Oxford : Facts on File, cl987. -322p : 24cm Includes index

ISBN 0-8160-1996-6 : fl2.95 : CIP rev. 1. Ti

428.24 - ENGLISH LANGUAGE FOR FOREIGN STUDENTS

428.2'4 - English language. Comprehension - For non-English speaking Student

Roberts, E.L.

Tactic 2/E.L. Roberts. - London : Macmillan [Workbook]. 1986. -40p : ill, Imap, ! Plan : 27cm

fantasy associated with the and production of alcohol as reflected in he magazines, newspapers, and literature of the English-speaking world/Emest L. Abel, Buffalo. NY: Prometheus Books, p. cm. Bibliography: p. [PE] 683.A24 1987] 1175.C35 1987] 1986-32206 ISBN 0-8204-0403-9 : 35.00

1. English language-Terms and pharases. 2. English language-Etymology Dictionaries. 3. Drinking customs-terminology. 4. Alcoholic beverages - Terminology. 5. Drinking customs. 6. Drinking of alcoholic beverages-Folklore. 1. Title CIARDI, John, 1916-

Good words to you: an all-new dictionary and native's guide to the unknown American language/John Ciardi. New York: Harper & Row, c 1987, p. cm. [PE2837.C54 1987] 1986-45647 ISBN 0-6-015691-0: 19.45 1. English language - United States- Dictionarias. 2. Americanisms -Dictionaries. I. Title.

HENDRICKSON, Robert,

422.03

The Facts on File encyclopedia of word and pharases origins/Robert Hendrickson. New York, N.Y.: Facts on File, c 1987.551p.:29 cm [PE 1689. H 47 1987] 1986-2067 ISBN 0-8160 -1012-9: 50.00

1. English language - Terms and phrases 2. English language -Etymology Dictionaries Facts on File. Inc. II. Title

ISBN 0-8160-1196-6 : F12.95 : cip REV. MAWSON. CO. Sylvester
I. Ti

B88-61681

428.2' 4-English Language - For non-English speaking students
New dimensions. - London: Macmillan Teacher's Book 3/Ann Ward & Jack Lonergan, - 1988. -112p : ill : 30 cm
ISBN 0-333-42340-2 (pbk) : f 2.95: CIP rev. 1. Ward, Ann, 1941- 2. Lonergan., Jack

B88-02088

4.28.2' 4-English language - Questions & answers - For non-English Speaking students
Harmer, Jeremy. 1950-
Meredian. - Longman, 1988
Test book 2. -15p
ISBN 0-582-57961-9. (pbk) : fl.70 l.Ti
4.28'4'07-Non-English speaking students. Education. Curriculum subjects: English language, Curriculum. Development

422.4

1870-1938. (Christographer Oriando Sylvester), The Harper dictionary of foreign terms: based on the original edition by C.O. Sylvester Mawson/ revised and edited by Engine Ehrlich 3rd Ed. New York: Harper & Row, c 1987, p. cm. Rev. ed. of: Dictionary of foreign terms, 2nd ed. 1975. Includes index. [PE 1670-M3 1987] 1986-40061
ISBN 0-06-181576-4: 19.50
I. English language -Foreign words and phrases -Dictionaries I. Ehrlich, Engine H. II Mawson,
C. O. Sylvester 1870-1938. Dicionary or foreign terms III. Title.
423 English Dictionaries

Providing feature headings is theoretically sound and extremely useful and it is done quite well in a printed catalogue or bibliography like BNB. But in a card catalogue, the breakdown of the class numbers into their hierarchical divisions would need too many cards for each entry. It sometimes diminishes its practical utility. Therefore, it has to be done with considerable imagination and caution. Feature headings should not be allowed to defeat their very purpose.

(ii) Alphabetical Index : This section is related to the word entries. All class directions, book directions and cross reference added entries are arranged in a single alphabetical order. This part functions as an index for the main classified part and alphabet. The alphabets or words are entered in the leading section of these entries.

This is a two-part complete catalogue by which all needs can be fulfilled. This catalogue comprises of merits of dictionary catalogue as well as classified catalogue.

Merits : The following are the merits of classified catalogue:

1. It is easy and convenient to use and arrange this two-part catalogue.
2. As the class numbers of the entries of the classification part are in the language of some recognised classification system, these are free from the limitations of national or regional languages.

   If a classification system of international standard is adopted with multilingual indexes, the search for the literature available in foreign languages becomes easier. This will overcome any language barrier and it will also facilitate international cooperation.
3. Classification order is very useful for those readers who are desirous of obtaining a book on a specific subject.
4. It gives an indication of the capability or incapability of the collection of reading material on a specific subject in the library. This is because the entries of the alphabetical part can quickly represent the number and the level of specific subject available in the library.
5. The arrangement of entries in the classification part is parallel to the arrangement of books in the shelves. This makes it easier for the users to find the book in the shelves.
6. The entries of the classification part are capable of fulfilling or of providing proper direction towards fulfilling all possible needs of the users.
7. The two parts of the catalogue are able and capable to fulfill the objectives of a library catalogue.
8. Any class or subject catalogue can be easily be printed whenever required.
9. This catalogue represents the ability or inability of the collection. This proves to be very helpful in book selection.
10. The classification part is helpful in compiling the bibliographical subject catalogue.
11. The rate of its growth is comparatively less.

Demerits : The following are the demerits of the classified catalogue:

1. This cannot be used with ease without having prior knowledge of the language of classification as the user is not well acquainted with the numerical-language of the classification. It is for this reason, the use of the classification part is not simple for general users.
2. The artificial language of the class number is complex and it creates a psychological obstacle in the mind of the user. Thus, it discourages the use of the catalogue.
3. It becomes necessary to form the alphabetical subject heading index entries of the class numbers for the classification part. This increases the size of the catalogue.
4. Usefulness of the classified part depends on the simplicity of classification language and its applicability.

Given below are samples of main entry for a classified catalogue and for a dictionary catalogue.

1. Main Entry for Classified Catalogue

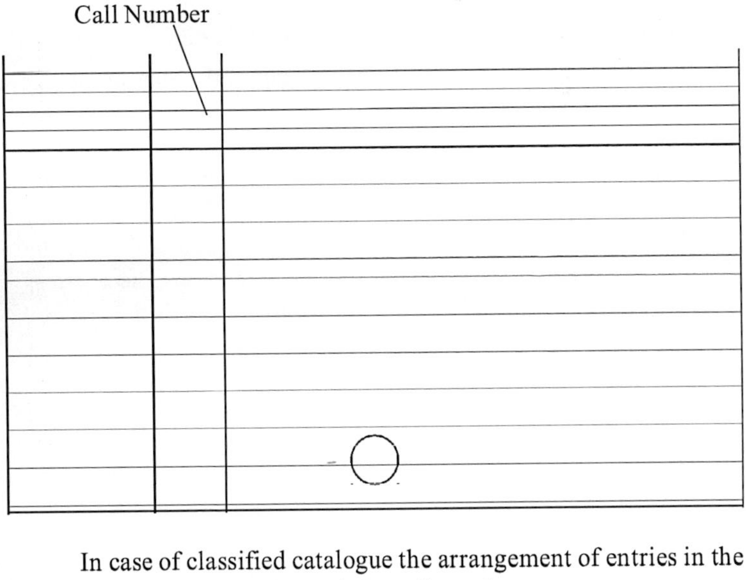

In case of classified catalogue the arrangement of entries in the classified part of the catalogue is by call numbers.

2. Main Entry of Dictionary Catalogue

Arrangement of entries in the dictionary catalogue will be according to the alphabetical order of the surname of the authors.

Comparison of Dictionary and Classified Catalogues

Out of the various types of catalogues, the classified and dictionary catalogues are the most important. The dictionary catalogue has superseded all other forms of alphabetical catalogues like author, title, subject and name catalogues. With elaborate cross references, it has increased its usefulness and capability to meet all the requirements of a library catalogue. On the other hand, the classified catalogue displaying its entries with a panoramic view of the subjects, incorporates many of the features of a dictionary catalogue in its 'alphabetical index'. Therefore, these two forms of catalogues have been adopted by most of the libraries.

A comparison of these catalogues is being made through following table :

Comparison between CC and DC

No.	*Features / Aspects*	*Classified Catalogue (CC)*	*Dictionary Catalogue (DC)*
1.	Preparation	From the point of librarian, it is simple to prepare because it utilizes the work already carried out in classifying the documents and its indexing proves easier as the collection grows.	Is equally simple to prepare but subject indexing gets complicated with the growth of a collection.
2.	Arrangement	Arrangement of entries in the classified part is the same as that of books on shelves. Arrangement in the alphabetical part is like a dictionary, which is easy to understand. Arrangement of multilingual entries does not present difficulties in the classified part but in the alphabetical part, multilingual entries can present difficulties.	Arrangement of entries is alphabetical like a dictionary, which is easy to understand. Multilingual entries can present difficulties.
3.	Logical and systematical order	A logical and systematic order is achieved in the classified part because the order is based on a scheme of classification. The order of the scheme of classification used in books and the classified catalogue being the same, users are likely to become more familiar with the shelf order of books, in case the library adopts the classified catalogue rather than the dictionary catalogue.	Owing to the natural order of alphabets, entries relating to the same subject would get scattered. For instance, subjects like *heat* and *magnetism* are related ones but in the catalogue, subject entries relating to these would get scattered,
4.	Subject approach	In case a user approaches through a specific subject, he has to consult the alphabetical part first, then he is directed to the classified part where he can find entries on the specific subject together, at one place, thereby requiring double action. As regards answering enquiries on various aspects of a subject, CC is certainly superior to DC because it brings together the material on a specific subject as well as on various aspects of a specific subject in its classified part.	It provides a direct approach to those who approach through a specific subject. Thus it is most suitable for answering enquiries under a specific subject and serves specific subject enquiries better than CC. It is difficult to consult for information on various aspects of a subject. In this type of enquiry it is slow as well as unsatisfactory in yielding information. For instance, material under various aspects of physics, like *electricity, heat, magnetism, nuclear physics,* etc., would get scattered due to the very nature of alphabetization. As a result, a

No.	Features/ Aspects	Classified Catalogue (CC)	Dictionary Catalogue (DC)
			user would find it difficult to know about material on all aspects of a given specific subject.
5.	Deeper function	Most users are not able to name exactly the specific subject of their interest. They are want to name a broader or narrower subject. A reader first consults the alphabetical part and then goes to the classified part where he finds the full field of his interest spread before him in a logical manner, becoming vaguely conscious of what he wants. The CC collates all material on a given topic and displays relationships between subjects in a way more useful to the user than any other kind of catalogue.	In it, there is an inevitable seattering of subjects and a large number of see also directions, which will virtually tire out the reader.
6.	Consultation	The CC is not really as difficult to consult as it appears to be. It does not require deep knowledge of the scheme of classification but it does sometimes set a psychological barrier in the mind of the users. Use of a large number of guides within and outside the catalogue, and training the users of the catalogue by the reference staff can be extremely helpful. In fact, once the basic structure of the catalogue has been understood, its use is likely to present fewer difficulties. Users who have used published bibliographies and catalogues will usually not find it at all difficult to use.	Easy to consult and outwardly simple to use, because it is usable like a dictionary. The complex system of subject entries creates hindrance in use, which at times can prove frustrating.
7.	Role of classification	Usefulness of CC depends upon the qualities of the scheme of classification though indexing and guiding can overcome the weakness to some extent. The scheme should be able to individualize each specific subject at book level, provide filiatory sequence and individualize various books.	Its usefulness does not depend upon a scheme of classification.
8.	Role of cross references	The number of cross references is less.Due to the presence of the classified arrangement,	For its ultimate success, it depends upon an elaborate scheme of references. Referen-

No.	*Features/ Aspects*	*Classified Catalogue (CC)*	*Dictionary Catalogue (DC)*
		the role of cross references is limited to referring from rejected headings to selected headings.	ces can often prove to be tiresome and there is always a possibility of missing one or more vital headings. They also multiply at a fast rate, making the catalogue difficult to use.
9.	Language barrier	In case an international scheme of classification like, the Universal Decimal Classification is used with its multilingual indexes, then literature scarches for foreign-language literature become easy. Thus international cooperation is possible.	International cooperation is difficult to achieve.
10.	Printing of a subject catalogue	Any class or subject catalogue can be printed at any time easily.	Subject catalogue is more difficult to print.
11.	Rate of growth	Overall rate of growth is slower.	Subject entries and references increase at higher rate than in CC. Rate of growth of the catalogue is high, making it difficult to use.
12.	Maintenance	The maintenance of subject entries in the alphabetical part is easier because replacing of old subject terms by new ones is easier as compared with DC.	Replacing of old subject terms by new subject terms is a tedious and time-consuming process.

So both these types of library catalogues should work reasonable well and within limits if worked and operated well. There is no absolute yardstick to measure their merits or demerits.

3. Alphabetico-Classed Catalogue

The alphabetico-classed catalogue is a combination or mixture of the best points associated with dictionary and classified catalogue. It represents an attempt to combine some of the advantages of a classified catalogue with the directness and ease of consultation for the alphabetical catalogue.

According to Hunter and Bakewell, an alphabetico-classed catalogue provides alphabetically arranged broad subject headings with alphabetically arranged "sub-divisions," whereas per, E.J. Coates, it is "A catalogue of this kind consists of an alphabetical sequence of mutually exclusive broad subject headings, under each of which appears of further alphabetical sequence of sub-headings." The process of alphabetical divisions can be carried down to the degree of minuteness required by the material being catalogue.

This type of catalogue must have an alphabetical index of specific subject for its successful operation.

The rearrangement of Dewey Decimal Classification Division of 600 Technology in an alphabetical order would yield the following.

Agriculture and related technologies (630)

Building (690)

Chemical and related technologies (660)

Engineering and allied operations (620)

Home Economics and family living (640)

Management and auxiliary services (650)

Manufactures (670)

Manufacture of product for specific uses (680)

Medicine (610)

Diseases (616)

of blood - forming, lymphatic, glandular system (614.4)

cardiovascular system (616.1)

digestive system (616.3)

of biliary tract (6 1 6.36)

of mouth and throat (616.31)

It is clear from above examples, the alphabetico-classed catalogue gets related subjects together in a way, but their alphabetical arrangement takes away the filiation of subjects. There are few examples of such catalogues today, because compromises are never entirely successful.

Parts of the original Museum subject index are the example alphabetico-classed catalogue.

Choice-of An Inner Form for A Library Catalogue

As can be seen from the above discussions of the inner forms of a library catalogue, no particular inner form would effectively and equally satisfy all the requirements of library catalogue. Therefore, choice or the selection of an inner form for a library, depends both on the technical soundness of an inner form of a library catalogue as well as some important management factors.

Choice of a catalogue by a library would depend upon certain factors—type of library, availability of printed catalogue cards, type of the catalogue used by neighbouring libraries, kind of training of the chief librarian, and altitude of authorities.

It is generally accepted that school and public libraries find the alphabetical form more suitable; and university, and research libraries prefer the classified catalogue. However, in practice a large majority of libraries use the dictionary catalogue, mainly because of lack of good schemes of classification.

Q. : Write short notes on Authority File.

Ans. A separate listing of entries and the authority on which they are based is commonly called an authority file. All decisions, which may later be questioned and the basis on which they were made must be recorded in some fashions if consistency of entries is to be maintained. In case the entries are derived from an authoritative source in the form of pre printed cards, photo reproductions of entries, prepared in advance by the authority, the file itself is the authority. Such files are commonly maintained for names, subject and series.

Authority file is the record of decisions taken by the cataloguer about individual items while preparing various forms of catalogue entries. Such decisions are helpful in maintaining consistency in the rendering of heading in different types of catalogue entries.

An authority file in just different from a staff mannal. A staff manual is the record the general instructions about different sections of a library. It also provides a broad guidelines of different activities being performed by the members catalogue department.

Whereas an authority file provides the detailed account of all such decisions, which are taken by the cataloguer, which do not find a place in the staff manual. Authority file is updated as and when a decision is taken by the cataloguer about an individual item, it may be due to variations, in the name of author, or interdisciplinary subject approach etc.

Different Forms of Authority Files

These are of following types.

(i) Name Authority File : Those libraries, which adhere to, the literary units principle, which would bring together all the works by an author, must rely on some authority for the establishment of the entry name. The 1941, ALA rules included authority files and rules for establishing them.

With the sale of Library of Congress Catalogue Cards, the practice of making authority files decreased, because the authority and style of entry were established at the moment the cards were obtained, and any further work would have been fruitless. Very few libraries would challenge the authority of the Library of Congress in its entry.

The literary units principle as it appears in the works of Seymour Lubetsky states that all the work of an author should be brought together in the catalogue under one form of his name, including works to which he has contributed as joint author, or joint editor and in analytical entries. To follow this rule, strictly would require a name-authority file. Authority Cards are made only when needed to resolve a problem of entry.

In case of Corporate Bodies, the changes in the name of a Corporate Body increases the difficulties if we follow the literary units principle. There would be good reason for not providing the history of the organisation in changes of names. It would be sufficient to adopt a rule that an organisation is considered defunct when its name changes and new name under the rule is applied to the new institution. But in case the library is not following such rules, it would be necessary to maintain a corporate entry name-authority file.

According to AACR 1, in a dictionary catalogue, author-heading is uniform in respect of all titles entered in the catalogue by the same author. But in case where the name of the author may be shown in various title pages of the books by the same author variantly because of the incidence of full name, initials, pseudonym, changes in names due to marriage, etc., or variations in spelling on account of transliteration from one language to another. All these variations are not shown while rendering the headings, but are brought through cross references.

The necessity of establishing authority of name is essential to ensure uniformity in the heading. The cataloguer is thus required to choose a particular form of name for rendering in the catalogue. This usually the form of the name widely known to the general public or academicians. Authority file in form of cards is helpful in achieving consistency in future.

(ii) Subject Authority File : Most of the libraries follow standard list for preparing subject entries. Also the libraries using Classified Catalogue Code, derive subject headings by the method of Chain Indexing as recommended by Dr. S.R. Ranganathan. Sometimes all the modifications which appear in the revised editions of the standard lists could not be employed by the libraries due to non-availability of these standard lists in the library. Many libraries maintain a card file of all subjects used in a catalogue, amended as changes occur. Unfortunately both the methods have several problems inherent in the arrangement and utilizations of authority file. Some of the libraries resolve these problems by making the addition of see references when a new subject is added.

In a Classified Catalogue Code, authority file is prepared to indicate which class index entries have already been made for each class number. In other words, subject authority card indicates the decision of the cataloguer regarding the choice of sought headings of a class number taken into account for preparing subject added entries or class index entries. Standard list of subject headings themselves can be regarded as an authority file. The headings and references, which have been already used are ticked off so that a cataloguer would immediately know, which headings and references have not been used. In case, the printed subject heading lists do not serve the purpose of a special library a separate subject authority file can be maintained to suit the needs of the library catalogue. Also all modifications in the printed list available can be recorded on the card form as a separate subject authority file.

(iii) Series-Authority File : Series authority files are used to maintain consistency of entry of series when the publisher changes the name of the series but continues the numbering or alters some part of the series tilling without, in fact, creating a new series. The series-authority file is, in fact, a decision file and this leads to the reason for maintaining any kind of authority file, especially those which are used to show the routing and treatment of periodicals.

Series added entries are made when the work is, in fact, a set rather than a series, but is treated as separate works and cataloged separately volume by volume. In this case, the series is reasonably considered a set and cataloged under one heading and classified together, that is when the series constitutes a subject entry where a choice is made whether to classify together or to treat on a more specific basis.

Advantages of Authority-File

(*i*) *Brings consistency and Uniformity :* It helps in bringing out consistency and uniformity in rendering of entry elements as headings in the library catalogue.

(*ii*) *Time-saving Device :* It is a time-saving device and is fit to explain the decisions taken in the problem areas of cataloguing from time to time.

(*iii*) *Serves as a supplement to Standard Lists of Subject Headings :* In small libraries, where every revised edition of standard list of subject headings cannot be procured, subject authority file serves the purpose of supplement to the standard list available in the library.

So, Authority files are usually time saving devices and are fit to explain the decisions which cannot be covered by others files. Authority file is an urgent tool for every library, may be big or small because it is a record of decisions taken for individual items or new coming problems in day to day cataloguing. In such cases authority files serves as a bacon-light for achieving the consistency and uniformity in rendering of entry elements in the catalogue. Moreover, the increasing concept of centralisation and computerisation has developed the need of central authority file for author's names, subject-heading and decisions regarding series. These will provide the maximum usefulness, if properly maintained.

3
Normative Principles

Q. : Describe in brief the Canons of Cataloguing.

or

Enunciate the 'Canon of Ascertainability'. Compare and comment on C.C.C. and A.A.C.R.-2 from the point of view of this canon.

or

Explain with examples the Canon of Sought Heading' and describe its implications in library cataloguing.

or

Explain with examples the 'Canon of Recall Value' and describe its implications in library cataloguing.

Ans. The Normative Principles of cataloguing have been recognized for a long time and have proved to be highly useful. These have provided a scientific basis to the field of cataloguing. These normative principles are useful for cataloguing in the following manner:

(i) These principles provide a fundamental base during the formation of 'Code'.

(ii) Critical study of the 'Code' can be made by these principles only.

(iii) Comparative study of different catalogue codes can also be made by these principles.

(iv) The definitions of the rules of 'code' can be presented in a scientific manner by these principles.

(v) These principles provide a guideline to the cataloguers.

Dr. Ranganathan evolved different normative principles at different levels. These are:

1. General Normative Principle (which have universal application);
2. Laws (at the discipline level, e.g. : Library Science);
3. Canons (at the subdiscipline level, e.g. : cataloguing); and
4. Principles (to assist in working with a subdiscipline).

1. General Normative Principles

Ranganathan calls the five laws of library science, *four general* be reorganized and recatalogued at a minimum cost, by the terms general *normative principles.* The general normative principles elaborated by Ranganathan in his works are detailed below.

(i) Laws of Interpretation
(ii) Law of Impartiality
(iii) Law of Symmetry
(iv) Law of Parsimony
(v) Principle of Local Variation
(vi) Principle of Osmosis

(i) Laws of Interpretation : Ranganathan refers to 1,008 principles of interpretation listed in the Nyaya-kosa. These have been evolved to a remarkable extent by the philosophers of the *purva-mimansa* and *Nyaya* school of Indian philosophy. According to Ranganathan, A catalogue code is like a legal document, therefore, it should be interpreted like a legal text. Some of the areas, where laws of interpretation may be made applicable are: (i) if there is a conflict between different rules, then the conflict should be resolved with the aid of the laws of interpretation; (ii) if a new kind of cataloguing problem comes up, then a solution should be obtained by means of proper interpretation of the rules of the code, keeping in view the laws of interpretation; (iii) the conflict between the law of parsimony, laws of library science and the canons of cataloguing should be solved by the aid of laws of interpretation. In such an eventuality, we should follow the principle: "the later the law, the greater its weightage". It has also been suggested by Ranganathan that the catalogue codes should be scrutinized from the angle of these laws of interpretation.

(ii) Laws of Impartiality : It directs that between two or more claimants (e.g. for use as heading), the preference should be made only on sufficient grounds, and not arbitrarily.

For example, in case of joint authorship, the law of impartiality recommends equal light to the names of all the authors for choice as heading.

(iii) Law of Symmetry : The principle states that of two entities in situations which admit of being regarded as symmetrical counterparts of each other, if one of the entities context, the other entry or situation should also be given a corresponding weight.

In case of a joint authors work, law of symmetry suggests that in the heading of the main entry, we are obliged to write the names of the two author is in the sequence in which they occur on the title page. CCC prescribed the rules at the directive of law of symmetry in case of joint authors. No other code made such a provision.

(iv) Law of Parsimony : This law directs that between two or more possible alternative rules bearing on a particular phenomenon, the one leading to overall economy of manpower, material, money, and time considered together with proper weightage is to be preferred.

For example, the practice of following canon of sought heading in choosing headings for class index entries leads to economy (*CCC,* p. 299), which satisfies the law of parsimony.

Application of the canon of sought heading to cross reference index entries reduces the number of entries, thus leading to the satisfaction of the law.

Law of parsimony would recommend unit-card system for printed cards. In this "a copy of the main entry card itself would be used as any specific added entry card, by merely inserting in the leading section the heading of the added entry" In case the card entry is handwritten or typed, then in each added entry, the information should be brief and notes are omitted in the added entries. This is called the multiple card system.

(v) Principle of Local Variation : This principle *(CCC,* pp. 65-70) recognizes a hierarchy of four codes—international catalogue code, national catalogue code, linguistic catalogue code, and local catalogue code. The principle prescribes that a catalogue code of higher level should mark out the factors to be left to the care of a code of next level. A national catalogue code should mark out the factors to be left to the care of each linguistic catalogue code in a multilingual country such as India. A national catalogue code or a linguistic catalogue code as the case may be should mark out the factors to be left to the care of the local catalogue codes in each individual library. The catalogue codes in each hierarchical line should be consistent with one another without any mutual contradiction and each lower link in each hierarchical line should be a supplement to all the upper links taken together.

(vi) Principle of Osmosis : This principle states that when a change in the catalogue code or in the scheme of classification becomes necessary in difference to the canon of context on and after a chosen data all the new accessions be catalogued and classified according to the new catalogue code and the new scheme of classification; just those of the old collections as are known to be in much use be recatalogued and "classified with an additional temporary staff, if necessary, during the first few months; the new accessions and the recatalogued and reclassified books be kept in a new collection and similarly their catalogue cards too kept in a new collection; the- rest of the old collection be kept as old collection and similarly their catalogue cards be kept as old collection. Readers' attention be invited by the Reference Librarian to the existence of the two collections; and if any book is taken out by a reader from the old collection, on its return by him, it be recatalogued and absorbed in the new collection and similarly with its catalogue cards.

Reclassification and recataloguing of the entire collection is not recommended because the cost of this is enormous. Further the entire collection is not going to be in active use, hence total reclassification and recataloguing would result to a criminal waste of library fund. The solution is Principle of Osmosis.

2. Five Laws of Library Science

These are specific normative principles which are applicable to any problem in the fields of library science, library practice, and library service. These laws are called as fundamental laws of library science. These five laws are :

First law	:	Books are for use
Second law	:	Every reader his/her book
Third law	:	Every book its reader
Fourth law	:	Save the time of the reader
fifth law	:	Library is a growing organism

The canons of cataloguing are the implications of the five laws. These canons are specific to the field of cataloguing. In case of a conflict between the canons, as appeal is made to the five laws of library science to resolve the conflict. Thus, five laws serve as a higher court. If there is a conflict between the canons of cataloguing and general normative principles, then a compromise can be achieved with the aid of the laws of library science.

3. Canons of Cataloguing

1. Canon of Ascertainability : This canon means that whatever information is given in the entries prepared by the cataloguer, that information should he specific.

According to C.C.C. "The choice and rendering of main entry and specific added entry and the heading and any other element in either entry should be determined by the information found in the title-page of the document and its overflow pages, in extreme cases information may be taken from the other pages of the work, but in no case from out of the work."

According to A.A.C.R., the entry is normally based on the description given on the title page of the document or instead, in some part of the document, but other descriptions that are clearly given should also be considered, such as title page, half title page, left-hand-side page of the title page etc.

In this manner, this canon is adopted in C.C.C. as well as in A.A.C.R.

Use of Canon in Catalogue Codes

This canon has been strictly adopted in C.C.C. It can be proven from the section number MD1 of the code that only that information, as entered in the book, can be used as the heading of the main entry. Considerable importance is also given to the cover page in the sections of chapter MD. In this manner, according to C.C.C., the information, which is to be entered in the entries is determined by the main page. This is the canon of ascertainability. However, there are certain exceptions to it. These are:

1. Summary note of the main entry, concluding note and related bibliographical note.
2. Leading section of the classified catalogue, directing section of

cross reference entry and subject analytical entry of the dictionary catalogue.

3. Heading and directing section of the class index entry of classified catalogue, specific subject entry and 'see also' entry of the dictionary catalogue.
4. Summary note for each book index entry, concluding note and headings taken from the related bibliographical note and directing section of the book index entry.
5. Directing section of the cross reference entry, except for the name entry.

This canon is adopted in A.A.C.R.-2. The information given in the preface, introduction or the main book is used for forming the main entry only when the information given on the title page is unclear or incomplete. Assistance is taken from external or other sources for forming the entry for unnamed documents.

According to A.A.C.R.-2, the entry of a document is normally based on the description available on the title page or instead, on the information available in some other part of the document. However, those descriptions that are expressed clearly should also be considered.

(ii) Canon of Prepotency : According to this canon, the potency (power or strength) to decide the position of an entry among the various entries in a catalogue should, if possible, be concentrated totally in the leading section. Within the leading section, as far as possible, it should be concentrated in the entry element. If total concentration in the leading section is not possible, the minimum possible potency should be allowed to overflow beyond it to later sections; and even this spillover should be distributed in the later sections in a decreasing sequence of intensity.

Thus, this canon is related with the placement of entries. The placement of entries in a catalogue is very important. The catalogues are arranged according to the potency. There should not be any mistake in the first word or number of potency, otherwise the entry becomes unnoticeable and it becomes very difficult to find it.

Use of this Canon in Catalogue Codes

According to C.C.C., "That group of words that has the more number of words than other word-groups from the elements expressed in multiwords and which we adopt as heading, should be formed as entry element."

In other words, those words or group of words should be adopted as heading, which include more words than other word-groups. Entry element should be adopted from the word-group that has more words. This will also increase the potency of placing an entry among the other entries will also increase. In this manner, only those words will be taken as entry element in various entries, whose probability will become less.

Names of bibliographical-series, monograph series, papers, publications etc. are normal words. These do not have any potency. Hence, it becomes necessary to add the name of the institution or administration with these to give them potency.

For example :

(i) American Chemical Society, Scientific monograph series

(ii) Geological Society of India, Special Paper

(iii) India, Education (Ministry of-), Publication

Main entry of the classified catalogue fully satisfies this canon. The call number is entered in the leading section in this catalogue. If the call number is not same for any two sub-classes, the complete potency of the entry gets collected in the leading section during its placement.

The class index entries of this catalogue fully satisfy this canon as well because no two class index entries are formed under the same heading. Thus, the complete potency gets collected in the leading section.

However, the cross reference entries of this catalogue are unsuccessful in satisfying this canon as only the class number is given in the leading section of these entries. Hence, there is very low potency in the leading section. The flow of potency gets transferred in the third section, where the call number of the book is given. This is also the case with the class reference index entries. The potency of placement flows to the title section in all the entries (main and added) of dictionary catalogue. Hence, this catalogue is unable to satisfy this canon.

(iii) Canon of Individualization : According to this canon, the name of any entity, which is used in an entry of the catalogue, should be fully individualized by the elements of individuality. This name of the entity may be of any type, whether it is the name of a person, geographical entity, corporate body, bibliographical series document, subject or the name of a language.

In other words, if the name of an entity (be it the name of a person, a geographical entity, a corporate body, a series, a document, a subject, or a language) used as a heading is not individualized, this will cause homonyms and the catalogue will become a mess. This will in turn mislead readers as well as librarians.

Use of this Canon in Catalogue Code

C.C.C.

Following rules of this catalogue code are associated with the canon of individualization:

1. Personal Name Rule Number JA-5 : The year of birth of the person should be added as the element of individualization after the name of the person.

The year of birth is used to individualise the homonyms that may be present in the names given in the headings of the entries. Such as: GUPTA (SK)(1917)

2. Geographical Boundaries: Rule Number JB-31: If two or more geographical units:

(i) Have same names,

(ii) Are located in different countries.

In such a case, the name of the country in which the geographical unit is located, shall be used as the element of individualization. Such as:

UXBRIDGE (Great Britain).

UXBRIDGE (United States of America).

Rule JB32, JB4 and JB41 are also associated with individualisation of geographical territories.

3. Corporate Body : Provision for individualization of corporate bodies has been made in rule JC4, JC5, JC65, JC71, JC72, JD72 and JE2.

Rule Number JC4: The name of the person who is chief executive of the administration will be given as the element of individualization in the form of second heading.

For example:

(i) PUNJAB, GOVERNOR (B D Pandey).

(ii) INDIA, PRESIDENT (K R Narayanan).

Rule Number JD2: If the name of the institution in itself is unable to individualise it following elements of individualisation shall be used to remove the homonyms:

1. Place, if it is local institution,
3. Country, if it is an institution of national level.
3. State, district etc. to whichever of these the institution belongs.
4. Head office if the elements given in above three (1 to 3) categories are not able to properly individualise the institution.

For example :

(i) LIBRARY (Public-) (Ajmer) (1993).

(ii) LIBRARY (Public-) (Ajmer) (1951).

Rule Number JE-2 : The name of the place where the conference was held, together with the year in which the conference was held, should be added with the name of the conference.

For example :

(i) LIBRARIAN (University conference) (Jaipur) (1964).

(ii) RELIGION (International Conference) (Varanasi) (1963).

Similar provision has been made in the rules, which can be used for individualizing series (JG7), document (JF8) and subject (K.K, KZD 496).

A.A.C.R.

Recommendations as follows have been made in rules of A.A.C.R.-2:

Personal names, Geographical names Names of Corporate bodies and Homonym Titles.

(iv) Canon of Sought Heading: This canon directs that "the decision whether an entry with a particular type of heading or with a particular choice for the heading, or with a particular rendering of the choice, or with a particular added entry arising out of it should be based on the answer to the question." Here reader or library staff is likely to look for a book under the particular type or choice or rendering of heading.

The application of this canon requires flair (natural aptitude) based on experience of reference service and book selection. The canon takes into consideration the approaches of users and will help in elimination of entries which are not going to be sought. Otherwise the number of possible entries can be very large.

The persons involved in preparing the catalogue codes must follow this canon so that it becomes easier for the cataloguers to form the catalogue. The direction for entering the authors' names by their surnames has been given in the catalogue codes due to the adoption of this canon only.

Such as, William Shakespeare is entered in the heading section of the entry as SHAKESPEARE (william).

The needs of the readers have been taken into consideration in this canon. At the same time, it also recommends removal of entries that are not needed for the readers. It is for this reason that the added entries are generally not formed by the names of the publishers or the place of publication etc. However, Dr. Ranganathan is not in the favour of forming the title entry according to this canon because in his opinion, the titles of the books are same and the readers are unable to remember them properly.

According to the canon of asceratinability no element, other than those given on the main page and its overflow pages, should be accepted as heading. On the other hand, according to the canon of sought heading the element, which should be taken in the form of the heading, that element is determined on the basis of the needs of the readers.

The cross reference index entries of the classified catalogue and the index entries of the dictionary catalogue affirm this canon. For example, many readers remember the pseudonym of the author, as this is the name printed on the book. However, it is also possible that some of the readers may also remember the real name also. Hence, it is necessary to create a reference in the real name. Such as:

DANNY (Frederic) and LEE (Manfred Bannington)

See

QUEEN (Ellery), *Pseud.*

Dr. Ranganathan has made use of this canon in his chain procedure also. As such, only the sought heading should be accepted as the class index entry as per this canon.

(v) Canon of Context : The canon prescribes that rules of a catalogue code should be formulated in the context of prevalent nature of cataloguing features of the book in relation to the mode of book production, prevalent nature of organization of libraries in regard to mode and quality of service, and existence of published bibliographies. Further, the rules should be revised from time to time, keeping step with the changing context.

Thus, the following points are taken into consideration while formulating the rules of catalogue code according to this canon:

1. *Mode of Book Production:* Dr. Ranganathan is not in the favour of giving too much description in the catalogue entries. According to him, there is no need to enter the year of publication, name of the publisher, number of pages, information related with illustrations etc. in the entry. On the other hand, directions are given in the A.A.C.R. -2 for including all these in the entry. Dr. Ranganathan also believes that the availability of books in the present age is not difficult because of the developments in the printing technology. The number of books in the earlier ages was very limited because the printing technology was not invented then. Hence, it was possible in that period to give a detailed description of the book in entries. This is not required in the present age.

2. *Organization of Libraries :* The information given in the catalogue entries also depend on the organization of the library. The organisation of the library is 'closed access' and 'open access'. today, open access system is more popular in present age where the reader is allowed to select and pick the book of his choice from the collection of the library without any restriction in this system. Hence, there is no need for giving too much information in the catalogue entries. In this manner, information should be entered in the catalogue entries with respect to the nature of the library organization.

3. *Published Bibliographies:* It is necessary to form subject analytical entries in the catalogue for fulfilling the needs of the researchers. The work of forming these entries is time consuming. However, many bibliographical lists are published in the present age by many international and national documentation centres etc. As such, there is no need to form subject analytical entries. Hence, there is no need to gives analytical descriptions if the bibliographical reference list is available in the library.

4. *Change in Context:* Changes are introduced from time to time in the books, libraries and the readers themselves. It is for this reason that the rules of catalogue code formulated once do not remain

practically useful over time. According to this canon, it is necessary to improvise the rules of catalogue code with the changes taking place from time to time.

(vi) Canon of Permanence: According to this Canon, "No element in an entry and the heading in particular should be subjected to change by the rules of a catalogue code except when the rules themselves are changed in response to the Canon of Context."

In this manner, the information given in the entry, especially the title should be permanent. However, the names of some persons, institutions and periodicals etc. change for some or the other reason. It becomes difficult to follow this canon in such circumstances.

Use of Canon

Cross reference index entries are given in the C.C.C. by using alternative names. According to its rule, whenever there is any change in the name of any person or corporate body, the headings in the entries of the related documents are not changed according to the new name. Instead, a cross reference entry is created to satisfy the readers.

However, the A.A.C.R. -2 does not follow this canon. According to this, a new heading should be given in the entry whenever there is any change in the name.

(vii) Canon of Currency : According to this canon, the terms used for expressing the subject in the class index entry of the classified catalogue and the subject entry of the dictionary catalogue should be popular terms.

The canon speaks about the use of the name of a subject. Current terminology indicating the specific subject should be used. A cross-reference be provided with the variant names.

For example, the term 'Political Economy' was used earlier for 'Economy', while 'Physical Science' was used for 'Physics'. It is proper to make necessary changes in the terms of the entries in case of these changed terms.

Canon of Currency v/s Canon of Permanence

Adhering to the canon of currency conflicts with the idea promoted in the canon of permanence. If we make a change in the entries then the canon of currency is satisfied but it is against the canon of permanency. Dr. Ranganathan has made a suggestion for overcoming the conflict between these two canons. According to him, the use of the canon of currency should be kept limited to the headings of class index entries and subject entries only while canon of permanence should be made for the name headings. Thus, the conflict can be overcome in this manner.

(viii) Canon of Consistence : The canon says that the rules of a catalogue code should provide for all the added entries of a document to be consistent with its main entry; and the entries of all documents should be consistent with one another in certain essentials such as choice, rendering, and style of writing of heading and other sections. It save time of the users and staff.

For the sake of consistency, is it essential that the main entry of documents should be of the same species. Besides, one species of entry should not be made to take the place of another. For the heading of one and the same entry, mixed species of main heading and subheading, such as author heading and subject subheadings, should not prescribed.

Use of Canon

This canon is completely adopted in C.C.C. This canon recommends that the name of the author should be given as the heading of the main entry. The only exception is when the author's name is absent.

However, this canon is ignored in the A.A.C.R. There are many such rules in the A.A.C.R. that flaunt this canon of consistence. Such as, the recommendation has been made to give the name of the subject heading as sub-heading in the main entries related with the documents written by author of administrative documents. Similarly, recommendation has been made to give a uniform title for religious books, unknown and title-less documents, collections of early period, peace treaties etc.

(ix) Canon of Recall-Value : This canon was propounded in 1969 by Ranganathan, which is the outcome of development research. The idea of recall value was mentioned by Ranganathan in his *Theory of Library Catalogue* but it is only later that it was raised to the status of a canon.

According to this canon, in case of multiword name of a person, an institution, conference or the multiword name of a division, a government, an institution or a conference, the word or group of words, which has the maximum recall-value will be made the first element in the heading section of an entry. This applies to the multiword title of a book, multiword name of a series and multiword name of a subject also, except for periodic publications. Dr. Ranganathan has defined this canon in the following manner–

1. In case of multiword name:

   (i) Person, (ii) Institution, (iii) Conference, and (iv) Administrative institution or conference.

2. In case of multiword title of document (except for the title of periodicals), the particular word or the group of words should be made the entry element, which has maximum recall-value.

The term 'recall value' refers to the quality of being called back to memory. Therefore, the canon directs that the entry element to be chosen should be the one having highest probability of being called back to memory by a majority of the readers. The canon is applicable for the rendering of names of entities in the heading of any entry.

The canon deals with rendering of pure names (full name remaining after removing of removable attachments) of persons, corporate bodies and titles of documents.

The need of the canon of recall-value is felt for the following reasons:

(i) Increase in number of names of a particular category that has to be memorized,

(ii) Growing trend of using mulitword names,

(iii) Increase in the categories of corporate bodies,

(iv) Increase in the number of corporate bibliographies,

(v) Increase in the number of homonyms or similar names to a large extent,

(vi) Increase in the number of alternative names, and

(vii) Tendency of changing names.

1. *Increase in the Number of Corporate Bodies* : It has become difficult for the readers to remember the names of the corporate bodies over the last many years as the number of these bodies has increased too much. In India itself, more than 30 such institutions come up every year. On the other hand, over 1700 such new institutions come into existence every year.

2. *Increase in the Categories of Corporate Bodies :* The categories of corporate bodies are also increasing with the increase in their number. It is for this reason that special type of approach is required with respect to these corporate bodies in order to give them individual identity. Dr. Ranganathan has divided the corporate body in the categories of government, institution and conference. However, a new 'Near sovereign body has evolved, such as the United Nations Organisation, Central Treaty Organisation etc.

3. *Homonyms of Corporate Bodies :* As many corporate bodies work in a single territory, their names are also found to be very similar. The readers find it difficult to obtain the document of their desired corporate body in such situation. It is worth noting that over 100 corporate bodies are operating in the world, just in the field of international matters.

4. *Multiword Names :* Due to the increasing number of corporate bodies, their names are also becoming multiword so as to give them individual identity. These names are made unique i.e., individualized by combining the correct subject, geographical area, nature of the corporate body etc.

5. *Alternative Names :* The names of many corporate bodies are well known by their abbreviations, such as FID, ILO etc. Hence this canon is required to fulfil the needs of this type.

Use of Canon

1. *Personal Names :* The western and the westernized family names i.e., the last word is taken as the entry element in catalogue code. The quality of recall value remains inherent in these elements.

For example:

(i) TALESARA (Dilip Kumar)

(ii) SHARMA (DK)

(iii) RUSSEL (Bertrand)

The quality of recall value is present in the given names in case of the South Indian names. Hence these names are used as entry elements.

For example:

(i) RADHAKRISHNAN (Sarvepalli)

(ii) RANGANATHAN (Shiyali Ramamrita)

2. *Corporate Names :* Dr. Ranganathan has divided corporate names in three categories:

(a) Government,

(b) Institution, and

(c) Conference.

(a) *Government*

(i) Administrative Department of Government : The administrative department of the government is rendered on the basis of the canon of recall value. According to rule number JC6, the word or the group of words that represents the scope of work of the administrative department of the government is taken as the entry element while rendering it.

For example:

INDIA, FINANCE (Ministry of-)

GREAT BRITAIN, EDUCATION (Ministry of-)

PUNJAB, AGRICULTURE (Department of-)

(ii) Temporary Organ of Government : Some time the government forms commission, committee etc. for fixed time duration from time to time to do a specific work. The recommendations of such commission and committee should be catalogued according to the rule number JC7 for the temporary organ of government while its entry elements should be rendered according to the rule number JC16 and its subsections, which is related with the administrative department.

For example:

(i) RAJASTHAN, PAY (Commission) (1958) (Chairman : JS Ranawat).

(ii) INDIA, FINANCE (Commission) (1951) (Chairman : KC Neogy).

(b) *Institution*

Readers are not able to remember the multiword names of the institutions and conferences in the exact order of the words that are used in these names. Hence, that word or group of words in these names must be decided, which have the maximum quality of recall value. It has been generally felt that the chances of recalling the word or group of words in the names of some corporate body are more for a reader when the reader is generally familiar with these word/s or when he is already in touch with these words.

According to rule number JD17, the words of the entry element related with the name of an institution that are accepted as the heading, must represent singularity. Thus, the words or the group of words used as the heading should be combined together as a singular entry element in a manner by which it represents a special characteristic about the subject of the institution or its scope of work. For example:

Indian Institute of *SCIENCE*.

American *LIBRARY* Association.

International Congress of *PHYSICISTS*.

In above corporate bodies, the words 'SCIENCE', 'LIBRARY' and 'PHYSICISTS' have more chances of being recalled by the readers. Hence these will be catalogued in the following manner: SCIENCE (Indian Institute of-). LIBRARY (American - Association). PHYSICISTS (International Congress of-).. According to rule number JD175, rule JD17 will not be applicable to university, college, school, laboratory, library, museum and any other such traditional institution and the order of the entry element will be 'university' etc. respectively.

For example:

(i) Yale University-UNIVERSITY (Yale-)

(ii) University of Delhi - UNIVERSITY (of Delhi).

(c) Conference

According to the rule number JE17, that word or group of words will be the entry element while rendering the heading of the name of a conference, which is indicative of the subject of the conference or its some other specific characteristic.

For example:

(i) MANAGEMENT SCIENCE (International Conference on-) (London) (1959).

(ii) LIBRARY (All India - Conference) (Varanasi) (1938).

(iii) FUEL (Conference) (London) (1928).

There are certain conferences that do not have any specific name and these are generally a group of some persons, which discusses the problems of its members, such as politicians, lawyers, workers of cloth mills etc.

According to the rule number JE4, if there is no specific name of a conference and it is not permanent in nature, then it should be given the name according to the group of persons who form it, such as citizens, Indian residents, women, traders, musicians etc. In this manner, the word or group of words that represent the class of the persons in the conference will be made the entry element.

For example:

(i) LIBRARIAN (University-s Conference) (Jaipur) (1964).

(ii) INDIAN RESIDENTS (Ceylon) (1978).

(iii) ORIENTALISTS (Conference of-) (Simla) (1933).

In this manner, the canon of recall value is very important. Dr. Ranganathan has stated that this canon is revolutionary, but this canon is contrary to the basic philosophy of Dr. Ranganathan himself. Ranganathan is not in the favour of giving liberty to the cataloguer. According to him, the rule of catalogue code should be such that it gives the same result when used by any person in any situation. Moreover, the rules of the catalogue code must be strictly followed.

4. Principles to assist Working

These principles include :

(i) Principle of Unity of Idea : A catalogue code should deal with the following elements:

1. Definition of cataloguing terms;
2. Interpretation of cataloguing terms in different contexts;
3. Choice of information for a section of an entry;
4. Rendering of it; and
5. Style of recording it.

The principle of unity of idea prescribes, "no rule in a catalogue code should deal with more than one of the elements mentioned above;, in respect of any problem." This principle has been dealt with in detail in the context of cataloguing by Bhattacharyya. However, it has not been mentioned in CCC as well as Ranganathan's *Cataloguing Practice.* Principle of unity of idea is a basic principle which should guide the work of formulation of rules in a code. The principle should also be used in the systematic organization of rules. In other words, rules should be organized into determination of authorship, rendering and recording (place of writing and style of writing) based on unity of idea.

(ii) Principle of Probability : The words forming part of a name of a person can be categorized into two groups. One group is more numerous than the other. In a modern Western name, a group consisting of family names is more numerous than the group of given names. However, reverse is the case for South Indian names. Thus, "making the word belonging to the more numerous group the entry word, increases the probability for satisfying the canon of prepotence." In other words, Principle of Probability indicates that a word belonging to the more numerous group if used as entry element, has a greater probability for satisfying the canon of prepotence. Thus, principle of probability taken along with canon of prepotence can be helpful in choosing the entry element for the heading of an entry. Principle of probability was introduced by Ranganathan in 1969 in one of his article. However, later literature does not indicate its application.

Relationship of Canon of Recall Value with Other Canons

1. Relation with Canon of Ascertainability : According to the canon of ascertainability, only that information should be entered in the heading section of the entries, which is given on the title page and the overflow pages of the document. This is the point from which scope of the canon of recall value begins, which states that those word or word-group should be selected as entry element that has maximum recall value. Hence, towards this end, the publisher should print that part of the author's name in bold or in thick letters by which the author wishes to be popularly known.

2. Relation with Canon of Prepotence : Both canons are associated with multiword names. Canon of prepotence states that such word should be made entry element by which maximum potency is gathered in the leading section and by which minimum potency is allowed to flow in subsequent sections. Further, this overflow of potency in subsequent sections should also be according to the principle of reducing sequence of potency. Although, the canon of potency and the canon of recall value appear to be similar but there are some differences in these. The canon of recall value stresses the use of that word or word-group as entry element, which has recall value. On the other hand, the canon of prepotence stresses the use of that word or word-group as entry element, which has maximum potency. Sometimes there can be a difference in these, such as in Association of Public Libraries. Here, *Public Library* will be accepted as the entry element according to the canon of prepotence and *Library* will be taken as the entry element according to the canon of recall value. Whenever there is such a contradiction in these two canons, preference should be given to the canon of recall value.

The differences in the two Canons are :

1. Canon of prepotence is mainly associated with the arrangement of entries while the canon of recall value is associated with the adoption of such an entry element in the heading section of the entry in which there is maximum recall value.
2. The canon of prepotence is satisfied by using the class number of the leading sections of C.C.C., while the recall value is related with the alphabetical value of the catalogue.

3. Relation with Canon of Individualization : Main objective of this canon is to remove the similarity and resemblance in the headings, no matter whether this heading is the name of a person, geographical territory, corporate body, bibliographical series, document or language. On the other hand, the scope of the canon of recall value is related with multiword names of persons or corporate bodies. The canon of individualization does not make any difference in the entries on the basis of words. On the other hand, canon of recall value is applicable to the multiword headings. The scope of the canon of recall value ends as soon as the word with maximum recall value is selected. While the canon of individualization is used for differentiating an element from other elements, such as in All India Adult Education Board and National Council of Adult Education, 'Adult Education' is the element of recall value. Hence, other words are minor terms that are written as the element of individualization.

4. Relation with Canon of Context : According to the canon of context, the rules of a catalogue code should be formed in the following context:

1. Popular nature of the special features of cataloguing of books, which should be related with the method of book publication.
2. Nature of the organization of libraries, which is popular in relation to the methods of library service, and
3. Existence of published bibliographical lists; and improvization of the rules in view of the changes in context, and amendment in the rules from time to time in tune with the changes in context.

Practically, the canon of recall value is a result of above changes.

5. Relation with Canon of Sought Heading : Canon of sought heading, canon of prepotence and the canon of recall value appear to be the members of the same family. According to the canon of sought heading, whether a specific added entry should be formed or not from a sought heading or from a specific derivation of that heading or from a specific rendering of that heading, which arises from it, depends on the answer to this question whether there is any possibility for the readers or the employees of the library to find a particular book by that specific heading or a specific derivation of that heading or form that specific rendering or under that specific entry.

In this manner, both canons give due importance to the needs of the readers from the catalogue. The objective of both canons is to provide the information desired by the readers in a quick, clear and easy manner. Fulfillment of both canons depends on the intelligence and general knowledge of the cataloguer. The experience of the cataloguer and his daily contact with the readers enable him to satisfy the needs, demands and the problems of the readers.

Although these two canons are similar, still there is a difference in the adaptation of these canons. The canon of recall value is much more mechanical than the canon of sought heading. This is because, although the cataloguers do not find any problem while working with the multiword names of the author but still they have to face peculiar problem at times. For example, Sheikh is the word with maximum recall value in Sheikh Mohammed Abdullah, while the person wants to be popularly known by the name of Abdullah. Hence, the cataloguer is forced to ignore the canon of recall value in such situations.

Effect of Canon of Recall Value on Library Catalogue

The detailed rules pertaining to the rendering of canon of recall value rules are broadly given in Cataloguing Practice. When this canon is implemented, it will create many other effects. The entries of the catalogue will also have to be changed when this canon is brought into practice. The principle of osmosis must be followed while practising this canon.

Possible Problems in Implementation : There are a few administrative problems in implementing this canon. These are:

1. It will add extra mental burden on the cataloguers because they

will have to find such words or word-groups that posses maximum recall value.

2. Some difference of opinion can also arise amongst the cataloguers in determination of the recall value of the words.
3. It is not necessary that the cataloguer and the readers have same opinion on the recall value of the word or group of words.

Suggestions : The following are some suggestions that may be used for overcoming the problems associated with the implementation of the canon of recall value:

1. The problems arising in cost decisions can be reduced to some extent. For example, directive principles can be formed for the cataloguers and such dictionaries can be compiled in which the extent of recall value of words is expressed.
2. Many of the libraries are small enough. As such, a duplicate sequence of the corporate authors can be created according to the most recent code. This action will offer the chance to carry out a comparative study of the new and the old methods of rendering the names of the corporate bodies. This type of research work can be carried out some time before the new code is brought into practice. A similar experiment was conducted by the School of International Studies, New Delhi, which showed that majority of the readers welcome the new method of rendering that is based on the recall value.

Conclusion : On the one hand Dr. Ranganathan has acclaimed this canon as revolutionary in the field of cataloguing, but this canon is in contrast with his own main ideology. Ranganathan is not in favour of giving liberty to the cataloguer. According to him, the rules of catalogue code should be such that these give same result when these are used anywhere by anyone. Moreover, the rules of the catalogue code should also be strictly adhered to. Its status should be like a 'legal' code. According to him, as far as possible, no decision should be left at the discretion of the cataloguer. This all is necessary in scientific methodology.

4
Kinds of Entries

Q. : Enlist the entries you will find in a catalogue according the C.C.C. Describe the role of each of these entries.

or

State the various kinds of entries according to C.C.C. and A.A.C.R.2. Discuss the different sections of main entry.

or

Enumerate and define the various kinds of entries that are prepared in a classified catalogue code along with their objectives.

or

Describe the role of each entry you will find in a dictionary catalogue.

or

What are the various parts of a main entry according to CCC? Discuss with examples.

Ans. Library catalogue is a record of the reading material available in a library which is formed to fulfil the needs of the readers. A number of 'Unit Records' are included in it. These unit records are called entries. Each entry is formed to fulfil a specific purpose. The usefulness and efficiency of a catalogue depends on the usefulness and efficiency of these entries only.

When a catalogue is prepared for a library collection, we have to follow a set of principles and rules to prepare the entries and to arrange and file them. Sets of rules that prescribe the various types of entries, their format and contents are known as catalogue codes.

The rules prescribed and followed for cataloguing documents in the library of the Popes (known as Papal Library) in the Vatican City of Italy is called "Bibliotheca Apostelica Vaticana". It is popularly known as Vatican Code. Rules prepared by Panizzi for cataloguing books of the British Museum (now called the British Library) and published in 1841 under the title "*Rules for Compiling the Catalogues in the Department of Printed Books*" are known as *British Museum Code.*

Cutter's *Rules for a Dictionary Catalogue,* which was in its fourth edition at the time of his death in 1903, was the first complete code for a Dictionary Catalogue. The Library of Congress was publishing its *LC Rules on Printed Cards* from 1903 to 1930s.

The Library Association of United Kingdom and the American Library Association in their joint efforts were publishing Rules for Cataloguing from time to time, leaving scope for some minor deviations in the two countries. The *Anglo-American Code* (1908) is also known as *Joint-Code. The American Library Association Rules* (1949) abbreviated as *ALA Rules,* 1949; the *Anglo-American Cataloguing Rules,* 1967 known as AACR-I, and the present AACR-2 are the results of such joint efforts.

Revision of AACR-1 was taken up in 1974 by a joint committee of representatives of the national libraries and national library associations of Canada, United Kingdom and United States of America. They wanted to standardize and reconcile the practices of those countries. Further, they wanted a wider international base for AACR so that other countries may also follow the Code. The revised Code known now as AACR-2 was published in 1978. But major national libraries had not followed it till January 1981. Revised edition of AACR-2 was published in 1988. In our country libraries were adopting either the British or the American practices. With the advent of AACR-2, many libraries preferred switching over to that Code Ranganathan published as Classified Catalogue Code *(CCC)* in 1934. The Code went through five editions during his lifetime. In present days, mainly two kinds of library catalogues are prepared. These are:

1. Classified Catalogue, and
2. Dictionary Catalogue.

Both of these types of catalogues are formed by different entries.

ENTRIES IN A CLASSIFIED CATALOGUE

In Ranganathan's Classified Catalogue we find the following entries.

1. Main Entry
2. Added Entries

(i) Cross Reference Entries.

(ii) Class Index Entries

(iii) Book Index Entries

(iv) Series Index Entries

(v) Cross Reference Index Entries

First two of the above are the entries with call or class numbers in their leading section. The other entries are word entries with alphabetical words in the heading section. Ranganathan's Classified Catalogue, thus basically, consists of two parts. They are known as Classified Part comprising of Main and Cross Reference Entries and Alphabetical Part consisting of the alphabetical index entries, namely, Class Index, Book Index and Cross Reference Index Entries.

Except main entry, all other entries are generally called as added entries.

(1) Main Entry : The main entry in the classified catalogue is formed from the call number of the book and it is arranged in the classified part of the catalogue according to class index. Call number is formed by the combination of three numbers;

(i) Class Number,

(ii) Book Number, and

(iii) Collection Number.

The class number represents the specific subject of the book. Hence these entries satisfy the subject-related needs of the readers. Since these entries are arranged according to the class index, all the reading material of the specific subject desired by the readers is presented at one time in a logical manner in the assisting index.

Different Sections of the Main Entry

Following six sections are included in the main entry of classified catalogue.

1. Leading Section,
2. Heading Section,
3. Title Section,
4. Note Section,
5. Accession Number Section, and
6. Tracing Section.

The first five sections of the above six are sequentially written on the front side of the entry-card but the sixth section is written on the back side of the card. These sections can be further understood by the figures given here:

Main Entry

(Front Portion)

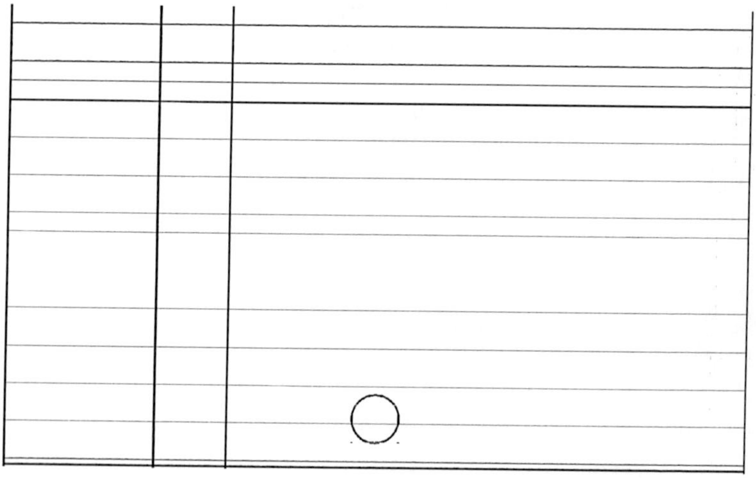

Main Entry

(Back Portion)

Tracing Section

Cross Reference Entry	Class Index Entries Book Index Entries Cross Reference Index Entries

1. Leading Section : This is the first section of the main entry. The call number, which is written on the inner page by the classifier, is copied in this section of the classified catalogue by the cataloguer. The call number (class number + book number + collection number) is written from the first vertical on the leading line and then the book number is written after leaving a space of two alphabets. If the collection number is also present then it is written above the book number. The call number is always written with a pencil. No 'full-stop' is marked after entering this information.

The information given in this section fulfils the subject-related needs of the reader and the class index entries are also derived from this section itself. This section also proves to be helpful for the readers in searching the books in shelves.

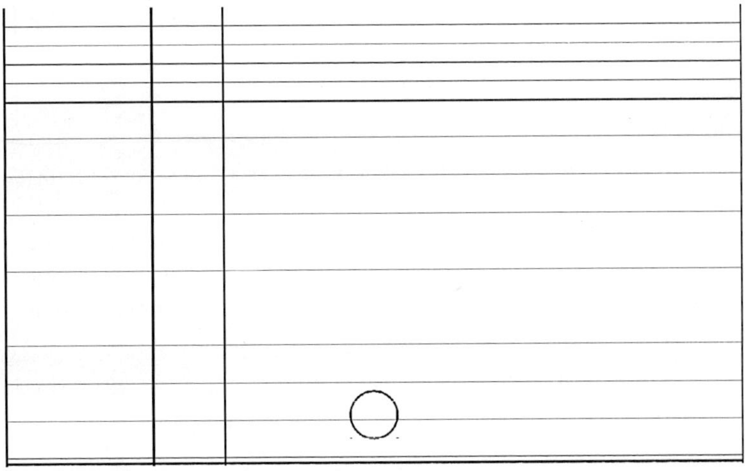

2. Heading Section : This is the second section of the entry. The information about the author is generally written in this. However, if the author is not present then the information about the collaborator or the title of the book is entered in this section according to the code of rules. The information is entered from the second vertical, but if it becomes necessary, then subsequent lines are started from the first vertical.

This section is considered to be the most important section of cataloguing from technical point of view. Most of the rules in all codes of cataloguing are related to this section. The information given in this section fulfils the author-related desires of the reader. In case when the call number is same for many entries, then these are arranged according to the information in this section only. At the same time, the author index entry is also derived from the information given in this section only.

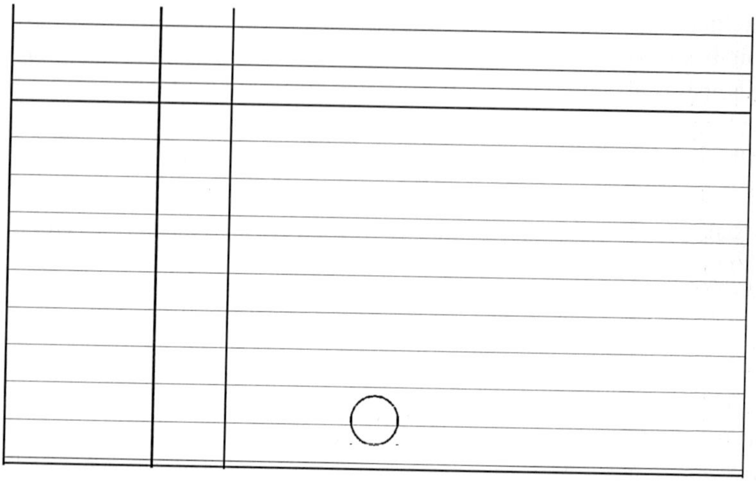

3. Title Section : The title section begins at the second vertical from the line next to the line at which the heading section ends. Subsequent lines begin from the first vertical. Title, sub-title, short title etc. of the book, its edition, information about the collaborator if it has not been already given in the heading section are entered in this section. The information is entered in following order.

- Title, sub-title or short title description,
- Description of edition (other than the first edition),
- Description of collaborator.

Articles such as 'a', 'an', 'the' or other such words written before the main title of the book are ignored before entering information in this section.

This section is important and for this reason it is also called the 'body' of the entry. Since this section contains the description of the book, the title and collaborator index entries are formed from it only.

4. Note Section : The note section begins at the second vertical from the line next to the line at which the title section ends. Subsequent lines begin from the first vertical. These notes are of many kinds and these provide additional information about the book. For this reason it is considered useful to enter the information of these in the entry.

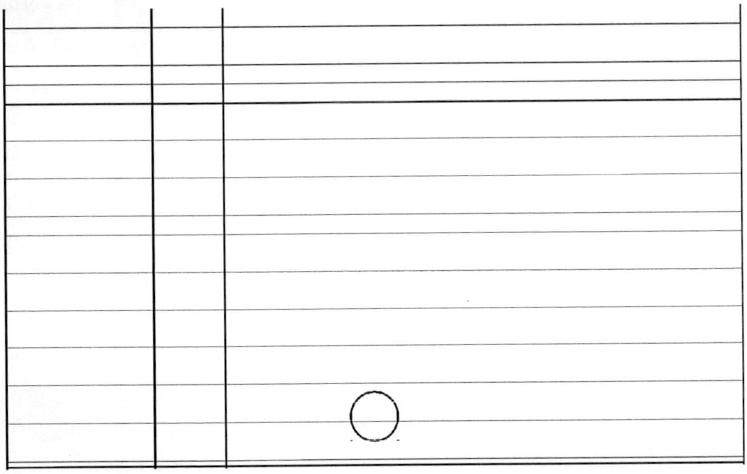

These notes may be of the following kinds:

(i) Series Note,

(ii) Pseudo Series Note,

(iii) Thesis Series Note,

(iv) Extract Note,

(v) Extraction Note, and

(vi) Change of the Title Note etc.

The most commonly used note of the above is the series note. The series note is further divided in following parts:

(a) Name of the Series,

(b) Name of the Series Editor and

(c) Volume Number of the Series

These notes which are entered in the main entry result in the formation of many added entries that are used for satisfying various demands of the readers.

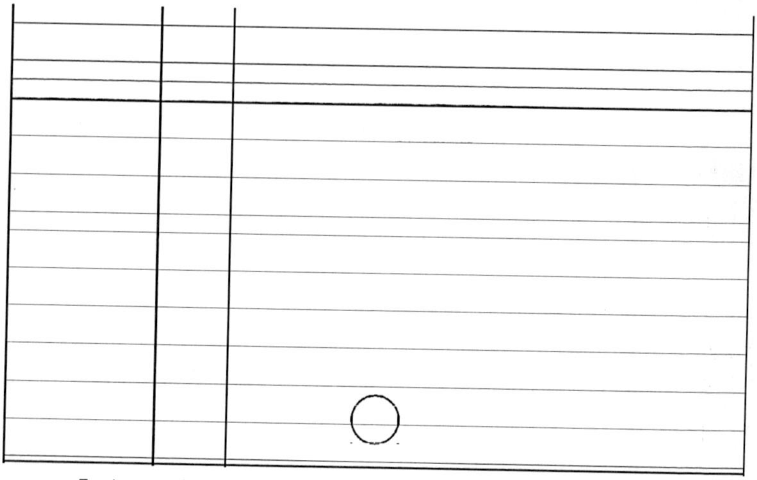

5. Accession Number Section : This section starts at the last line of the card from the first vertical. The accession number of the book is entered in this section. "Full-stops" i.e., period is not marked after entering the information. It is this section that forms the co-relation between the book and the card.

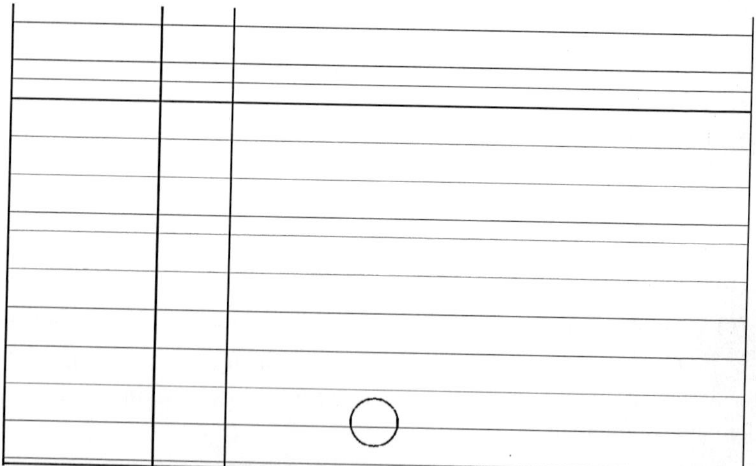

6. Tracing Section : This is the last section of the main entry. The titles of all the additional entries that are formed for a book are marked in this section as indication. The information of this section is entered on the back side of the main entry card as this information is not for use by the readers, this gives the knowledge to the employees of the library about the total number of additional entries for a particular book that have been arranged in the catalogue. However, if the complete information cannot be entered in the back section then this information can be entered on the front part of a continued card. The back side of the card is considered to be divided in two parts i.e. the left half and the right half, for the purpose of entering information. Information of the cross reference entries is made in the left part while the right half is further assumed to be divided in three parts and information of the following entries is entered in these:

- Class Index Entry,
- Book Index Entry, and
- Class Reference Index Entry.

For Example:

Cross reference entry	Classified catalogue code with additional rules for dictionary catalogue code. Cataloguing, Library Science. Library Science. Ranganathan (Shiyali Ramamrita (1892-1972) Neelameghan (A) (1927), Assist. Sarda Ranganathan Endowment for Library Science.

(2) Added Entries

Main entry is used for satisfying most of the needs of the readers but still the needs of the readers may be different. Hence, added entries are formed to satisfy such different needs of the readers. These entries are derived from the main entry itself. Thus, those extra entries that are formed other than the main entry for satisfying the needs of the readers and which are derived from the main entry itself, are called additional entries. These may specific or general, numeric or alphabetic entries.

The following kinds of added entries are formed in a classified catalogue:

(i) Cross Reference Entry,

(ii) Class Index Entry,

(iii) Book Index Entry,

(iv) Series Index Entry, and

(v) Cross Reference Index Entry.

(i) Cross Reference Entry : "A Cross Reference Entry enters a document under one or other of the classes other the then the dominant focus or class". It indicates towards the subject described in the main book from the class number of a section of the book. Being a numeric entry, it is arranged in the classified section of the classified catalogue. These entries satisfy the subject-related needs of the readers. Main entries are related to the specific subject of the whole book while these entries are related to the specific subject of the individual sections of the books.

The number of entries that should be formed for a book in the library depends on the nature of the library:

A cross reference entry is divided in following sections:

1. Leading Section,
2. Second Section,
3. Locus Section,
4. Call Number Section,
5. Heading of the main entry of the book, and
6. Title of the book and source of procuring it.

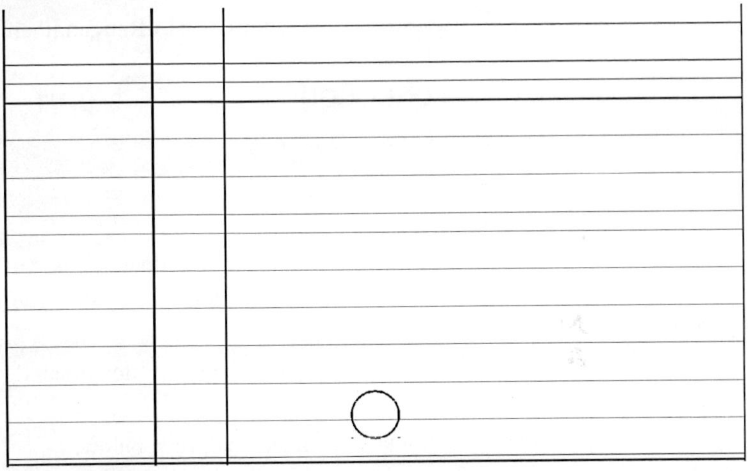

(ii) Class Index Entry : The particular general alphabetic entry of the classified catalogue, which indicates towards the class number from the name of the class, is called class index entry. This is general type of entry. Main entries and the cross reference entries are formed to satisfy the subject-related needs of the readers, but the specific subject of the book in these is in the form of the class number and it cannot be understood by the readers. Hence, it is necessary to form certain entries that can be easily understood by the readers to satisfy their subject-related needs. These entries are formed by entering the specific subjects of the books in natural language in order to satisfy the subject-related needs of the readers.

The headings for these entries are formed by the chain-process of forming headings, which was developed by *Dr. S.R. Ranganathan.*

The number of these entries depends on the class number of the book. Since the class index entry can be used for all the books that have the same class number, these are formed only once. Although, one class index entry for at least one book must be formed. These entries serve as an index of the classified catalogue.

The following three sections are included in the class index entry:

1. Leading Section,
2. Directing Section, and
3. Index Number Section.

For example, for the Classified Catalogue Code by Ranganathan Class Index Entries are provided as:

CLASSIFIED CATALOGUE CODE	2:55 N3
CLASSIFIED CATALOGUE	2:55
CATALOGUE, LIBRARY SCIENCE	2:5
LIBRARY SCIENCE	2

All Class Index Entries carry the statement "For documents* in this Class and its Sub-divisions, see the Classified Part of the catalogue under the Class Number".

(* Earlier the word 'books' was used but the word 'documents' is relevant now).

An example for one of the above subjects is given below.

Class Index Entry

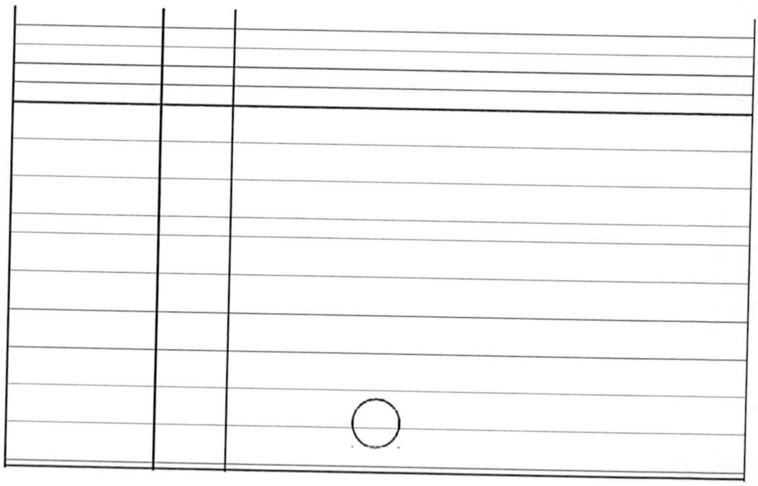

Here, Library science is written in Leading section; Directing section is represented by phrase For documents ... Class number and 2 is the Index number.

Similar entries are given for the other subjects stated above. These entries are General Added Entries and they are filed in the Alphabetical Part of the Classified Catalogue. It may be noticed that they are similar to the subject Added Entries in the Dictionary Catalogue. In the Dictionary Catalogue, details of document that is being catalogued are given in the entry, but a Class Index Entry indicates the Class number under which documents on a particular subject are classed.

(iii) Book Index Entry: The specific assisting alphabetic entry of the classified catalogue is called book index entry. It is a specific alphabetic entry in the catalogue. These entries are formed with an objective of providing guidance to the reader in locating the book of his choice, provided he has correct and clear knowledge about the author or co author, collaborator, title or the series etc. Generally an entry is known by the same name as the particular need of the reader which it fulfils. This name is entered in the leading section of the entry. These entries can be of the following types:

1. Author Index Entry,
2. Joint Author Index Entry,
3. Commentator Index Entry,
4. Editor Index Entry,
5. Illustrator Index Entry,
6. Reviser Index Entry,
7. Translator Index Entry,
8. Assistant Index Entry,
9. Compiler Index Entry,
10. Title Index Entry, and
11. Series Index Entry.

Although following four sections are included in a book index entry, but only first three sections are normally used for the general books:

1. Leading Section,
2. Second Section,
3. Index Number Section, and
4. Note Section.

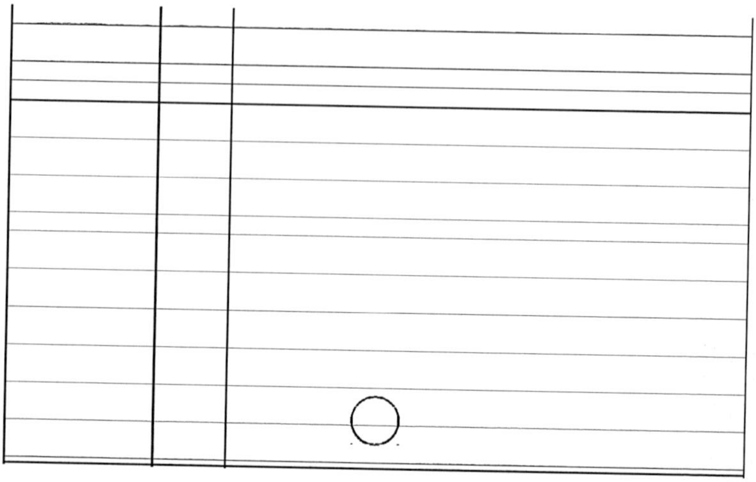

(iv) Series Index Entry : The objective of forming series index entry is to provide assistance to those readers who try to find the books on the basis of the name of the series. Thus, if some reader finds that some book of a particular series is interesting then he wants to read other books of the same series also. Information of all the books belonging to a specific series in the library is made available at a one place by formation of the series index entries. As a result, the information about which books of some specific series are available in the library, is quickly given to the readers.

Following three sections are included in this entry:

1. *Leading Section* : The original name of the series is entered from the first vertical in capital letters at the leading line in this section.
2. *Second Section* : The volume number of the series or, in absence of the volume number, the year of publication is entered in this section. This number begins at the first vertical. Thereafter, the personal author's name as used in the heading of main entry or two personal co-authors; names and complete name of the collaborator are entered. This information begins from the second vertical and the abbreviated title and short description of the edition is entered after marking a':' (colon).
3. *Index Number Section* : The call number of the book is entered on the right side of the entry in this section. Such as:

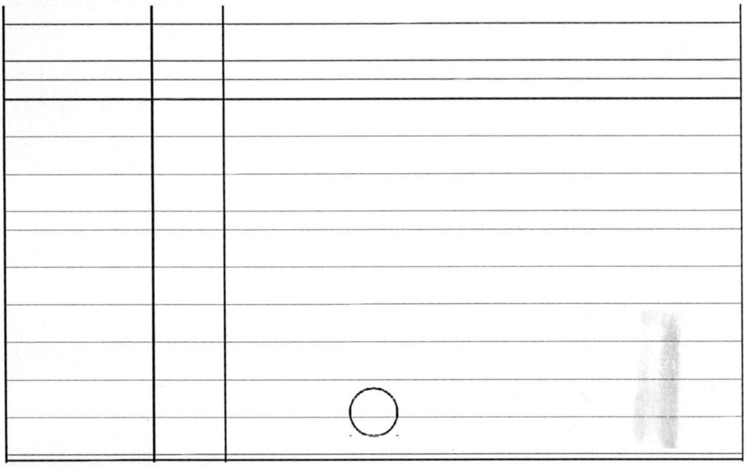

(v) Cross Reference Index Entry : The cross reference entry is defined as follows in the Classified Catalogue Code:

"General added entry referring from one word or set of words to another synonymous word or set of words."

This is a general entry. Since this entry begins with words, it is placed in the alphabetic part of the classified catalogue. It is not the object of this entry to provide actual information about the books to the reader, but the object of this entry is to direct the attention of the reader to some synonymous set of words or title of similar subject matter for which the reader is searching for on the basis of a word or a set of words. In this manner, the entry guides the reader to the subject matter he is looking for.

As this entry belongs to the category of general entries, a single entry proves to be useful for many books. This is the reason for which the call number, title, author's name or the accession number etc. are not mentioned in it. The directions given in these entries do not provide any specific information, but these direct the readers to the place from where they can receive the information they are looking for. Formation of these entries reduces the number of added entries.

There are many kinds of cross reference index entries; of which following five kinds are the main:

1. Alternative Name Entry,

2. Variant form of Word Entry,
3. Pseudonym-Real-Name Entry,
4. Editor of Series Entry, and
5. Genetic Name Entry.

The success of the catalogue largely depends on these entries. If these entries are not made in a library then many readers will not be able to get the reading material of their choice even when it is available in the library. Moreover, a lot of time would be wasted in searching for the desired books in absence of these entries.

Following three sections are included in a cross reference entry:

1. Leading Section,
2. Directing Section, and
3. Reference to Heading.

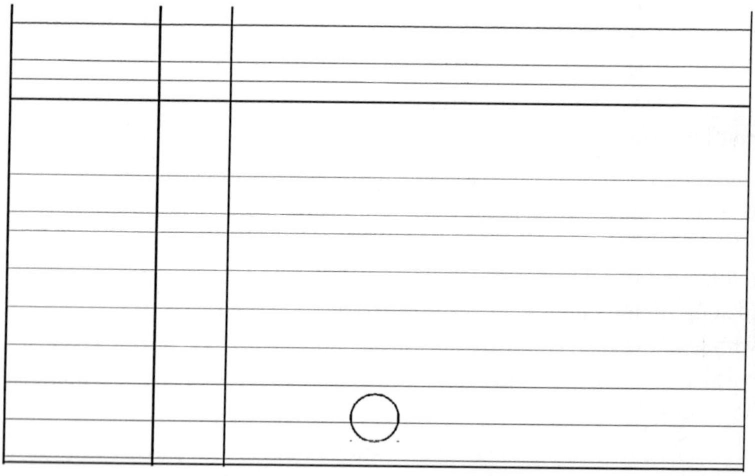

ENTRIES IN A DICTIONARY CATALOGUE

Dictionary catalogue is that catalogue in which all the entries are alphabetic and all these are arranged in a single alphabetical order, just as in a dictionary. In this manner, it is a single volume catalogue.

In a Dictionary Catalogue we normally provide.

1. Main Entries (under the author, collaborator or title; if the author is not known authorship is diffused, or if the item is not produced under editorial direction that item will be entered under the heading for the title of the book).

2. Collaborator Added Entries (for persons or institutions or organizations or societies, etc., associated with the creation of the work).
3. Subject Added Entries (for the subject or subjects dealt with the document).
4. Title Added Entries (for title of the work and also for alternate title if there is one). Sometimes added entry is also provided for a sub-title of the work if there is a sub-title and it is so distinct that an added entry for it may be helpful.
5. Cross Reference Entries.

The entries except the main entry, are generally known as added entries.

Main Entry

The main entry in this catalogue is generally formed on the basis of the author's name. But in the absence of the author's name, main entry is formed on the basis of the collaborator or title or the subject. Hence, this entry is helpful in finding the books to those readers who have correct information about the author, collaborator or the title. This entry provides maximum information about the books to the readers.

Following sections are included in the main entry of the dictionary catalogue:

1. Heading Section,
2. Title Section,
3. Note Section,
4. Index Number Section,
5. Accession Number Section, and
6. Tracing Section.

Five of the above six sections are entered in sequence on the front side of the card while the sixth section is entered on the back side (verso) of the card.

Front Portion of Main Entry

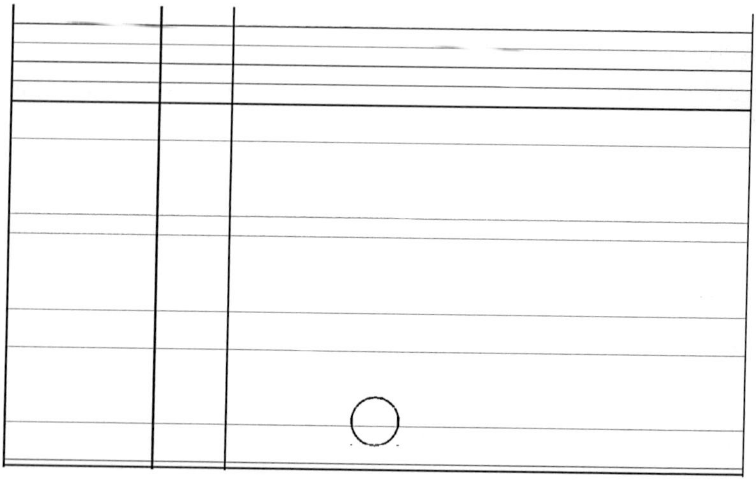

Back Portion of Main Entry

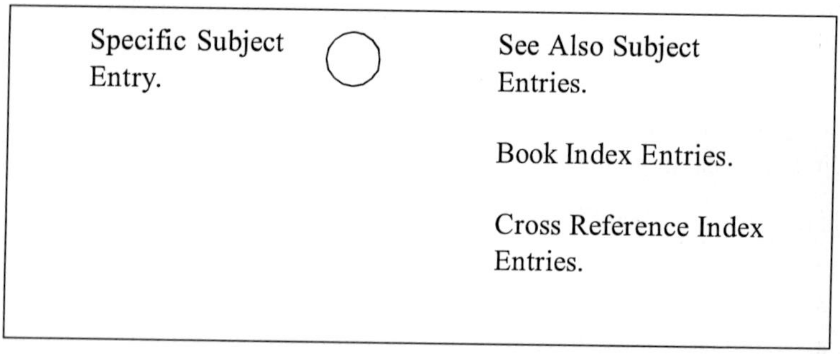

1. Heading Section : This is the first section of the dictionary catalogue. Generally the author's personal name or the pseudonym is entered at the leading line from the first vertical and the subsequent lines are also entered from the first vertical. The sequence of entering the author's name is as follows:

Family name (Personal name) (Year of birth and death)

RANGANATHAN (Shiyali Ramamrita) (1892-1972).

This section fulfils author-related need of the readers.

2. Title Section : Title of the book, its sub-title, description of the edition and collaborators are entered in this section. This section begins at the second vertical from the line next to the line at which the heading section ends. Subsequent lines begin at the first vertical. Information is entered in this section in the following sequence:

Title : Sub-title. Description of edition. Description of collaborator e.g.,

Classified Catalogue Code with additional rules for dictionary catalogue code. Ed5. Assisted by A Neelameghan.

3. Note Section : Note section begins at the line next to the line at which the title section ends from the second vertical and the subsequent lines begin at the first vertical. Notes may be of many types. These are used for providing additional information about the books. It is for this reason that information of these notes be also included in the entry. Notes are of mainly six types. But the series note is the most commonly used. There are three sections of the series note, which are entered in the following sequence respectively:

(Name of the series, name of the series editor, volume number of the series or year of publication), e.g.,

(Sarda Ranganathan Endowment for Library Science. Ed. by A Neelameghan. 1964).

Information of the note is entered in circular brackets '( )'.

4. Index Number Section : If space is available in the same line where the note section ends, then entry is made in this line with pencil. Otherwise, entry is made in the next line on the right side of the card. The class number is entered first in this section. Next, the book number is entered after leaving space of two digits in the following manner:

2 :55N3   qN64

5. Accession Number Section : This section begins at the last line of the card from the first vertical. Accession number of the book is entered in this section.

6. Tracing Section : This is the last section of the main entry. Headings of all added entries formed for a book are entered as indication in this section. This information is entered on the back of the card. It is assumed that the back portion of the card is divided in two parts. The headings of the specific subject and subject analyticals are entered in the left part while the right half of the card is further assumed to be divided in three parts from top to bottom. The headings of the see this also subject entries, book index entries and the cross reference index entries are entered in the top, middle and the bottom portions respectively.

Information of all the books and their editions/translations that are written by the same author or collaborator or have the same title, is made available in one place in the catalogue by the main entry.

The last section of the main entry, i.e., the tracing section, gives information about the added entries. This information is used to remove all the cards of such books from the catalogue that are damaged, lost or withdrawn from the library for some reason.

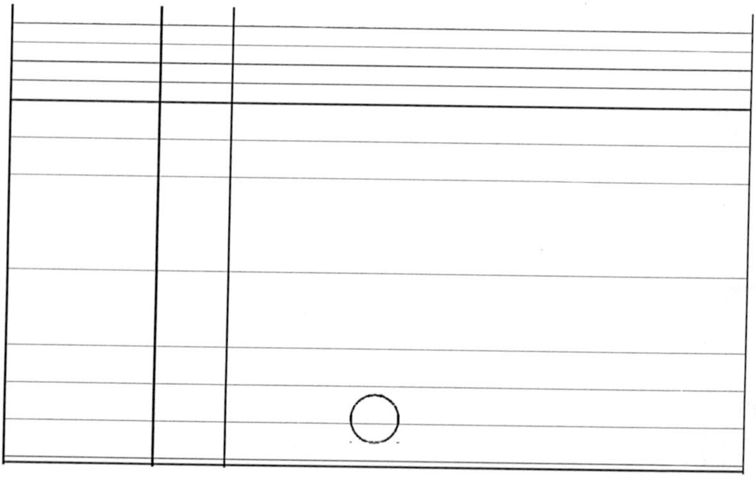

Classified Cataloguing Code.
Cataloguing Library Science.
Library Science.

Ranganathan (Shiyali Ramamrita) (1892-1972).
Neelameghan (A) (1927), *Assist*
Sarda Ranganathan Endowment for Library Science.

Gopinathan (MA), *Ed.*

Added Entries

There are many kinds of added entries, which fulfil different needs of the readers. Generally, the information that is entered in the heading section of the entry on the leading line, fulfils the needs of the readers and it is given the same name as the particular need it fulfils. These are formed from the main entry itself. These entries in the dictionary catalogue are normally alphabetic.

According to *Dr. S.R. Ranganathan* :

"Entry other than main entry is added entry". According to *C.A. Cutter* :

"Added entries, a second entry, i.e. any other than a main entry."

Kinds of Added Entries

It is necessary to form these entries to satisfy the different needs of the readers. Generally, following types of added entries are formed in a dictionary catalogue:

(i) Subject Index Entry,

(ii) Book Index Entry,

(iii) Cross Reference Index Entry.

(i) Subject Index Entry : This is an assisting alphabetic entry in the dictionary catalogue, which provides the information about the subject of the book. Dr. S.R. Ranganathan has further sub-divided this entry in following three types:

1. Specific Subject Entry,
2. Subject Analytical Entry, and
3. See also Subject Entry.

1. Specific Subject Entry : The specific word entry that is related to the subject or the class of the book described in the catalogue is called 'Specific Subject Entry'. The subject of the book is entered in natural language in the leading section in these entries and other necessary information about the book is entered under it. Thus, if a reader has the knowledge of the specific subject of a book, then these entries can provide the information whether a particular book on the subject is available in the library or not? At the same time, information about the particular books and how many books of the desired subject are available in the library is also obtained from these entries.

In the language of cataloguing, the specific subject of a book is known by the class number. Heading for the specific subject entry is obtained by chain process. Main heading of for the specific subject heading is formed by the last number of the last searched link of the class number. Following are the three sections of this entry:

(i) Leading Section,

(ii) Locus Section: It includes three sections: Heading of the book + short title of the book + description of edition,

(iii) Index Number.

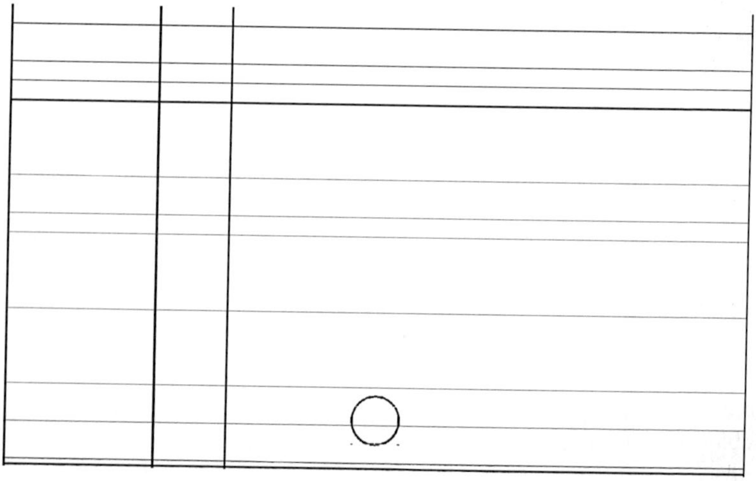

2. Subject Analytical Entry : These entries refer to those entries of the dictionary catalogue in which the subject of the book is described in a subsidiary way. The subject analytical entries also serve the similar purpose as the specific subject entries. The only difference is that the specific subject entry describes the specific subject of the complete book while these entries describe the specific subject of a particular part or section of the book. It is necessary to form such entries for multi-focal books.

The information of the pages, chapters etc. in which the subject is described, is entered in the locus section of this entry after the description of the edition of the book. This is the only difference between specific subject entry and this entry, otherwise both of these entries are formed in the same manner.

3. See Also Subject Entry : These entries are formed to provide the information of all reading material related to the subject desired by the reader. Main objective of these entries is only to direct the reader from one subject to another related subject. This is a general assisting entry of the dictionary catalogue that directs the name of a subject to the name of another subject. 'See also subject entry' is formed by all necessary links of a chain other than the link used for the heading of the specific subject entry. The structure of this entry is similar to that of the cross-reference index entry. Following sections are included in this entry:

(i) Leading Section,

(ii) Directing Section, and

(iii) Referred to Heading Section.

For example:

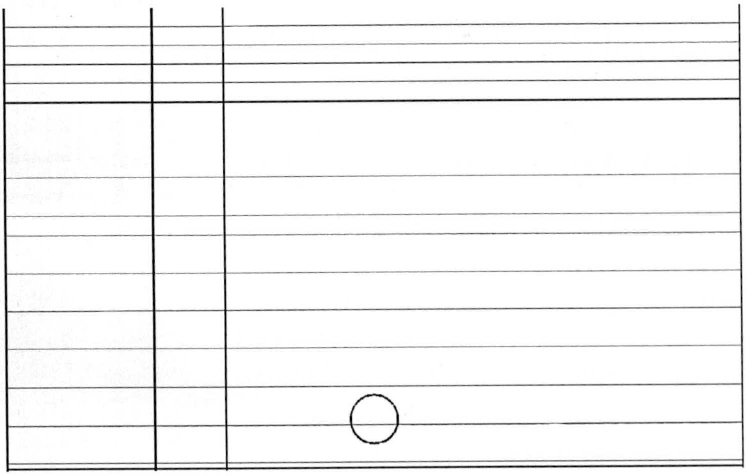

(ii) Book Index Entry : A specific assisting alphabetic entry in the dictionary catalogue is called 'Book Index Entry". Following four kinds of book index entries are formed in this catalogue:

(i) Joint Author Index Entry,

(ii) Collaborator Index Entry,

(iii) Title Index Entry, and

(iv) Series Index Entry.

The information about the author or collaborator or title is entered in natural language in the heading section of main entry of the dictionary catalogue. Hence no added entry is formed from this section, however, only if there are two joint authors then the 'Joint Author Index Entry' is formed. Four sections are included in this entry of the dictionary catalogue also, similar to the book index entry of the classified catalogue. Moreover, the structure of these entries is also similar. All the book index entries that are formed in the classified catalogue are also formed in the dictionary catalogue. These are:

(i) Leading Section,

(ii) Secondary Section,

(iii) Index Number Section, and

(iv) Note Section.

For example:

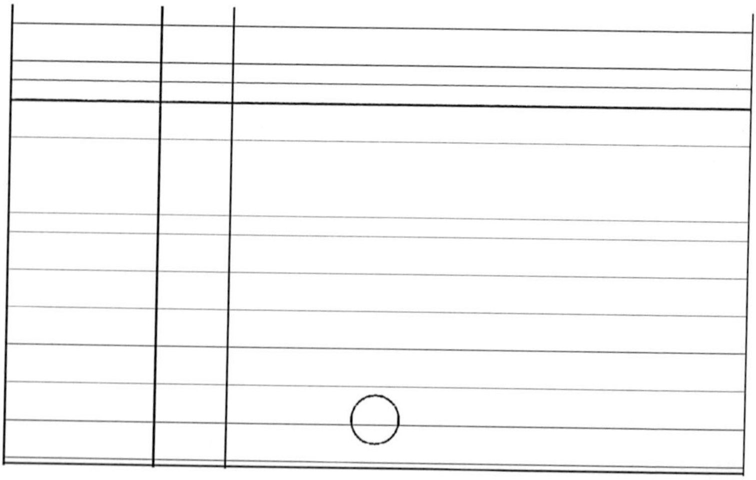

(iii) Cross Reference Entries : In a library where a Dictionary Catalogue is maintained we see entries of the type known as 'References' and also of the type known as 'Analytical Entries'.

A library catalogue tries to help the user to the maximum extent possible as a search tool. So, any difficulty we can visualise on the part of the user is to be countered by some kind of an entry in the catalogue. Similarly, any additional information found necessary and useful is to be provided by appropriate entries.

Uniformity is an essential feature in library cataloguing.

Therefore, when there are several variations in the spelling of a name of a person or corporate body or when a term used as heading is having two or more synonymous terms, there is a need to accept one particular form of the name or heading uniformly throughout the catalogue. On such occasions, to help the user, we will have to provide a *Reference.*

References are of two types; *'See'* Reference and *'See also'* Reference.

"See reference": The function of a see reference is to direct the user of a catalogue from a form of the name of a person or a corporate body or the title of work that might reasonably be sought to the form that has been chosen as a name heading or a uniform title. A see reference says to the user, "No. you won't find what you're looking for here; but if you will look under..... you will find something".

For example,

A personal name like RANGANATHAN can be written as :

RANGANATHAN

RANGANADAN

RANGANATHAN and the like.

In our catalogue entry we prefer only one of these forms, but a user may search the catalogue under one or the other forms mentioned above. If there is no entry under the form in which the user is searching the user may get disappointed thinking that there is no book by that particular author in the library. In such cases, we provide an added entry of the type and similarly for other variations also, e.g.,

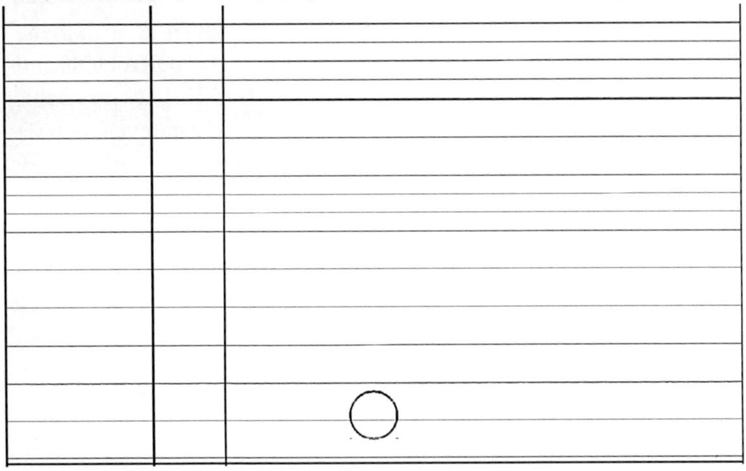

"See also" references : *See also* References are provided when there are entries in a catalogue under both Referred-from and Referred-to heading forms. The function of a see also reference is to direct the user from one name heading or uniform title to another that is related to it. A *See* also reference says to the user, "Yes, there is some information here and you may also be interested in related information that you can find under...". For example, we are following both two terms–

'Interior Decoration' as well as 'Home Science' in our catalogue. Then entries will be made as follows :

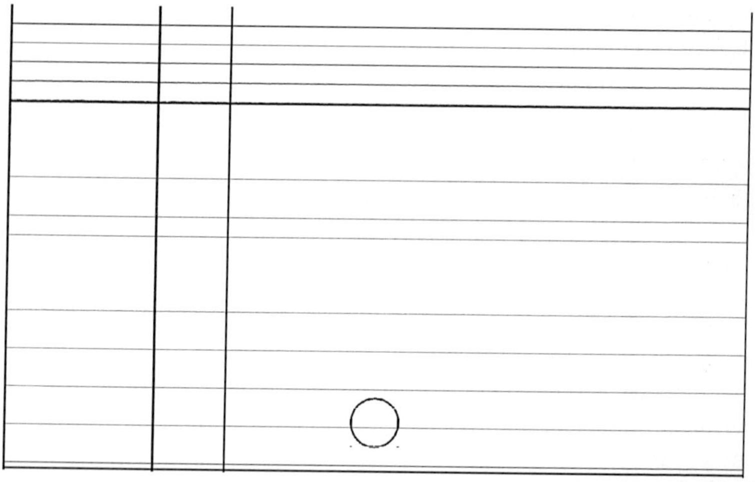

Such an entry indicates that there are entries in the catalogue both under the *Referred-from* heading INTERIOR DECORATION and also under the *'Referred-to'* heading HOME SCIENCE. The entry helps the user to find the related material. In a *'see also'* reference, entries should be given for both headings. In the above example another entry will be:

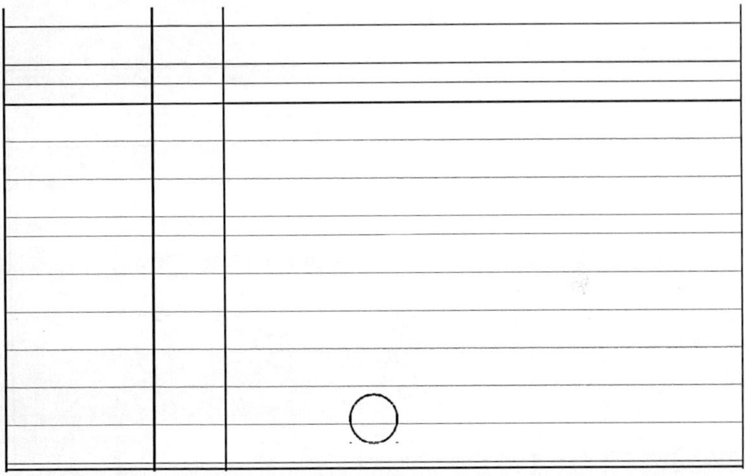

Besides, there are analytical entry also. An analytical entry can be defined as, an entry of a part (like articles in periodicals, contributions to conference proceedings and collections, etc.) of a document referring to the document which contains it. In other words, an analytical entry is "an entry for a work of part of a work that is contained in a collection, series, issue of a serial, or other bibliographical unit for which another comprehensive entry has been made. Analytical entries may be either separate, self-contained entries or added entries that are part of the cataloging of the larger work.''

There are three kinds of analytical entries, namely, author analytical, title analytical, and subject analytical. The sample entries are as follows:

Author Analytical "is a Specific Added Entry referring from the name of the Author and the title of a contribution occurring in a host document, to its locus, that is, the host document and the place of occurrence in it".

Example given in CCC for this is:

Author Analytical

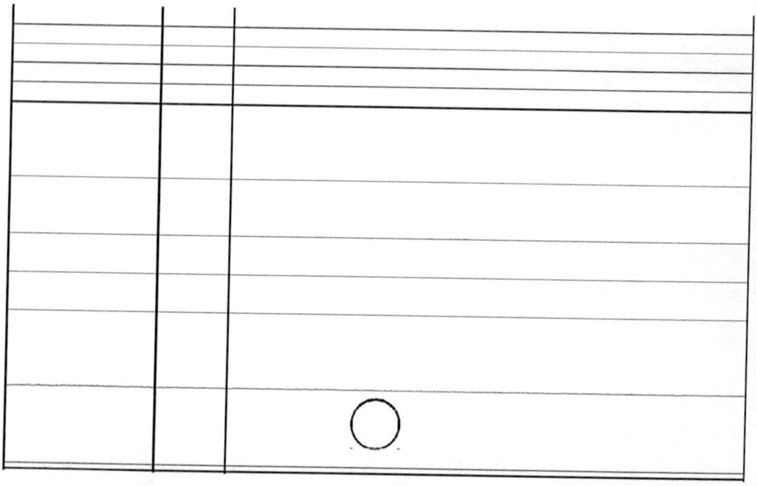

Title Analytical is a "Specific Added Entry referring from the title of contribution occurring in a host document, to its locus, that is the host document and the place of occurrence in it".

Title Analytical for the above contribution will be :

Title Analytical

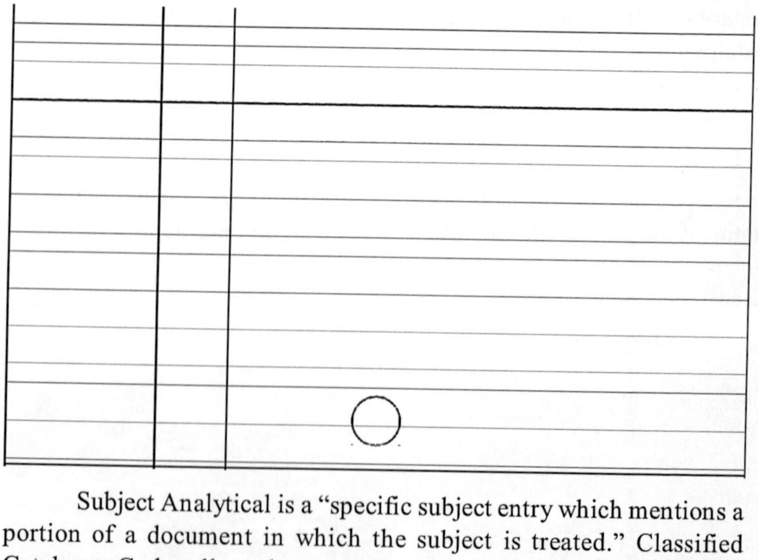

Subject Analytical is a "specific subject entry which mentions a portion of a document in which the subject is treated." Classified Catalogue Code calls such a type of entry as "Cross Reference Entry".

It can be understood by following example –

In the book,

'COLLECTED PAPERS

OF

SRINIVASAN RAMANUJAM

Edited by

G.H. HARDY

P.V. SESHU AIRYAR

and

B.W.WILSON'

published in 1927 in its introductory pages from xi to xix, the biography of Srinivasan Ramanujam was given. This part of the book was very valuable at that time because that was the only biography of the great mathematical genius of India available then. So, a Subject Analytical Entry (or what is known in CCC as Cross Reference Entry) is provided for the biography part constructing as Class Number for it. The entry is as follows:

Subject Analytical Entry

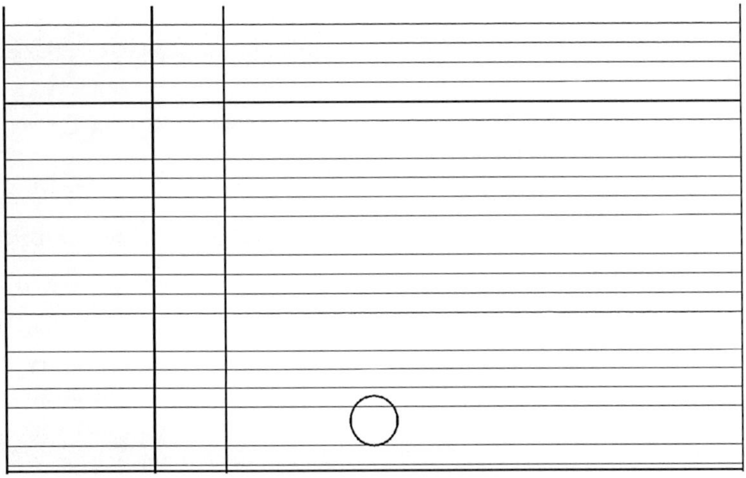

A.A.C.R.–2

A.A.C.R.-2 is a proper code for the dictionary catalogue. A dictionary catalogue is a catalogue in which all the entries (author, title, subject, series etc.) and the directions related to these are arranged in the normal alphabetical order, but there may be some difference in sub-arrangements i.e., sub-headings etc. In this manner, all the entries and all related directions are arranged in the same order in a dictionary catalogue.

According to A.A.C.R. -2, following entries are included in a dictionary catalogue:

(i) Main entry,

(ii) Added entries,

(iii) References and cross references.

(i) Main Entry : Main entry is "the complete catalogue record of an item, presented in the form by which the entity is to be uniformly identified and cited. The main entry may included the tracings of all other headings under which the record is to be represented in the catalogue". Each document gets one main entry. It is usually an author's entry, with sometimes title occupying heading of a main entry. The last section may contain the tracings, which indicate headings under which added entries have been prepared for a given document.

The International Standard Bibliographic Description (ISBD) has identified the following eight areas for the description of a document:

1. Title and statement of responsibility area
2. Edition area
3. Material (or type of publication) specific details area
4. Physical description area
5. Series area
7. Note area
8. Standard number and terms of availability area

Even though AACR-2 provides for the eight areas of description and for certain elements of information in each area, it is not necessary that every document catalogued should be provided with all the areas of description. Nor is it necessary to provide all the data elements in any area of description. Layout for basic constituent elements for a printed monograph along with required punctuations is given below :

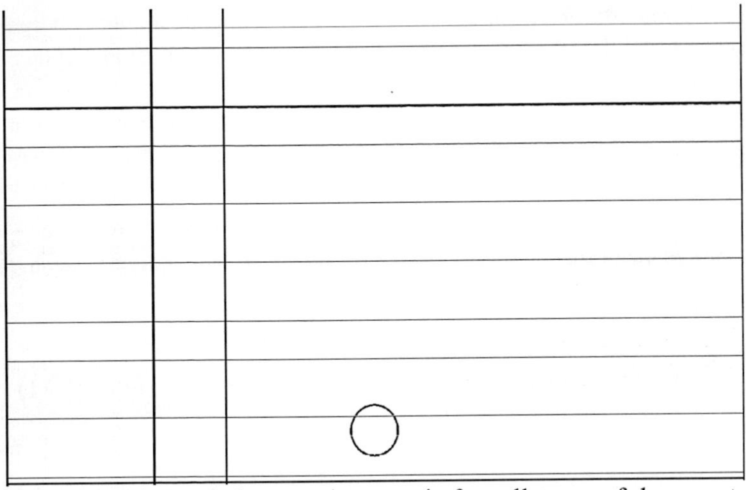

The above skeleton main entry is for all types of document. Brief rules the making a main entry, are provided as under :

Chief source of information : The chief source of information for printed monographs is the title page or, if there is no title page the source from within the publication that is used as a substitute for it...If information traditionally given on the title page is given on two facing pages or on pages successive leaves, with or without repetition, treat those pages as the title page (AACR2, rule 2.0 B1).

Prescribed sources of information : The prescribed source(s) of information for each area of the description of printed monographs is set out below. Enclose information taken from outside the prescribed source(s) in square brackets *(AACR2,* rule 2.0 B2).

Area	*Prescribed sources of information*
Title and statement of responsibility	Title page
Edition	Title page, other preliminaries, and colophon
Publication, distribution, etc.	Title page, other preliminaries, and colophon
Physical description	The whole publication
Series	The whole publication
Note	Any source
Standard number and terms of availability	Any source

Punctuation : Precede each mark of prescribed punctuation by a space and follow it by a space, except for the comma, full stop, hyphen, and opening and closing parentheses and square brackets. The comma, full stop, hyphen, and closing parentheses and square brackets are not preceded by a space; the hyphen and the opening parentheses and square bracket are not followed by a space.

Elements within areas are divided by punctuation. For instance, a statement of responsibility is always preceded by a diagonal slash.

Example :

Cataloguing of Non-book Material/Anil

Kumar Dhiman (rule 1.1 A1)

Punctuation for publication area are:

Place of publication: Publisher, Date of publication

Example:

New Delhi : Ess Ess, 2004.

Indicate an interpolation (i.e. data taken from outside the prescribed source(s) of information) by enclosing it in square brackets. Indicate the omission of part of an element by the mark of omission (...).

An additional unit of title information is preceded by a colon.

Example:

Thinking and reasoning : selected readings

Long titles may be abridged without loss of essential information. However, the first five words are not omitted. An omission is indicated by means of three dots.

Capitalization : The general rule for titles in English language is that first letters of all proper names are capitalised and first letter of a title is also in capital.

Title and statement of responsibility area : Transcribe the title proper exactly to wording, order and spelling, but not necessarily as to punctuation and capitalization.

Examples:

The materials of architecture

Introduction to science

Fourteen hours

Statement of responsibility, which are preceded by a diagonal slash, are recorded in the form they appear in or on the item (rule 1.1 F). e.g.,

British India / by Sanjay Gosain

Handley Cross: a sporting tale / by the author of "Jorrocks' jaunts and jollities"

The Oxford book of English verse / chosen and edited by Sir Arthur Quiller—Couch

Map catalogue / Ordinance Survey

Common service book of the Lutheran Church / authorized by the United Lutheran Church of America

George Cross and R.L. Birrell : their friendship and correspondence/edited, with an introduction, by Royal C. Ball

Modern mathematics/A.L. Norman, N. price, R.L. Flinn

Add an explanatory word or short phrase to the statement of responsibility if the relationship between the title and the person(s) or body (bodies) named in the statement is not clear (*AACR2,* rule 11F8).

Examples :

Baijun ballads / [collected by] by Chet Williams

If there is more than one statement of responsibility, record them in the order indicated by their sequence on, or by the layout of, the chief source of information *(AACR2,* rule 1.1 F6). Statements of responsibility subsequent to the first one are introduced by a semicolon.

Examples:

Bits of paradise: twenty-one uncollected stories / by F. Scott and Zelda Fitzgerald; selected by Scottie Fitzgerald Smith and Matthew J. Bruccoli; with a foreword by Scottie Fitzgerald Smith.

Letters from AE / selected and edited by Alan Denson; with a forward by Monk Gibbon

The diary of a country parson, 1758-1802 / by James Woodforde; passages selected and edited by John Beresford.

When a single statement of responsibility names more than three persons or corporate bodies performing the same function, or with the same degree of responsibility, omit all but the first of each group of such persons or bodies.

Examples :

America's radical right / Raymond Wolfinger...[et al.]

Dickens 1970 : centenary essay / by Walter Allen...[et al.]; edited by Michael Slater

Edition Area

2nd ed.

[Rev. ed.]

When statement of responsibility relates only to particular editions and not to all editions of an item, then it must be included in this area.

Introduction to chemistry / by R.S. Jain. —Rev. with additional chapters / by A.C. Sharma

An issue statement may be given in addition to an edition statement if the reissue contains changes (*AACR2,* rule 1.2 D) 4th ed., repr. with additions and amendments

Publication, Distribution, etc. Area : Generally, the first named place of publication and first named publisher are given but subsequent places of publication and names of publishers are included if given prominently by the layout of the source of information or if located in the home country of the library/ agency cataloguing the publication.

Examples :

London; New York : Longmans, Green

(for a cataloguing agency in the United States)

New York; London: McGraw-Hill

(for a cataloguing agency in the United Kingdom)

New York: McGraw-Hill

(for a cataloguing agency in India)

London : Benn; Chicago : Rand Mc Nally

(for a cataloguing agency in the United States)

The name of a publisher, distributor, etc. are given in the shortest form in which it can be understood and identified internationally (*AACR2,* rule 1.4 D2).

Examples :

: Penguin *not* : Penguin Books

: W.H. Allen *not* : Allen (Avoids confusion with other publishers called as Allen)

Physical Description Area : This area is preceeded by a full stop, space, dash, space or start a new paragraph. Here later prescription has been used. Precede other physical details (i.e., other than extent or dimensions) by a colon. Precede dimensions by a semicolon.

Examples :

x, 165 p. : ill.; 18 cm.

271 p. : col. ill. ; 28 cm+3 maps

Series Area : Series area is preceded by a full stop, space, dash, space. Series statement is enclosed in parentheses.

Examples :

(Business management series ; 2)

(Environment science research ; v. 6)

(Popular science series ; no. 7)

Statements of responsibility appearing in the chief source of information are provided if regarded necessary for the purpose of identification of series.

Examples :

(Research monographs / Institute of Economic Affairs)

(Technical memoranda / Beach Erosion Board)

Notes Area : Notes are used to amplify or clarify the more formal elements of the description.

Examples :

Bibliography : p. 250-291

Originally published : London : Gray, 1871

Revision of: 3rd ed. London : McMillan, 1953

Choice of Access Points : Having described an item, in the next step headings and/or uniform titles are normally added to the standard description to obtain different kinds of entries. Headings provide access points in the catalogue. A heading can be a word, name or phrase placed at the head of a catalogue entry. However, in case an entry is created under title proper, then entry may be made under the first words of description.

Rules are provided for determination of choice of access points (headings) under which a bibliographic description is entered in the catalogue. One of the access points is chosen as the main entry heading. The main entry is the one presented in a form by which an item can be identified and cited. The other access points are used as added entry headings.

Main Entry Headings : The main entry heading consists of the name of a person, the name of a corporate body, or title.

In case of a name of person, the code directs that a "personal author is the person chiefly responsible for the creation of the intellectual or artistic content of a work". If there are more than one personal author, then the question of shared responsibility arises. A work is entered under the heading for the corporate body in following categories :

(a) those of an administrative nature dealing with the corporate body itself...

(b) some legal and governmental works...

(c) works which record the collective thought of a body...

(d) those which report the collective activity of a conference ..., of an expedition, or event...falling within the definition of a corporate body...

(e) sound recordings, films and videorecordings resulting from the collective activity.

A work is entered under its title when :

(a) the personal authorship is unknown, diffuse, or indeterminable,

(b) it is a collection or a work produced under editorial direction,

(c) it emanates from a corporate body but does not fall into one or more of the category (a) to (e) above and is not of personal authorship and

(d) it is accepted as a sacred scripture by a religious group.

Main Entry

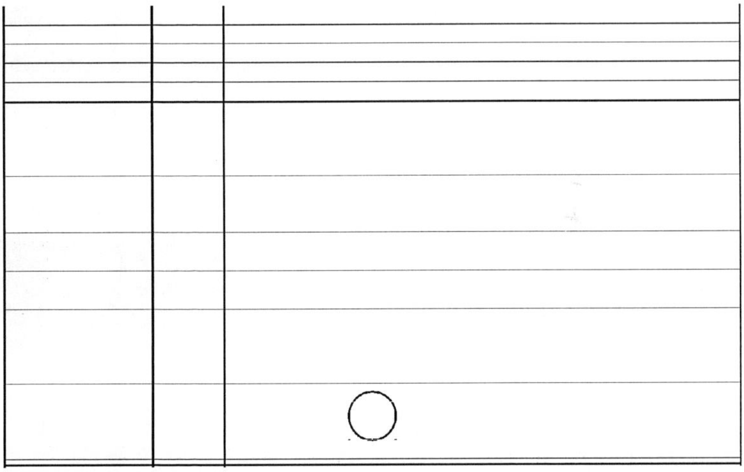

(ii) Added Entries : Added entry is an entry other than the main entry, which presents a bibliographic entity in the catalogue.

Added entries complement the main entry and fulfil different needs related to the documents. These added entries are known as secondary entries and have their own importance. These are formed for joint authors such as co-author, editor, co-editor, translator, illustrator etc.

Provision for guiding rules for these entries is not made in the A.A.C.R. -2, but rules for these have been determined in A.A.C.R. -1.

The added entries in AACR-2, are prepared through unit card system. In this, the main entry and the added entries carry the same information about the document. The only difference between them is that each added entry will have the approach element at the top of the entry starting from the second indention. In such cases, the main entry is known as 'Unit Entry'.

For example, main entry is :

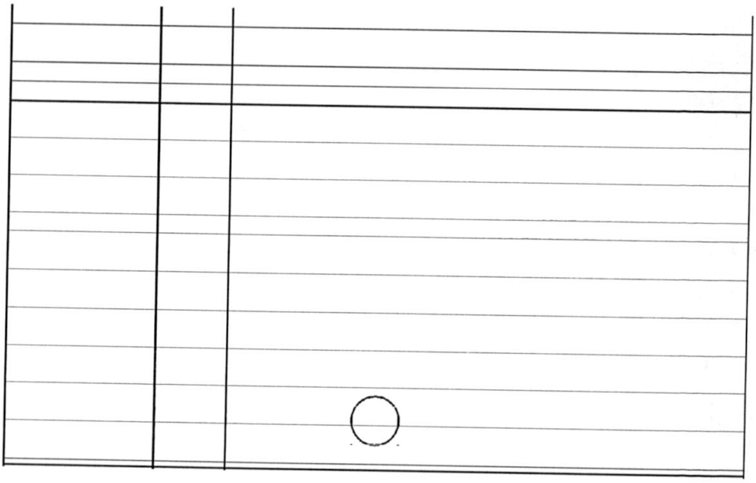

Title Added Entry under Unit Card System will be as under :

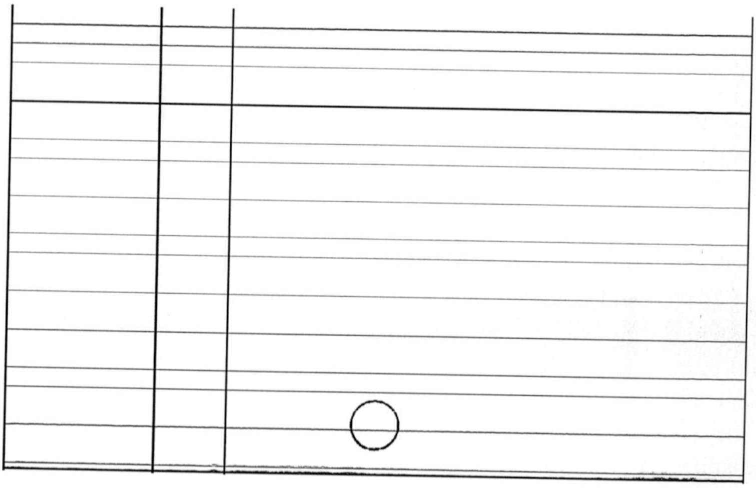

Subject Added Entry (Unit Card System)

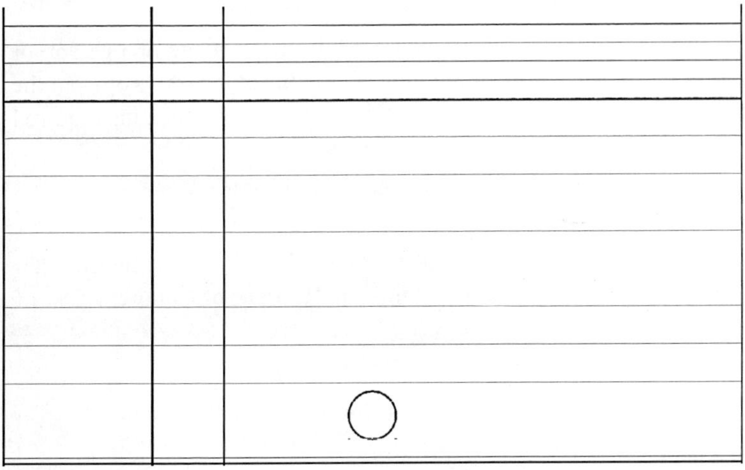

When the information given in the added entry is brief, the above subject heading which is added to the entry looks like the one below :

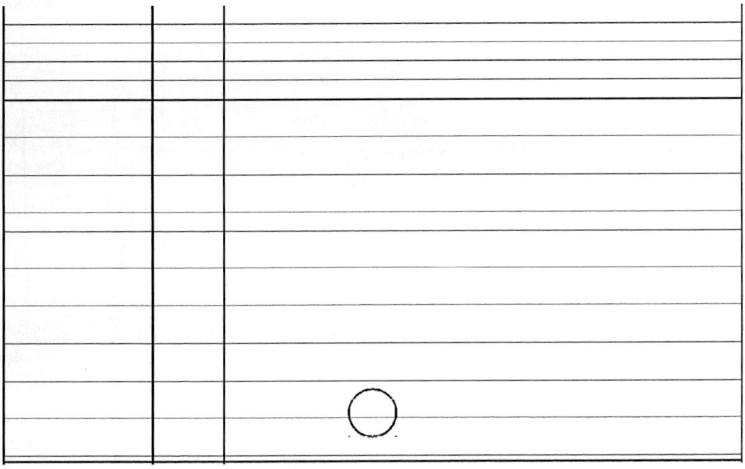

In this type of brief added entry, only the Call Number , author, title and year of publication are given. Sometimes, even the year is omitted. The main line is now occupied by the added entry element but this element starts from the second indention, which indicates that the entry is not a main entry.

(iii) References : 'References' is to direct from one heading or entry to another heading or entry.

'See references' directs a reader from the name of a person or title of the book heading of the subject or name of the series or from the general title to the place or point of the catalogue at which the required information has been provided by the cataloguer.

'See also references' directs the reader from one heading to another related heading.

Guidance about the subject-related directions is received from the 'Sears List of Subject Headings' or 'Library of Congress List of Subject Headings'.

Reference (Editor Series)

McGregor, John P. *ed.*
see Scientific monograph series (American Chemical Society)

Reference (Alternative form of Name)

Demombynes, Maurice Gaudefroy-
see Gaudefroy-Demombynes, Maurice

Reference (Subject)

ASPHYXIATING AND POISONOUS GASES
see GASES, ASPHYXIATING AND POISONOUS

Reference (Series)

American Chemical Society. Scientific monograph series
see Scientific monograph series (American Chemical Society)

5
Structure of Names

Q. : Write an essay on structure of Indian names.

or

Write an essay on the personal names for a library catalogue.

Ans. The author or the subject of a book can be based on the name of the person. The names of the person may be included in heading, title and the series section.

It is necessary for the cataloguer to be acquainted with the different cultures while considering the structure of personal names. Otherwise, the cataloguers will generally face difficulty.

Types of Personal Names

1. Given Name : The name that is given to a person after birth by the parents or the guardian.

2. Family Name : This normally includes the name of the person's forefathers or family. This is the 'Surname'.

3. Based on Person's Qualities : The names also become popular due to the qualities of a person. These qualities can be as follows:

(i) Educational and professional qualifications,

(ii) Military, civil or other specialties,

(iii) Commercial specialties,

(iv) Communal qualities based on religion, thought or caste.

Family names carry more importance in China, Japan and the western countries. The reason behind this being that the family name is chosen from a large group while the given name is chosen from a smaller group. However, given names are more important than the family names in Myanmar (Burma), Sri Lanka and South India. Given name is also given more stress in Muslim names.

(1) Western Names

Surnames are common in all European languages. However, there are surnames with prefixes, compound surnames with or without a hyphen, surnames with place names, titles of nobility and terms of honour. There are also names of royalty, popes and other ecclesiastical officials.

English (Indo-European) Names

1. English names consist of forename (s) and a surname, e.g.,

   W. Somereset Maugham

   Logan Pearsall Smith

2. There are surnames with separately written prefixes such as De, Le, Du and De la. e.g.,

   Thomas De Quincy

   John Le Carre

   Daphne Du Maurier

   Walter De la Mare

   There are other prefixes which are neither articles nor prepositions, e.g.,

   David FitzGerald

   William Macdonald

   Henry O'Neil

3. Compound surnames, with or without a hyphen, e.g.,

   Mark Bonham Carter

   Cecil Day-Lewis

   David Llyod George

   Henry Smith-Dorrien

   Married women with compound names consisting of maiden name and husband's surname, e.g.,

   Harriet Beecher Stowe

4. The names with British titles of honour, Sir, Dame and Lady, e.g.,

   Sir John Suckling

   Dame Rebecca West

Other Western Names

1. Names containing a surname, e.g.,

Danish	:	Hans Christian Andersen
French	:	Albert Camus
German	:	Sarah Bernhardt
Polish	:	Jan Henry Kowalski
Portuguese	:	Joaquim Pedro Ferreira

2. Compound surnames, hyphenated or not, e.g.,

Czech	:	Jankovic Mirijevaski, Teodor
Danish	:	Friis Moller, Kai
Dutch	:	Huber Noodt, Ulrich
French	:	Martin-Mery, Gilberte
German	:	Meyer-Lubke, Wilhelm
Hungarian	:	Konkoly-Thege Sandor (no comma)
Italian	:	Rosmini-Serbati, Antonio
Polish	:	Jodko-Nakiewicz, Witold
Russian	:	Rimski-Koraskov, Andrej Nikolaevic
Yugoslav	:	Petrovic-Njegos, Petar

3. With place name, e.g.,

   Heinrich Muller-Breslau

4. Surnames including an article or preposition or combination of the two e.g.,

   Afrikans (Dutch of South Africa) : under the prefix

   Van der Post, Christian Willem Hendrik

   Czech and Slovac : under the part following the prefix

   Zerotina, Karel Z

   Dutch : under the part following the prefix unless the prefix is ver.

   Aa, Pieter van der

   Drioessche, Albert van

   Ver Boven, Daisy

   French : under the prefix consisting of an article or of a contractions (du, des)

Le Rouge, Gustac

La Bruyere, Rene

Du Bellay, Joachim

Des Granges, Charles-Mare

Otherwise under the part following the preposition (d', de)

Aubigne Theodore Agrippa d'

Musset, Alfred de

La Fontaine, Jean de

German: same as in French (under an article, but not under a preposition)

Am Rhyn, August

Zur Linde, Otto

Goethe, John Wolfgang von

Italian: under the prefix

A Prato, Giovanni

D' Arienzo, Nicola

Portuguese: under the part following the prefix

Fonseca, Martinho Augusto da

Rego, Jose Lins do

Scandinavian languages (Danish, Norwegian, Swedish): under part of the name following the prefix

Hallstrom, Gunnar Johannes of

Linne, Carl von (of German origin)

under the prefix, if the prefix is the Dutch de or of another origin

De Geer, Gerard (Dutch de)

La Cour, Jens Lessen (of French origin)

Spanish: the prefix consists of an article only,

Las Heras, Manual Antonio

- **Married woman:** The surname of a married woman consists of surname before marriage and husband's surname.
- **Name with titles of nobility,** e.g.,

Abrantes, Laure Junot, dechess d (French)

Bismarck, Otto, Furst von (German)

Covour, Camillo Benso, conte di (Italian)

Lopez de Mendoza, Marques de (Spanish)

– **Royalty** (all Western names): e.g.,

John, King of England (state)

Clovis, King of the Franks (people)

– **Popes:** e.g,

Pius XII, Pope

John, XXIII, Pope

– **Bishops:** e.g.,

Joannes, Bishop of Ephesus

John, Abbot of Ford

– **Identical Names:** There are two or more identical names with different person's dates (birth, death) e.g.,

Smith, John, 1924-

Smith, John, 1837-1896

(2) Hindu Names:

Family Name:

(i) Sub-cast: Garg, Goyal etc.

(ii) Place name: Multani, Gokal, Siyal etc.

(iii) Business: Chopra, Dewan, Munshi, Pathak, Seth etc.

(iv) Forefather name: Chowdhary etc.

Given Name:

(i) Name of object: *Paani (*water), *Jhanda (*flag) etc.

(ii) Colour: *Kaala* (black), *Laal* (red) etc.

(iii) Season: *Basant* (spring) etc.

(iv) Month: *Chait, Saavan* etc.

(v) Psychological quality: *Dheeraj* (patience), *Himmat* (courage) etc.

(vi) Physical quality: *Chhota (small), Mota* (fat) etc.

(vii) Taste: *Meetha* (sweet), *Khatta* (sour) etc.

(viii) Plant,

(ix) Flower,

(x) Birds and animals,

(xi) Stone,

(xii) Star,

(xiii) Gods and Godesses,

However, no uniform pattern can be seen in North India. Some persons are not using the name of their caste. As a result of this, only the personal name remains. Other than this, there are certain words that are used as the complementing word as well as the family name.

Bengali Names : The name of the caste is given after the personal name in Bengali. Such as, *Ram Mohan Roy, Ramesh Chandra Dutta, C.R. Das* etc. Here *Roy, Dutta and Das* are the cast names.

Tamil Names – : Personal name of father is added before the name of a person. Name of the birth place or the native place of the forefathers is added before the name of father. Such as:

(i) N.K. Sundaram, here Narayanan is father's name.

(ii) C.V. Raman, here Chandrashekhar is father's name.

(iii) S.R. Ranganathan, here Shivyali is the place name, Ramamrita is father's name and Ranganathan is personal name.

Kannada Names : Name of the native place of forefathers is added before the personal name in Kannada. Such as,

Sabur Mangesa Rao, here the first word is place name and the last two words form the personal name of the person.

Telugu Names : Family name is added with the personal name. Such as,

S. Radhakrishnan, here first word is family name and second word is the personal name of the person.

Malayalam Names : Family name is added before the personal name. Such as,

V.K. Krishna Menon, here first word is the family name, second word is father's name, third word is the personal name and the last word is the caste name.

Gujarati Names : Generally two names are included before the family name. Such as, Mohandas Karamchand Gandhi, here first word is the personal name, second word is father's name and third word is family name.

Marathi Names : Personal name is followed by father's and family name. Such as, Bal Gangadhar Tilak, here Bal is the personal name, Gangadhar is father's name and Tilak is the family name.

Parsi Names : Personal name is generally followed by the father's name. Such as, Mankerasha Bajajai Meghora, here Mankerasha is personal name, Bajajai is father's name and Meghora is family name.

Sikh Names : Personal name is generally formed of two words. e.g., Sukhvir Singh, Amrita Kaur. Second word is Singh and Kaur, which is used for men and women respectively.

(3) Muslim Names

Muslim names are of following kinds:

1. Conventional or professional title or laqab: e.g., Hakim, Qazi, Maulvi, Sardar, Syed, Khaja, Aga, Mir, Mirza etc.
2. The personal name or ism or alam: It is of several types as given below:

   Biblical names from the Quran (Ibrahim, Sulaiman, Yakub, Musa etc.) Arabic adjectives or substantives (Ahmad, Ali, Hasan, etc.).

   Compound names (Abd-al Aziz, Asrar-ul-Haq, Nur-al-Hasan, Nur-un-Nabi, Nazr-al-Islam, etc.).
3. The paternal or matronymical name or Kunniyat: Normally it consists of the word Abu or Ben meaning 'father of' followed by the name of the oldest son or daughter, e.g. Abu Musa Ali (meaning Ali Father of Musa), Abu'l Fadal (meaning father of merit), Ibn-I-Insha (meaning son of literature), Ibn-I-Batuta (meaning son of Batuta), etc.
4. Conferred title or laqab: It is a name other than that which the holder received at birth and yet not substituted for it. It is omitted, e.g. Badr-ad-Din (full moon of faith), Saraj-ad-Daula (lamp of the state), Allama (Great scholar), Najmudda-ula, Dabirul-mulk, etc.
5. Nick name or urf: It is used as an alternative name or as a pseudonym, e.g. Mirza Nausha.
6. Relative name of nisbat: It usually has ending in I or y. e.g. al-

Qurashi, al-Hashmi, al-Baghdad, Abidi, Chisti, Naqvi, etc.

7. Literary name or takhallus (i.e. pseudonym): It occurs at the end, e.g. Firdawsi (the paradise), Ghalib, Jigar, etc.

Concludingly, it can be said. Hindu name have different forms and values in different parts of India. It is necessary to become familiar with the different cultures before forming and rendering them. Same suggestion applies to the other cultures also. Following are some suggestions that may be used for overcoming any difficulty related with names:

(i) Dictionaries of personal names should be prepared for each and very linguistic area of the world. This work can be completed with the cooperation of literary societies or bodies.

(ii) Standardized title page should be adopted. It should be mentioned behind the standardized title page, by typing, which element of the person's name is entry element and which is the sub–element, by which these can be adopted in the heading. This information can also be alternatively given in other parts of the document.

Besides there is need for in-depth research in the field of personal names.

6
Comparative Study of AACR and CCC

Q. : Describe in brief the different kinds of authors. Compare the rules for cataloguing pseudonymous books in C.C.C. and A.A.C.R.-2.

or

Write briefly on the choice and rendering of personal names in AACR–2 And CCC.

or

Discuss the treatment of Shared Authorship in AACR-2. How does it differ from the treatment of joint authorship in CCC ?

Ans. There is one or the other author of every document. It is impossible to create a document without the author. Generally, the term 'author' is used for the originator of the document.According to Dr. S.R. Ranganathan, an author in,

Sense 1: "Person creating the work, that is the thought and the expression constituting it."

Sense 2: "Corporate body owning responsibility for a work that is for the thought and expression constituting it."

According to Anglo American Cataloguing Rules I "Author is the person or corporate body chiefly responsible for the creation of the intellectual or artistic content of work e.g. the writer of a book, the compiler of a bibliography, the composer of a musical work, the artist who paints a picture, the photographer who takes a photograph."

Thus, that person or corporate body, who creates the book and is completely responsible for the ideas and expressions in it, is called the 'author'.

Types of Author

Generally, authors are of two types:

(i) Personal Author, and

(ii) Corporate Author.

(I) Personal Author

Meaning and Definition : When one or more persons are responsible for the creation of a book and the expressions made in it, they are called personal author.

According to Dr. S.R. Ranganathan, "Person as author, is the responsibility for the thought and the expression consisting the work resting solely on his private capacity and not on the capacity of any office being held by him within a corporate body, nor on the capacity of the body."

According to A.A.C.R. -2, "The person chiefly responsible for the creation of the intellectual or artistic content of a work."

Types of Personal Author : The personal author can be divided in the following categories:

1. *Single Personal Author* : When only one person is responsible for the creation of a book and its contents and expressions, he is called 'Single Personal Author'.
2. *Joint Personal Author* : When two or more than two persons jointly create a book, they are called 'Joint Personal Author'.
3. *Pseudonymous Author* : When the author uses a false name i.e., a name other than his real name in the works that he creates, he is called a 'Pseudonymous Author'.
4. *Anonymous Author* : There are many books whose authors are not known. Such books are called anonymous books. Most religious books fall in this category.
5. *Editor, Compiler and other Collaborators* : Certain books are created by collecting material from independent writings, essays, poetry etc. The person who creates such books is called editor or compiler. All other persons who contribute in creation of this type of books such as, assistant, illustrator, translator, etc. are called collaborator.

(II) Corporate Author

Meaning and Definition : In the present times, there are many books published other than those written by personal authors in which the name of some administrative department, institution etc. is written as author's name. This type of author is included in the category of corporate author.

According to Dr. S.R. Ranganathan, "Corporate body as author, the responsibility for the thought and expression constituting the work resting solely on it or any organ of it, and not on the private capacity of any person or persons forming part of or holding office in or in any other way connected with that body."

According to A.A.C.R -2 corporate author is "An organisation or group of persons that is identified by a particular name and that acts, or may act, as an entity. Typical examples of corporate bodies are associations, institutions,- business firms, non-profit enterprises, government, government agencies, religious bodies, local churches and conferences." According to Jolly, "A work is said to be of corporate authorship when the responsibility for its contents, expression and opinion rests with a society, institution, government or other corporate body and not with a personal author."

Thus, such a document that describes the functioning or other related matters of a corporate body or expresses its ideas as a whole falls under the category of corporate authorship. Generally reports, books containing rules and codes of the corporate body, reading material about the corporate body, minutes of the meetings etc. fall in this category.

Types of Corporate Author : Dr. Ranganathan has divided corporate author in following categories:

1. *Government* : When the Government or its organ is responsible for the expressions and the contents of a book, such book is called a government publication.
2. *Institution* : Just like the government, an institution is also one of the categories of the corporate body and the books created by it are known by the name of the institution itself. The institution is responsible for the ideas expressed in institutional publications and it is known as the author of such books.
3. *Conference* : The authors of many publications are conferences,

seminars, conventions etc. These publications contain the report of conference, the decisions made in the conference, results of the seminars and other similar type of reading material.

AACR-2

CHOICE AND RENDERING OF HEADINGS : PERSONS

Choice and rendering of headings for the persons involve the study of the choice of access points/headings for the works of personal author and joint authors/shared responsibility.

I. Choice of Headings

1. Single personal author, works of -

Definition : "A personal author is the person chiefly responsible for the creation of the intellectual or artistic contents of a work." (AACR2, p. 284).

Rule 21.4A

"Enter a work, a collection of works, or selection from a work or works by one personal author (or any reprint, reissue, etc., of such a work) under the heading for that person whether named in the work or not."

Example:

Glimpses of world history, by Jawaharlal Nehru

Main entry under the heading for Nehru

More stories from Tagore

Main entry under the heading for Tagore

Cataloguing of Non-book Materials by Anil Kumar Dhiman

Main entry under the heading for Dhiman.

2. Joint authors/shared responsibility, works of Joint author

Definition : "A Person who collaborates with one or more persons to produce a work in relation to which the collaborator perform the same function." (AACR2 Glossary, p. 567).

Shared responsibility

Definition : "Collaboration between two or more persons or bodies performing the same kind of activity in the creation of the content of an item,. The contribution of each may form a separate and distinct part of the item, or the contribution of each may not be separable from that of others." (AACR2 Glossary, p. 570).

The choice of heading for joint authors/shared responsibility is as under :

(a) Principal responsibility Indicated (Rule 21.6 B) : If the principal responsibility is indicated either by wording or the layout of the chief source of information, then the entry is made under the heading for that principal person or body, e.g. :

Building Construction

by

SAT PAUL VIJ

Assisted by

R.M Malik and L.M Goyal

Main entry under the heading for Vij.

If the principal responsibility is indicated to two or three persons or bodies, then main entry is prepared under the heading for the first named person or body, e.g :

PRACTICAL CHEMISTRY

BY

R.N.MEHTA, Surinder Kumar And S.S. Bajwa

Main entry under the heading for Mehta. Added entries under the headings for Surinder Kumar and Bajwa.

(b) Principal responsibility not indicated (Rule 21.6 C) : If there are two or three responsible persons or bodies and the principal responsibility is not indicated, then main entry is made under the named first person or body and added entries for others are prepared accordingly, e.g:

ACADEMIC LIBRARIES

by

Anil Kumar Dhiman

and

S.C. Sinha

Main entry under the heading for Dhiman. Added entry under the heading for Sinha.

HEALTH FOR EFFECTIVE LIVING

BY

Edward Johns

Wilfred C. Sutton

Lloyed E. Webster

Main entry under the heading for Johns. Added entries under the heading for Sutton and Webster.

If there are more than three persons or bodies and no principal responsibility is indicated, then main entry under the title and added entry for the named first person or body are made, e.g :

ELEMENTS OF GEOGRAPHY

Physical and Cultural

Vernor C. Finch

Glenn T.Rewartha

Edwin H.Hammond

Arthur H.Robinson

Main entry under title. Added entry under the heading for Finch.

3. Mixed responsibility, works of -

Definition : "A work of mixed responsibility is one in which different persons or bodies contribute to the intellectual or artistic content by performing different kinds of activities (e.g. adapting, or illustrating a work written by another person)" (AACR2 Glossary, p. 568).

(a) Illustrated texts (rule 21.11)

Example: THE VILLAGE IN TOWN

by J.ROBINSON Illustrated by D. WILSON

Main entry under the heading for Robinson.

Added entry under the heading for Wilson, because the illustrator's name is given in equal prominence.

(b) Adaptions of texts (Rule 21.10)

Example:

Adventures of Tom Sawyer

by

MARK TWAIN

rewritten for young readers

by

Felix Sutton

Main entry under the heading for Sutton.

Added entry (name-title) under the heading for Twain i.e. Twain, Mark. Adventures of Tom Sawyer.

(c) Translated texts (Rule 21.14) : The translated work is entered under the heading appropriate to the original. An added entry is recorded under the heading for translator as per instructions of rule 21.30 Kl.

Examples:

(i) For not more than once translation in the same language:

The Revenue Stamp: an autobiography

AMRITA PRITAM

Translated from the Punjabi by Krishna Gorowara

Main entry under Amrita Pritam.

(ii) From the layout as the translator is author:

The Short Stories of Tolstoy

Translated by

Aylmer Maude

Main entry under the heading for Tolstoy.

Added entry under the heading for Maude.

(iii) For more than once translation in the same language :

GODAN By Prem Chand; translated by William Robinson

Main entry under the heading for Prem Chand.

Added entry under the heading for Robinson.

(d) Art works (Rule 21.16):

Example :

PRACTICAL FLOWER ARRANGING

by

Jean Taylor

Photographs by Doughlas Rendall

Main entry under the heading for Taylor.

Added entry under the heading for Rendall.

II. Form of Heading

Form of heading for an item may vary, but the consistent use of one form of heading is desirable. AACR 2 chapter 22 deals with the problems of heading for persons.

Heading for Persons:

Rule 22.1. General Rule.

Entry is made under the name by which he or she is commonly identified. This may be the person's real name, pseudonym, title of nobility, nickname, initials or other appellation.

Examples :

Jimmy Carter	not James Earl Cater
P.N. Kaula	not Prithvi N. Kaula
H.D.	not Hilda Doolittle
Prem Chand	not Dhanpat Rai
George Bernard Shaw	not Bernard Shaw

Rule 22.2 : Choice among different names :

22. 2A. Predominant names :

If one name or form of name predominates and is clearly the name by which a person is most commonly known, entry is made under that name. Otherwise, one name or form of name is chosen according to the following order of preference:

- name appearing most frequently in the person's works,
- name appearing most frequently in reference sources,
- the latest name

Example:

The comedian and author Terene Alan Miligan is commonly known as Spike Miligan, entry heading is made for Spike Miligan.

22. 2.B. Change of name :

If the name of a person undergoes a change by the title of nobility or the adoption of a new married name or by any other reasons, entry is made under the latest name, or form of name or title, unless there is a reason that an earlier name is expected to continue to be better known.

Example:

Dorothy Belle Hungher

not Dorothy Belle Flangen

(Maiden name used in works before author's marriage)

Rule 22.2C. Pseudonyms :

Definition : Pseudonym is "a name assumed by an author to conceal or obscure his or her identity". (AACR 2 Glossary, p. 569).

22.2C1. One Pseudonym : If a person always uses one pseudonym, entry is made under that pseudonym and reference entry is made from his real name.

Example:

Prem Chand *not* Dhanpat Rai

22.2 IC 2. Predominant name : If a person uses several pseudonyms or real name and one or more pseudonym(s). Entry is made under the predominant name and reference entries are made from other names, e.g.:

Mistinguett *not* Jeane Bourgeois

Howard Fast *not* E.V. Cunninghon

not Walter Ericson

22.2 C3. No Predominant name : If there is no predominant name, each item is entered according to the name appearing in it. References to connect the names to and from the various headings are also made.

22.2 C4. Different name in editions of the same work : If a person uses different names in the editions of the same work, entry is made under the most often used in editions of the work. If that is not determined, entry is made under the name appearing in the latest editions of the work. Name title references from the other name(s) are also prepared.

21.6 D. Shared pseudonym : If two or more than two persons use one pseudonym in the works, entry is made under the pseudonym. References from their real names to the pseudonyms are also prepared, e.g. :

Haunted House by Frederick Evans

(Frederick Evans is a joint pseudonym of Robert Smith and Manning Bonn).

Main entry under Frederick Evans.

References from Robert Smith and Manning Bonn.

Rule 22.4 Entry Element : If the name of a person consists of several parts, the entry element should be that part of the name under which the person is cited in authoritative alphabetic lists in his or her own language or country.

22.4 B. Order of elements : If the entry element is the first element of the name, the name is entered in direct order e.g.:

Krishan Kumar

Girja Kumar

If the first element is a surname, then it is a followed by a comma, e.g.:

Chiang, Kai-Shek

(Name: Chiang Kai-Shek)

(Sumame: Chiang)

If the entry element is not the first element of the name, the elements are transposed preceding the entry element. Secondary element is to be preceded by a comma, e.g.:

Srivastva, Ashok Kumar

Dhiman, Anil Kumar

22.5 C3. Hyphenated Surname : Entry is made under the first element of hyphenated surname, e.g.:

Day-Lewis

Carr-Saunders, A.M.

22.5 D. Surnames with separately written prefixes : Entry of English name is under the prefix, e.g. :

De La Mare, Walter

Le Gallienne, Richard

22.5C. Compound surnames : These refer to surnames consisting of two or more proper names. Rule 22.5C2 instructs that entry is made under the element by which the person prefers to be entered or, if this is unknown, under the element under which it is listed in reference sources in the person's language or country of residence.

22.6. Entry under title of nobility : A nobleman is entered under the title of nobility when he or she use his or her title of nobility rather than the surname in his or her works or when such a person is listed by title in reference sources. Then title of nobility is followed by the personal name (excluding unused forenames) in direct order and by the term of rank in vernacular, e.g. :

Wellington, Arthur Wellesley, *Duke of*

22.18 and 22.19. Additions to distinguish identical names : If the heading is identical one to another, it is to be distinguished by adding dates or distinguishing terms, e.g. :

Jones, William, 1815-1871

Jones William 1897-1954

Brown, George, Captain

Brown, George, Rev

22.25. INDIC NAMES : The authorities before the middle of 19th century are entered under the first word of personal element name, leaving honorific terms (Sri, Shri, Swami, Acharya, Muni, etc.), if these are not appearing with the names in reference sources, e.g.:

Kalidasa

Panini

Sankaracharya

22.25B. Modern names : Entry is made under the surname or the name that the person is known to have used as a surname, e.g. :

Ranganathan, S.R.

Mittal, R.L

Navlani, K.

Dhiman, A.K.

CCC

CHOICE AND RENDERING OF HEADINGS: PERSONS

I. Choice of Heading

1. Single Personal Author

Definition : "Person as author, the responsibility for the thought and the expression constituting the work resting solely on his private capacity and not on the capacity of any office being held by him within a corporate body, nor on the capacity of that body. (CCC, Rule FC 31).

Example :

Sacred Plants and their Medicinal Uses

by

Anil Kumar Dhiman

Daya Publishing House

Delhi

Main entry under the heading for DHIMAN (Anil Kumar)

The name of personal author is chosen as the heading of the main entry as it occurs in the title page or its substitute.

2. Joint Authors

Definition : "Two or more authors, personal or corporate, sharing responsibility for the thought and expression constituting the work, the portion for which each is separately responsible not being either specified or separable" (CCC Rule FC 5).

Rule MD 32 : If the title-page contains the names of two and only two joint authors, both the names are to be used as the heading with the conjunction 'and' connecting them.

Example:

An Introduction to Statistical Methods

by

G.B. Gupta and Vijay Gupta

Main entry under the heading for Gupta (G B) and Gupta (Vijay).

RULE MD 33 : If the title page contains the names of three or more joint authors, the name of the first mentioned author alone is to be used as the heading and the word 'etc'. is to be added there after.

Example :

Foundation of Physics

R.S. Gambhir D. Banerjee

M.C.Durgapal

Main entry under the heading GAMBHIR (R S) etc.

3. Mixed Responsibility

CCC discusses the problem of mixed responsibility under the Chapter 'G', 'Conflict of authorship between Person Vs Person, Person Vs Corporate body, etc.' The conflict of authorship between two persons are grouped into following categories :

- Spoken words
- Correspondence
- Maps and atlases
- Dependent works

The original author is to be taken as the author for the dependent works; abridgement, adaptation, paraphrase, revision, selection and translation. However, for the dependent works like commentary, dramatisation, index, novelization, etc., the author of the dependent work is to be taken as the author.

Example :

The Revenue Stamp

an autobiography

by

Amrita Pritam

Translated from the Punjabi by Krishna Gorowara

Main entry under the heading AMRITA PRITAM.

Book Index entry under the heading GOROWARA (Krishna), *Tr.*

II. Rendering Of Heading

Rule JA 2 : "If the back of Title-Page of the book conforms to the Standard for Entry Statement for Author mentioned in Sec FR77 the Entry Element is to be the Word(s) printed in a dominant typeface in the Entry Statement for Personal Author; the Secondary Element is to be the rest of the Word(s) in it ; and the further individualizing element is to be the Year(s) mentioned in it."

One-Worded Name : Rule JA 3 : "The rendering of a Title-Page Name consisting of one word only is to write it as it occurs in the Title-Page."

Example :

KALIDASA

VALMIKI

Multi -Worded Name : Rule JA 6 : "For the rendering of a Title-Page Name consisting of two or more words, it should first be reduced to the Entry Name, and the Entry Element and the Secondary Element should be separated out with the aid of the Definitions and the Section of part H and in particular the chapter HE and HF. The rendering is to consist successively of the

– Entry Element;

– Secondary Element; and

– Year(s) of the person.

Example:

ADAMS (Mary) (1898)

DAS GUPTA (Sachidulal) (1912)

RANGANATHAN (Shiyali Ramamrita) (1892-1972)

Pseudonymous Author

Definition : "An author assuming a false or fictitious name or any other specificate different from the real name. A pseudonym may also be given by others to an author or it may even get started in a casual way, either in his own time or in later-times" (CCC, FC6).

Rule MD 41 : If the title page gives only a pseudonym in the place of the author's name, pseudonym is to be used as the heading followed by the descriptive element, "*Pseud*".

Example:

TWAIN (Mark), *Pseud.*

Rule MD 421 : If the real name of the author is also given in a subordinated manner, it is to be added in circular brackets after the descriptive element "*Pseud*". The real name of the author is to preceded by the symbol "i.e.". The bracket is to be preceded by a comma and words in the real name are to be written in their natural sequence.

Example:

LIBRA, *Pseud*, (i.e., Shiyali Ramamrita Ranganathan).

Rule MD 422 : In case the title page gives the real name of the author and adds the pseudonym; in a subordinated manner, the former is to be chosen for the heading and the latter is to be added after it and enclosed in circular bracket. The descriptive element "*Pseud*" as to be added with the brackets and the bracket is to be preceded by a comma.

Example :

RANGANATHAN (S R), (Libra, *Pseud*),

Rule MD 423 : If the title page gives only a pseudonym, but the real name of the author found from outside the work, the real name is to be added in square bracket. Example :

LIBRA, *Pseud*, [i.e., Shiyali Ramamrita Ranganathan].

Rule MD 424 : If a pseudonym represents two joint authors and if the real names of the authors are also known, the symbol "i.e." which comes after the pseudonym is to be followed the real names of both the authors. Their names are to be written in the natural sequence with conjunction "and".

Example :

EVANS (Frederick), *Pseud*, (*i.e.*, Robert Smith and Manning Bonn)

Rule MD 425 : If a pseudonym represents three or more than three authors and the real name known, the symbol "i.e." which comes after the pseudonym is to be followed by the real name one of the authors alone which itself is to be followed by the word "etc."

Rule MD 43 : "If there are two or more pseudonyms occurring in the place of author's names, they are to be connected by the conjunction 'and'.

Example :

JKFRS and SA.Sc, *Pseud*, [i.e., James Keir].

Indic Names

There are no specific rules for the choice and rendering of headings of Indic Names in CCC. However, one can find a detailed study of Western, Muslim, Indic name patterns in part H "Name of the Person "for the choice of heading and in chapter J A for rendering of heading.

Examples :

DAS GUPTA (Sachidulal) (1912)

QUILLER-COUCH (Arthur Thomas) (1863-1944)

MUHAMMAD IBN ALI (Abu Abdulla)

Q. : Compare the treatment of Government as corporate author in C.C.C. and A.A.C.R. –2.

or

Compare the treatment of Conference as a corporate author in C.C.C. and A.A.C.R.–2.

or

Compare the treatment of Institution in C.C.C. and A.A.C.R.–2.

or

What do you understand by 'Corporate Author'? Discuss the rules for choice and rendering of heading either for 'Conference' or for 'Institution' as corporate Author according to C.C.C. and A.A.C.R.–2.

or

Write briefly on choice of heading of Corporate Authors in CCC and A.A.C.R.–2.

or

What do you mean by Corporate Authorship ? How they are rendered in CCC or A.A.C.R.–2.

Ans. A work is said to be the work of a work of corporate authorship, if (i) it indicates somewhere in itself the name of a corporate body, (ii) there is internal evidence of corporate authorship, (iii) the title page mentions the name of a corporate body and (iv) the content is of deliberative, legislative, directive, judicial, administrative or of routine character. Governments and government organs (agencies, according to AACR-2R), institutions and their affiliates, and delegations to conferences are-viewed as corporate bodies by CCC.

CHOICE OF HEADINGS: CORPORATE BODIES (AACR 2)

Choice and rendering of headings for corporate bodies involve the study of choice of access points/headings for the works which fall into one or more or more of the categories stated below:

(a) those of an administrative nature dealing with the corporate body itself.

(b) legal and administrative works of certain types (See 21.31-21.36 rules of AACR-2).

(c) those works which record the collective thought of a body.

(d) works which report the collective activity of a conference, of an expedition, or of an event falling within the definition of a corporate body, provided that is permanently named in the item being catalogued.

(e) sound recordings, films and video recordings from the collective activity of a performing group as a whole where the responsibility of the same goes beyond that of mere performance, execution etc. (rule 21.1 B2).

Works of single corporate body (Rule 21.4 B)

"Enter a work or collection of works, or selection from a work or works emanating from one corporate body (or any reprint, reissue, etc. of such a work) under the heading for the body if the work or collection falls into one or more of the categories given in 21.1 B2."

Examples :

(i) International Conference on Cataloguing Principles, Paris, 9th-18th October, 1961 : a report.

Main entry under the heading for Conference.

(ii) Universities Handbook : India, 2002-03. Association of Indian Universities.

Main entry under the heading for the Association.

(iii) Library, University of California, Berkeley. Author title Catalog.- Boston : G.K.Hall

Main entry under the heading for the Library.

Works of Shared responsibility (Rule 21.6 B)

21.6 B.1. Principal responsibility indicated : If the principal responsibility is indicated either by the working or the layout of the chief source of information, the entry is made under the heading for that principal person or body.

If the principal responsibility is indicated to two or three persons or bodies, then main entry is made under the heading for the first named person or body.

21.6C. Principal responsibility not indicated : If there are two or three responsible persons or bodies and the principal responsibility is not indicated, then main entry is made under the name of first person or body and added entries for others are prepared.

If there are more than three persons or bodies and no principal responsibility is indicated then main entry under the title and added entry for the named first person or body are made.

Rendering of Heading for Corporate Bodies

Geographic names : In the rendering of headings for corporate bodies, the basic problem relates to the rendering of geographic names. Chapter 23 of AACR2 provides guidance for "Geographic names", the 'places' which commonly constitute essential elements in headings for corporate bodies. Generally these are required (i) to be used as headings for governments, (ii) to be used in addition to corporate bodies (e.g. for conferences) and (iii) to differentiate bodies with identical names.

Rule 23.2A : The rule instructs that English form of name in general use of a place is to be used after being determined from gazetteers and other reference sources, e.g. :

Sweden *not* Sverize

Rule 23.2B: If the English form of name is not in general use, the form in the official language of that country is to be used, e.g. :

Livomo *not* Leghorn

Rule 23.4 : If it is required to differentiate bodies with identical names, the name of larger geographical entity in which the place is located is to be added in parenthesis, e.g. :

Bangor (Gwynedd)

Bangor (Northern Ireland)

Rule 23.5 : If the first part of the place name begins with a term indicating a type of jurisdiction, then entry is made under the element commonly found as the entry element in lists published in the language of the country in which it is located, e.g. :

Kerry (Ireland) not Country Kerry (Ireland)

Different Categories of Corporate Bodies : Corporate bodies may be grouped into three categories:

(i) Government,

(ii) Societies and institutions, and

(iii) Conferences

(i) Rendering of Heading for Governments

AACR 2 footnote provides that "the word government is used to mean the totality of corporate bodies (executive, legislative and judicial exercising the powers of jurisdiction)".

Rule 24:3E directs for the use of the conventional name of a government unless the official name is in common use. The conventional name of a Government is the geographic name of the area over which the government exercises jurisdiction, e.g. :

'India' rather than the Republic of India.

Government bodies and officials : Rule 24 17 instructs that a government agency is entered under its own name if its name is unique and does not contain terms that suggest dependent status, e.g :

University of British Columbia

not British Columbia University

Government agencies entered subordinately : Rule 24.28 directs that a government agency is entered subordinately if it belongs to one or more of the following types :

Type 1. Containing the term as department, division, section, branch, e.g. :

Uttar Pradesh. *Department of Technical Education*

Type 2. Containing the term Committee, commission or the like, e.g.:

India. *Planning Commission,*

Type 3. An agency with a name that has been or is likely to be used by other governments, e.g.:

United States. Environment Protection Agency.

Type 4. An agency that is ministry or the like e.g. :

India. *Ministry of Finance.*

Type 5. Legislative bodies, e.g.:

India. *Parliament.*

Type 6. Courts e.g. :

India. *Supreme Court.*

Type 7. Principal armed services, e.g.:

India. *Air Force.*

Type 8. Chief of State and Heads of Governments, e.g.:

India. *President. 1969-1975 (V.V. Giri)*

Type 9. Embassies, Consulates, etc. e.g. :

India. *High Commission (Bangladesh).*

Type 10. Delegation to international and intergovernmental bodies, e.g.:

United Kingdom. *Delegation to the United Nations.*

Additions : 24.6 B and 24.6 C

Examples : Cork (Cork, Ireland)

Cork (Ireland : Country)

Berlin (Germany : East)

Berlin (Germany: West)

Changes: A new heading for a new name of the body is required.

(ii) Societies and Institutions

Entry is made under the name of the body as determined from items issued by the body in its own language, e.g. :

Aslib

British Museum

National Science Foundation.

Exception is for the subordinate, body where it is entered under a higher body, e.g.,

HNB Garhwal University. *Department of Library and Information Science.*

When the name of the corporate body changes by way of amalgamation or otherwise, a new heading is required for the new name.

Additions : In case of two or more bodies having the same name, the name of place or the year of founding is added to distinguish them, e.g. :

Loyola University (Chicago)

Loyola University (New Orleans)

Ommissions:

(i) Initial articles unless required for reasons of grammar are ommitted, e.g.:

Library Association *not* The Library Association

(ii) Incorporations or Limited (Ltd.) etc. are ommitted unless they are integral part of a name or they are needed to make clear the body, e.g. :

Cecil E.Walts Limited *not* Cecil E. Walts

(ii) Conferences

Definition : "1. A meeting of individuals or representatives of various bodies for the purpose of discussing and activing on topics of common interest. 2. A meeting of representatives of a corporate body that constitutes its legislative or governing body." (AACR2 Glossary, p. 565).

Rule 24.26 : "Enter a delegation, commission, etc., representing a country in an international or intergovernmental body, conference, undertaking etc., as a subheading of the heading for the country represented."

Example : United States. *Mission to the United Nations.*

Ommissions (Rule 24.7 A) : The words denoting the number, frequency or year of convocation are ommitted, e.g. :

Louisiana Cancer Conference....................

not Biennial Louisiana Cancer Conference......................

Additions (Rule 24.7 B) : Add to conferences, etc. headings, the number of the conference, etc., the year and the place in which it was held as follows :

Louisiana Cancer Conference (2nd : 1958 : New Orleans)

CHOICE AND RENDERING OF HEADING : CORPORATE BODY IN CCC

Definition : In CCC Corporate body has been defined in two senses:

Sense 1. A number of persons taken collectively usually as united, or organized, or coming together informally in a common cause or for common action such as governmental business, or commercial or industrial or service political or any other business, or for deliberation, or for collective expression of opinion or statement.

Sense 2. A number of corporate bodies, in sense 1, taken collectively usually as united, or organized or coming together informally, in a common cause or for common action such as governmental business, or commercial or industrial or service or political or any other business, or for deliberations, or for collective expression of opinion or statement. "(CCC, Rule FC2).

Any organ, may be constitutional, administrative, or executive, is also itself a corporate body.

Broadly, corporate body has been categorised into three types :

(i) Government

(ii) Institution

(iii) Conference

(i) Government as Author

Rule JC 1 Whole Government : If the corporate body is a government as a whole, the name of the territory of the government is taken as a heading.

Example :

INDIA is the heading for "Government of India".

Rule JC 2 Organ of Government : If the corporate body is an organ of a government, a multiple corporate heading is to be used in which second heading is to be the name of the organ.

Example :

INDIA, LOK SABHA

Rule JC 4 Head of the Government : If the second heading is the head of the government, the name of the occupant of the office is used as an individualising element.

Example :

INDIA, PRESIDENT (APJ Abdul Kalam)

Rule JC 6 Administrative Department : If the entry element is the name of an administrative department of a government, it is to be the word or word -group denoting its sphere of activity.

Example :

INDIA, FINANCE (Ministry of-)

Rule JC 7 Temporary Organ : If the entry element is the name of a temporary organ of a government, it is to be rendered on the analogy of section JC 6 and its sub-divisions for the administrative department.

Example :

INDIA, EDUCATION (Commission) (1964) *Chairman*: D S Kothari).

(ii) Institution as Author

Rule JD 1 : This rule prescribes that the name to be used in rendering the name of an institution is to be the one in the shorter form found in the title page; or half-title page; or any other part of the document.

Rule JD 11 : If the name of an institution occurs in two or more languages, the name in the language occuring earliest in the scale of languages of the library is to be used for rendering the heading.

Rule JD 12 : The initial article is to be omitted, while rendering the name of an institution.

Rule JD 13 : Every honorific word, not forming an inseparable part of the name is to be omitted, while rendering the name of an institution, if found either at the beginning or at the end ,or in other position in the name.

Rule JD 17 (Amendment to CCC) : The entry element in the name of the institution in the heading of any entry is to consist of the word or word-group denoting the subject or any other speciality forming the purview of the institution, in its singular nominative form.

Example :

LIBRARY (lndian Association).

JD 171 (Amendment to CCC) : The secondary element in the heading is to consist of the rest of the word(s) occurring in the name of the institution written in the sequence of their occurrence in it.

JD 175 (Amendment to CCC): The Rule JD 17 is not applicable in the case of the name of a university, college, school, laboratory, library, museum and any similar traditional institution. The entry element should respectively be university, etc.

Example :

UNIVERSITY (Gurukul Kangri)

Rule JD 2 Individualising Element : If the bare name of an institution does not individualize it, the individualizing element to be used for resolving the homonym is to be the term denoting its place, if it is a localized institution; country, if it has a national status; constituent state, country, district, taluk etc. if it is a state, country, district, taluk etc. institution and headquarters, if it cannot be individualized conveniently by any of the terms mentioned above.

Example :

LABOUR PARTY (Canada)

LABOUR PARTY (Great Britain)

GENERAL POST OFFICE (Mumbai)

GENERAL POST OFFICE (Kolkata)

If the name of an institution does not individualize as per Rule JD 2, the year of foundation of the institution is to be used as a second individualizing element.

Example :

STATE AGRICULTURAL SOCIETY (South Carolina) (1839)

STATE AGRICULTURAL SOCIETY (South Carolina) (1855)

Rule JD 3 Organ of an Institution : The rendering of the name of any organ of an institution is to be made on the analogy of Rule JD 2 to JC 8, as discussed earlier under the heading "Government As Author".

(iii) Conference As Author

Rule JE 1 : The name to be used in rendering the name of a conference is to be the one in the shortest form found in the title page; or half title page; or any other part of the document and in accordance with the following additional rules.

Rule JE 2 Individualizing Element : The name(s) of the place(s) of a conference and the year of its holding are to be added as individualising elements, but not for the conference held periodically.

The entry element in the name of a conference in the heading of any entry is based on the analogy of JD 17.

Examples : LIBRARY (All India-Conference) (Varanasi) (1938).

ECONOMIC (International-Conference) (Paris) (1952).

Rule JE 3 Diplomatic Conference : In case of a diplomatic conference the name of the place of the conference is to be prefixed to the name of the conference not held periodically, so as to form a word group, if it is not already in the name of the conference; and the year(s) of the conference is (are) to be added as individualizing element.

Example : PARIS PEACE CONFERENCE (1919).

Rule JE 4 Without Specific Name : In case of a conference, not being held periodically, without a specific name, the word or word group denoting the class of persons is to be the entry element.

Rule JE 6 Organ of Conference : The rendering of the name of any organ of a conference is to be made on the analogy of Rule JC 2 to JC 8, as discussed earlier under the heading "Government as Author".

Q. : What do you understand by Anonymous work ? How these are rendered in AACR – 2 or CCC.

or

Write an essay on the treatment of Anonymous work in CCC or AACR–2.

Ans. An Anonymous work may be defined as the work of uncertain or unknown authorship, or by an unnamed group. Most of the sacred books and many old and medieval texts are anonymous works.

1. Treatment in AACR–2

(i) If a work is of unknown or uncertain personal authorship, or if it emanates from a body that lacks a name, enter it under title :

Personal

The secret expedition : a force (in two acts) as it has been represented upon the political theatre of Europe.

(Author unknown entered under the title)

Corporate

A memorial to Congress against an increase of duties on importation's. (by citizens of Boston and vicinity)

Orthogonal expansions and their continuous analogues: proceedings of a conference held at Southern Illinois University;

Edwardsville, April 27-29, 1967 (edited by Deborah Tapper Haino)

(ii) If such a work has been attributed to one or more persons or corporate bodies, enter it under title and make added entries under the headings for these persons or bodies: e.g.,

The law of serutiny; or, Attornies guide

(variously attributed to Andrew Carmichael and William Noreott)

Main entry under the title and added entries under

Carmichael, Andrew

Noreott, William

La Capucisere, or, Le bijan enleve a la course, poem

(possibly by Pierre-Francois Tissot erroneously attributed to Pierra- Jean Baptiste Nougaret)

Main entry under title as above

Added entries

Tissot, Pierre-Francois

Nougaret, Pierre-Jean-Baptiste

(iii) If reference sources indicate that a person is the probable author of such a work, enter it under the heading for that person; and make an added entry under title.

A true character of Mr. Pope

(Author uncertain; generally attributed to John Dennis) Main Entry under Dennis, John

Added entry under title as above

Portrait of Andrew Jackson

(Once attributed to Mathew Brady, but generally thought to be by Edward Anthony)

Main entry under Anthony, Edward

Added entries under Brady, and title as

Brady, Mathew

Portrait of Andrew Jackson

If the name of a personal author is unknown and the only indication of authorship is the appearance in the chief source of information of a characterizing word or phrase or a of a phrase naming another work by the person, enter it under that word or phrase; and make an added entry under title :

Memoir of Bowman Hendry by a Physician

Enter under the Physician

Physician

Memoir of Bowman Hendry

Added entry under title Memoir of Bowman Hendry

The unveiled heart: a simple story by the author of Early impressions

Enter under the phrase

Author of Early impressions

Early impressions, Author of

Added entry under title

The Unveiled heart: a simple story

If the only indication of authorship is a predominantly non-alphabetic and non-numeric device, enter it under title. Do not make an added entry under the device :

Angry thoughts by x!x!x!

Enter under title as,

Angry thoughts

Enter anonymous works in scripts other than Greek or Roman, under their established titles in English. For example:

Arabian Nights

Book of the Dead

When an anonymous work is known to be written by a particular author, enter it under the name of the author:

A Tale of a Tub

(Published anonymously by Jonathan Swift)

Enter under Jonathan Swift as,

Swift, Jonathan

Added, entry under title

A Tale of a Tub

2. Treatment in CCC

An anonymous work is treated in two ways in CCC viz.,

(i) those that are with collaborators and (ii) those that one not with collaborators.

(i) In the first type the name of the collaborator is chosen as the heading, if the title page of a document gives the name of the collaborator.

For examples :

Bhagwat Gita

Translated from the Sanskrit by

Juan Mascaro

Main entry under the heading MASCARO (Juan). *Tr.*

In the second type, the title page does not carry any name, the heading gives the title of the book.

Example : ANGLO ASSAMESE (Dictionary, etc.) Ed 10.

Q. : What do you understand by uniform titles? How they are treated in AACR–2 And CCC.

or

Defining uniform title, discuss how they are treated in AACR-2 and CCC.

Ans. A uniform title is the particular title by which a work that has appeared under varying titles is to be identified for cataloguing purposes. It is also a conventional collective title used to collocate entries for publications of an author, or corporate body, containing several works, or extracts from several works, e.g. complete works in a particular literary form. So, the purpose of using uniform titles is to avoid dispersal in a catalogue of the entries of the various editions of the same work due to their varying titles. It is also the purpose of uniform titles to collocate the entries of publications of an author containing several works in a particular literary form. It is then the means for bringing together all the catalogue entries for a work when various editions and other manifestations of it have appeared under various titles. Uniform titles also facilitate identification of a work when the title by which it is known differs form the title proper of the item being catalogued. Use of uniform titles depends upon:

- how well the work is know;
- how many manifestations (editions, translation, etc.) of the work are involved;
- whether another work with the same title proper has been identified;

- whether the main entry is under the title;
- whether the original work was in another language and
- the extent to which the catalogue is used for research purposes.

TREATMENT IN AACR-2

The basic rule about uniform titles in AACR-2 prescribes selection of one title of a work if its manifestations have appeared under several titles.

The uniform title is to be enclosed in square brackets and given before the title proper. Thus,

Dickens, Charles

(Martin Chuzzlewit)

The life and adventures of Martin Chuzzlewit... 1868

Dickens, Charles

Martin Chuzzlewit...1899

Dickens, Charles

(Martin Chuzzlewit)

Martin Chuzzlewit's life and adventures...1910

In the above example, three different editions of Charles Dicken's Martin Chuzzlewit are appearing under three different titles i.e., the proper. This work is popularly known as Martin Chuzzlewit, which title, then, is used as the uniform title for the work. The uniform title chosen for the cataloguing purpose and the title proper of the 1899 edition of the work are identical and so the title is not enclosed in square brackets in that case. Where the two are different, the uniform title is enclosed in square brackets and is followed by the title proper, as in the case of the two editions of 1869 and 1910 in the example. The uniform title used here serves the purpose of bringing together all editions of Martin Chuzzlewit under the heading for Dickens. The uniform title in this example is not used as main entry heading. In the following example, the uniform title is used as heading

Blind date

Chance meeting

(Motion picture issued in Britain as: Chance meeting

Later issued in the U.S. as Blind date).

Thus, the two manifestations of the same work-in this case, Blind date-are brought together under the uniform title.

When a work is entered under a uniform title, it is necessary to make an added entry under the title proper of the item being catalogued. Thus, in the above case,

Chance meeting

See Blind date

If a work is entered under a personal or corporate heading and a uniform heading is used, make a name-title (author's name and title) reference from variants of the title;

Dickens, Charles

The life and adventures of Martin Chuzzlewit...1868

See Dickens, Charles

Martin Chuzzlewit...

If a later manifestation of a work is a revision or updating of the original work, a uniform title is not be used. Instead, on the entry for the revision or updating a note should be provided, giving the title of the earlier edition. For example,

Scott, Franklin D

The United States and Scandinavia-1950

Scott, Franklin D.

Scandinavia... Rev. & enl. ed.... 1975

Note : previous ed, published in 1950 as: The United States and Scandinavia

Richardes, George

A Treatise on the Law of Insurance..... 1892

Rochards, George.

Richards on the Law of Insurance...5th ed./by Warren Freedman...1952 (Fifth revision)

Note : First-3rd eds. Published as : A treatise on the Law of Insurance.

Works after 1500 : While cataloguing works created from 1501 A.D., the title of a work in the original language by which it has become known through use in its manifestations is to be used. For, example,

Jonathan Swift's *Travels into several remote nations of the world by Lemuel Gulliver* has become known as *Gulliver's travels*, and *An almanac for the year of our Lord* has become known as *Whitaker's almanac*. Thus, *Gulliver's travels and Whitaker's almanac* become uniform titles respectively.

Swift, Jonathan

(Gulliver's travels)

Travels into several remote nations of the world by

Lemuel Gulliver...1726

Whitaker's Almanac

An almanac for the year of our Lord...

If no one title of the several titles of a work is best known, use the title proper of the original edition, omitting introductory phrases and articles :

Wodehouse, P.G.

(Ring for Jeeves) (the title of the original ed)

The Return of Jeeves.....

Treatise of a Galaunt

Here begynneth a treatise of a Galaunt

(Introductory phrase, begynneth, is omitted)

If a work is published simultaneously in the same language under two different titles, use the title of the edition published in the home country where the cataloguing is being done. If it is not published in the home country, use the title of the edition received first in the library.

For a cataloguing agency in the United Kingdom :

Joesten, Joachim

Denmark's Day of Doom.– London... 1939

Joesten, Joachim

[Denmark's Day of Doom]

Rats in the Larder : the story of the Nazi influence in Denmark New York... 1939

In the above case, the title of the British edition became the uniform title. In an agency in the United States, Rats in the Larder would be the uniform title.

Works before 1501 : Use as well-established English title for a work originally written in classical Greek. If there is no English title, use the Latin title. If neither exists, use the Greek title :

English :

Aristophanes

(Birds)

not Aves

not Ornithes

Homer

[Iliad]

not Ilias

Homer

[Odyssey]

not Odyssey

not Odysseia

Plato

[Republic]

not Republica

not Politeia

Additions to Uniform Titles : Add in brackets an explanatory word, brief phrase, or other designation to distinguish between two identical uniform titles:

Genesis (Anglo-Saxon poem)

Genesis (Book of the Bible)

France

[Constitution (1946)]

France

[Constitution 1958)]

Translations : If the item being catalogued is a translation, add the name of the language of the item to the uniform title:

Goncourt, Edmond de

[Les freres Zemganno, English]

The Zemganno brother...

(An English translation of a French novel)

If the item being catalogued is in two languages, name both. If one of the languages is the original language, name it second :

Caesar, Julius

[De bellow Gallico, French & Latin]

If the item is in three or more languages, use the term Polyglot, unless it is originally in three or more languages in which case name all languages

United States

[The Declaration of Independence, Polyglot]

The Declaration of Independence of the United States in ten languages.

Parts of a Work : If a separately catalogued part of a work has a title of its own, use the title of the part by itself as the uniform title. Make a 'see' reference from the heading for the whole work. Make an explanatory reference, when necessary. Thus:

Tolkien, J.R.R.

(The Two Towers)

see reference: Tolkien, J.R.R.

1. The Lord of the Rings. 2 The Two Towers

see Tolkien, J.R.R.

(The Two Towers)

(Sindbad the Sailor)

explanatory ref : Arabian Nights

For separately published stories from this collection, see

Ali Baba

Sindbad the Sailor

[etc.]

Several Parts of a Work : If the item being catalogued consists of consecutively numbered parts of a work, use the designation of the parts in the singular as a sub-heading of the title of the whole work.

Homer

[Iliad. Book 1-6]

For non-consecutive parts, the title of the first part becomes the uniform title for the item:

Homer

[Iliad. Book 1 English]

Iliad. Books I and VI

Added entry under. Homer. Iliad. Book 6 English

Extracts : For extracts from a work, use the title of the work as a uniform title followed by the term 'selections'.

Gibbon, Edward

[The History of the Decline and Fall of the Roman Empire.

Selections]

Two Works Issued Together : If an item being catalogued contains two works of an author, use the uniform title of the work that occurs first in the item. Make a name-title added entry using the uniform title of the Second work:

Enter Dickens' new stories, which contains his two works, viz., Hard times and pictures from Italy, as follows:

Dickens, Charles

[Hard Times]

Dickens' new stories

(contains Hard Times and Pictures from Italy)

Added entry : Dickens, Charles

[Pictures from Italy]

Dickens' new stories

(contains Hard tines and Pictures from Italy)

Complete Works : Use the collective title Works for an item that consists of, or purports to be, the complete works of a person:

Maugham, W. Somerset

[works]

Complete Works...

For complete works of a person in one particular form:

Maugham, W. Somerset

[plays]

Collected plays....

Maugham, W. Somerset

[short stories]

complete short stories...

Selections : Use the collective title Selections for items consisting of three or more works in various forms, or in one form if the person created works in one form only, and for items consisting of extracts, etc., from the works of one person.

Maugham, W. Somerset

[selections]

The Somerset Maugham pocket book...

(Contains: Cakes and Ale, The Circle, Short Stories, Travel Sketches, Essays)

Maugham, W. Somerset

[selections]

Wit and Wisdom of Somerset Maugham

Maugham, W. Somerset

[Novels, Selections]

Selected novels.....

Laws (Legal Material) : Use the term Laws, etc. for complete or partial collections of legislative enactments other than compilations on a particular subject:

United Kingdom

[Laws.etc]

Halsbury's Statutes of England

United States

[Laws, etc]

United States Code...

Compilations on a particular subject:

California

[Agricultural Code]

West California Agricultural Code...

United Kingdom

[Licensing Acts]

Paterson's Licensing Acts-85th ed., 1977

Single Laws:

United Kingdom

[Field Monuments Act 1972]

India

[Income Tax Act 1961]

Maharashtra

[Public Libraries Act 1967]

Treaties : Use Treaties, etc., as a uniform title for collections of treaties between two parties. Follow the uniform title by the name of the other party:

India

[Treaties, etc.]

Use Treaties, etc. alone, if the collection contains treaties between a single party and two or more other parties;

India

[Treaties, etc].

If a collection of treaties, etc., signed at the same time, is identified by a name, use that name followed in brackets by the year of signing. Make 'see also' references from the title of the collection to the headings of the single treaties:

Treaty of Utrecht (1713)

see also

Fiance Treaties, etc. Prussia...

Spain Treaties, etc, Great Britain...[etc.]

For single treaties between two parties, use Treaties, etc. as the uniform title followed by the name of the other party and the date of signing the treaty:

Denmark

[Treaties, etc. United Kingdom, 1966 Mar.3]

Conventions : Use a the uniform title for a treaty, etc. between four or more parties the name by which the treaty is known. Add the year of signing:

Universal Copyright Convention (1952)

Sacred Scriptures : Use as the uniform title for a sacred scripture the title by which it is most commonly identified.

Avesta

Bible

Jaina Agama

Koran

Talmud

Tripitaka

Vedas

Aranyakas

Brahmanas

Upanishads

A part of a scripture should be used as a sub-heading of the scripture and a part of that part as a sub-heading of the part :

Avesta.Yasna

Avesta.Yasna. Gathas

Bible O.T. (Old Testament)

Bible. N.T. (New Testament)

Bible. O.T. Ezra

Bible. N.T. Revelation

Bible. O.T. Ecclesiastes III, 1-8..

Bible. N.T. Epistles of John (1-3 John)

Jaina Agama. Anga

Jaina Agama. Anga. Acaranga

Tripitaka. Abhidharmapitaka

Tripitaka. Vinayapitaka. Pratimoksa

Vedas. Rigveda

Vedas. Atharvaveda

Vedas. Samaveda

Vedas. Yajurveda

Aranyakas. Aitareyaranyaka

Brahmanas. Satapathabrahmana

Upanisads. Chandogyopanishad

References : Refer from the title of parts that are entered as sub-headings of the larger works to the work e.g.

Ezra (Book of the Old Testament)

see Bible. O.T. Ezra...

Abhidhramapitaka

see Triptiaka. Abhidhramapitaka

Atharvaveda

see Vedas. Atharvaveda

Chandogyopanisad

see Upanisads. Chandogyopanisad

Acaranga

see Jaina Agama. Anga. Acaranga

Language: Add the name of the language of the item after the designation for the scripture or its part being catalogued.

Bible. English

Bible O.T. English

Bible O.T. Genesis. English

Vedas. English

Vedas. Rigveda. English

Vedas. Yajurveda (Vajasaneyisamhita). English

All appropriate additions regarding versions or nature of content must follow after the name of the language.

Bible. Latin . Vulgate

Bible. N.T. Corinthians. English. Authorised.

Vedas. Rgveda. English. Selections.

Vedas. Yajurveda (Vajasaneyisamhita) English. Selections.

TREATMENT IN CCC

Uniform title in CCC is described as follows:

"Title uniformed by popular or cataloguing usage in lieu of listless, and often unintended, variants of the title of one and the same work in different editions or the titles of different volumes of one and the same work."

The annotation to the above description given above say "...It is helpful to use one uniform title for a document in the place of its variants. Generally, a Sacred Book of Religion is given slightly varying titles from time to time, without any significance. There is therefore, a need for adopting a Uniformed Title for it. Bible, Vedas, and Talmud are examples of such Uniformlized Titles. The same thing happens also in the case of Classics and Works of Literature. Many governmental and annual reports change their titles routinely. For example, it may be *Administrative report on agriculture* in one year, *Annual report on agriculture* in a still another year. This is a case where a Uniformized Title is called for. Uniformity of the title may also be necessary in respect of a periodical conference. This is a case in which the Canon of Ascertainability is not followed rigidly."

Examples of books calling for title as heading.

Reference Works

COLUMBIA Viking Desk Encyclopaedia. Ed 2.

SCIENTIFIC (Van Nostrand's - Encyclopaedia etc.). Ed 2.

Sacred works of religions, such as Vedas, Upanishads, Bible. New Testament, Kuran, etc., are treated as if they were a class or subject. To distinguish them from a normal class or a subject, they are called a quasi-class or quasi-subject.

Similarly, works of literature such as Ramayana, Sakuntala, Iliad, Hamlet, etc., are also treated as if they were a quasi-class or quasi-subject.

Classical works such as Aristotles' Poetics, Newton's Principle, Marx's Capital are also treated as a quasi-class or quasi-subject.

In CCC cataloguing of translations, parts of a work, extracts, two works together, complete work, selections, legal publications, are not discussed under uniformized titles. They are treated under the respective heads in different chapters, unless such works come under the categories mentioned above.

Q. : Write briefly about treatment of composite book in CCC.

or

What do you understand by composite books? Giving their types, discuss their treatment in classified catalogue code.

Ans. According to Classified Catalogue Code, there are two types of composite books –

— Ordinary composite books

— Artificial composite books

An ordinary composite book is defined as "Composite book provided with a single, generic title to denote all the contributions collectively".

Some of the books which fall under the category of ordinary composite books are anthologies, christomathy hymn-book, prayer book, symposium, festschrift etc.

Besides, there are cases when a publisher has issued two different books bound together with two separate titles. Some individuals or even libraries bind two or more different books in one cover. Such types of books are called as artificial composite books.

The cataloguing of an ordinary composite book does not pose any problem. It is dealt with as a simple book ignoring the names of the contributors except for Book Index Entries. However, whenever needed Author and Subject Analytical entries can be provided. Such entries are to be prepared with caution. Wherever there are published bibliographies which cover the composite books, Analytical Entries need not be prepared. When a book covers several contributions, making subject and author analytical in addition to Class Index Entries may tend to bulge the catalogue and go against the Laws of Library Science.

In other ordinary composite books, the Main Entry is simple and explanations are required only if we have to prepare Analytical Entries.

Example

The poet's Craft
Verses selected
By
Helen Fern Daringer
and
Anne Thaxter Eaton
Illustrated
By
Helen Carter
Books for Libraries Press
Freeport N.Y.

Other information :

Call No. 0111, 1× L2

Acc. No. 5853

Date of publication. 1972

There is a series : Granger Index Reprint Series.

The relevant entries are worked out below :

Main Entry

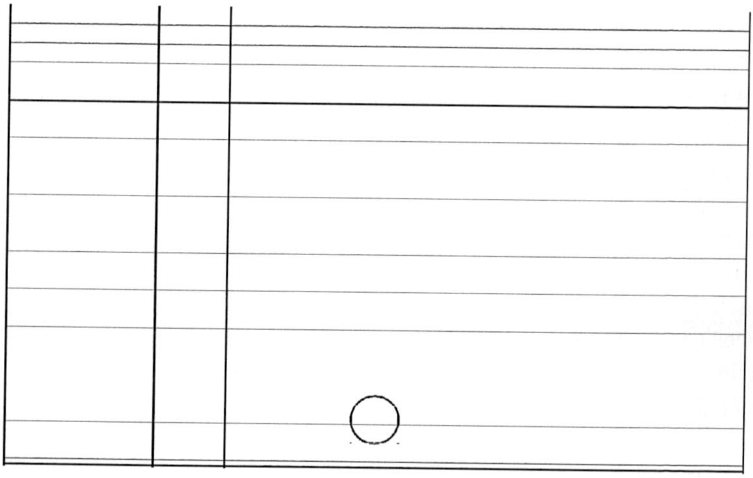

Chain Index :

O = Literature

O111 = English literature

O111,1 = English poetry

O111, 1x = Collection of English poetry

Class Index Entry

Other Class Index Entries are :

POETRY, ENGLISH.

ENGLISH, LITERATURE.

LITERATURE.

Book Index Entry (Joint Compilers)

Book Index Entry (Joint Compilers)

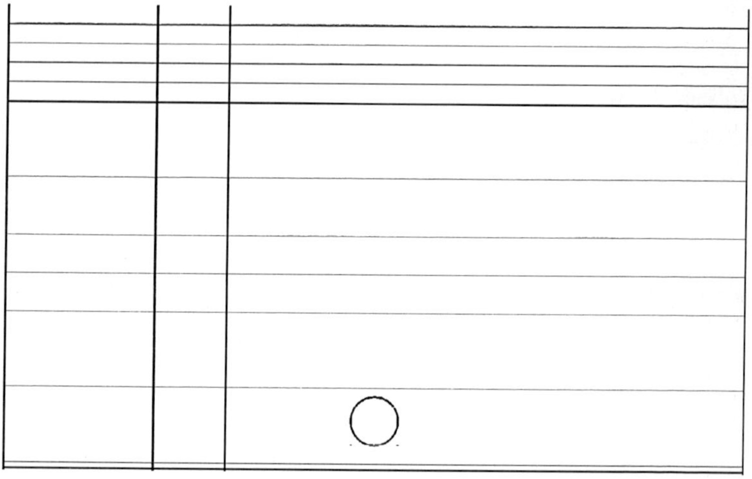

Book Index Entry (Illustrator)

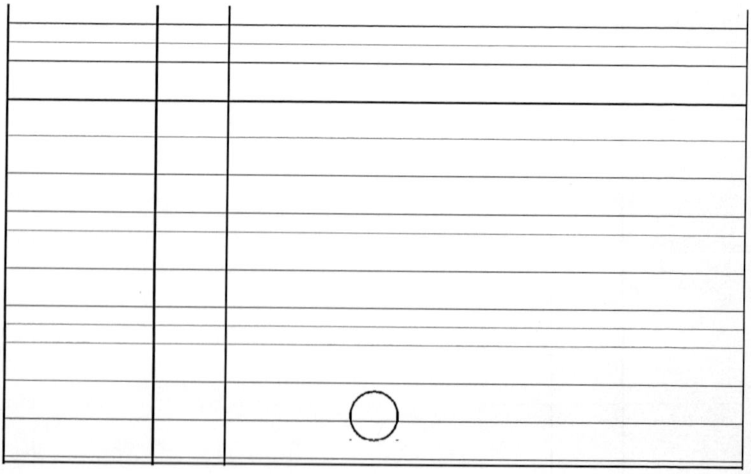

Book Index Entry (Title)

Book Index Entry (Series)

Tracing

Collection, Poetry, English. English, Poetry. English, Literature. Literature. Daringer (Helen Fern) and Eaton (Anne Thaxter), *Comp.* Eaton (Anne Thaxter) and Daringer (Helen Fern), *Comp.* Carter (Helen), *Ill.* Cranger index reprint series.

Coming to another example, some explanation is called for our above worked out example. We have given a descriptive element to the two collaborators who are responsible for the publications of the work. From the title page we can make out that they have selected several verses and compiled a book. Hence, instead of designating them as editors, we have stated them as compilers, which is more appropriate. In the book there is no number provided for the series and according to the books accessioned in the library, we have provided a number for their series. In CCC we do not usually provide Title entries, but this is a case where a reader is likely to remember such a title. Title entries are provided when the book has

(i) a fanciful title.

(ii) contains a proper noun.

(iii) treated in usage as a proper noun provided it has not been used as the Heading in the Main Entry or it is not eligible as the Main Heading of a Class Index Entry.

Artificial composite Books

The cataloguing of artificially composite books is not so simple. By themselves they may be simple books but the problem arrises when they are bound together. CCC has provided some rules to catalogue such books. This has been explained by a example. Below are reproduced the two title pages of the two books bound together.

Marlowe's Dr. Faustus

J.P. Brockbank

Arnold

London

Other information:

Call No. O111.2J64, D:g K6

Acc. No. 5990

Date of publication. 1966

There is a series under the name Studies in English Literature. This is a small book containing only 64 pages which has been bound in the library with another book the details of which are given separately. There is no accession number for the second book.

Second book bound with the previous book:

Ben Jonson's

Bartholomew fair

Edited by

G.R. Hibbard

Earnest Benn

London

Other information:

Call No. O11, 2J72, B L7.

Date of publication. 1977

It is obvious that cataloguing the two books separately will not cause any problems as, both are simple books. Now, because they are bound together as one book, special treatment is required. The classification numbers are also to be provided according to their subjects.

We will first work out the example and then you will be in a position to know how to catalogue such books. CCC calls this type of book an artificial composite book.

Main Entry

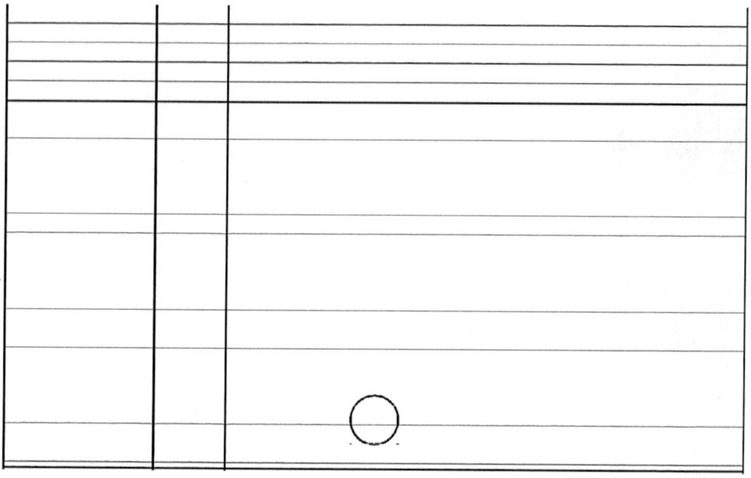

Chain Index :

O	= Literature
O111	= English Literature
O111, 2	= English Drama
O111,2J64	= Christopher Marlowe, Drama
O111,2J64,D	= Dr. Faustus, Marlowe
O111,2J64,D:g	= Criticism, Dr. Faustus, Marlowe
For the second book	
O111.2J72	= Ben Jonson, Drama
O111,2J72,B	= Bartholomew fair, Ben Jonson

Class Index Entry (for the 1st book)

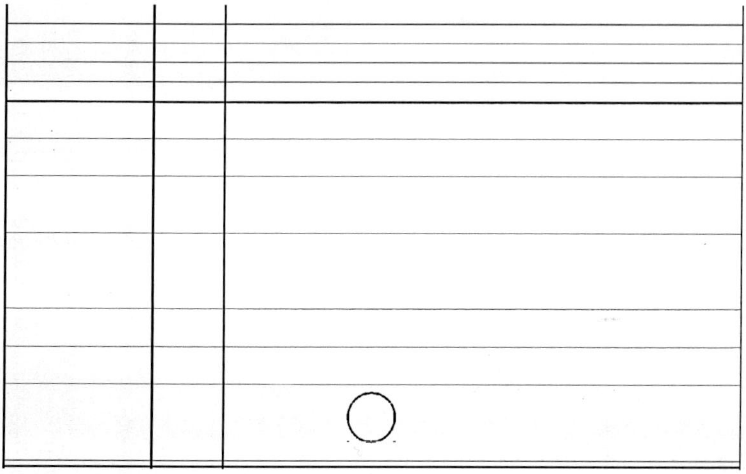

Other Class Index Entries for the first book are :

DR. FAUSTUS, MARLOWE (Christopher)

MARLOWE (Christopher), DRAMA.

DRAMA, ENGLISH.

ENGLISH, LITERATURE.

LITERATURE.

Book Index Entry (Author)
Constituent work – I

Book Index Entry (Series)

Entries for the second book are :

Class Index Entry

Other Class Index Entry is :

JONSON (Ben), DRAMA

Special Cross Reference Entry

	O111, 2J72, B L7	
		Jonson.
		Bartholomew fair. Ed by G R Hibbard.
		Bound as part 2 *with*
		O111, 2J64, D : g K6
		Brockbank.
		Marlowe's Dr. Faustus.

Book Index Entry (Editor)

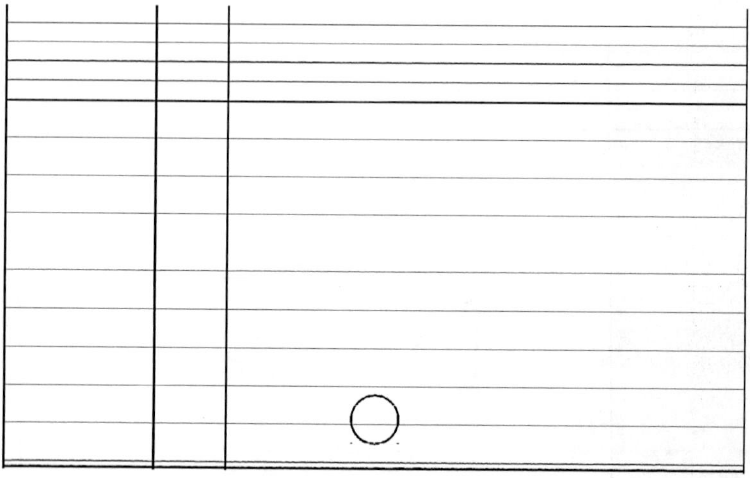

Book Index entry (Author)
Constituent work – II

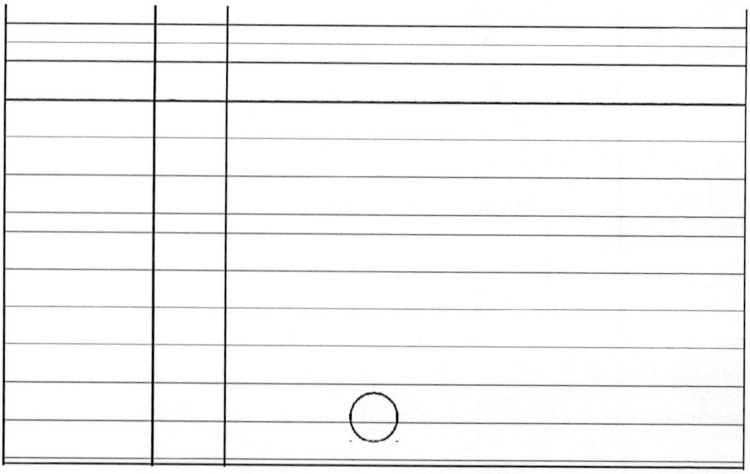

Tracing

O111, 2J72, B	Criticism, Dr faustus, Marilowe (Christopher). Dr. Faustus, Marlowe (Christopher). Marlowe (Christopher), Drama. Drama, English. English, Literature. Literature. Bartholomew fair, Jonson (Ben). Jonson (Ben), Drama. Brockbank (JP). Studies in english literature. *Continued in the next card.*

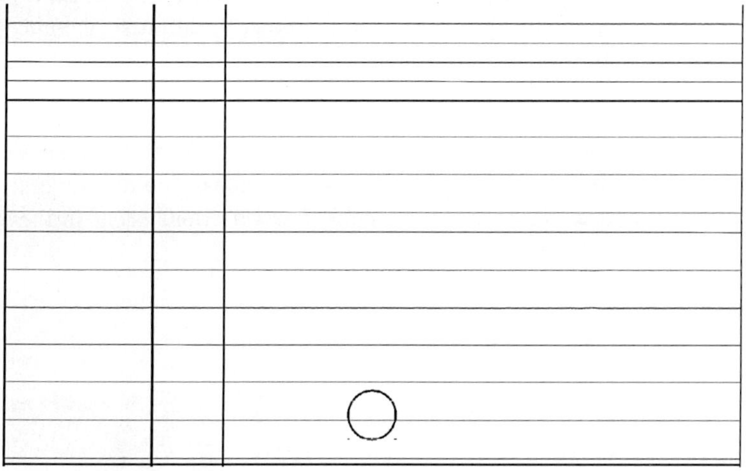

When two books are artificially bound or printed together, the Main Entry is to be made for the first book. In the Main Entry, after the call number, it is to be stated as Composite book. The second book should be written as 2 and then the details are given. The second book receives its own call number. All the Class Index Entries derived from both the class numbers are to be worked out. A special Cross Reference

Entry is to be provided and to be stated that it is bound as part 2 with the first book.

Q. : What do you mean by a multivolume book? How they are treated in AACR – 2, discuss briefly with examples.

Ans. Generally books are published in a single volume, but when thought content cannot be accommodated in one volume of reasonable size, it is published in more than one volume. The AACR-2 calls multivolumes as multiparts and define it as "a monograph complete or intended to be completed in a finite number of separate parts".

Multivolume books may be published in various ways, such as:

(i) the title page common to all the publications,

(ii) each volume has its own title besides the common title to all the volumes,

(iii) all volumes may have continuous pagination or separate pagination for each volume,

(iv) all volumes may or may not have the same publication date.

Besides, the authors or editors of each volume need not be same. The sequence of publication also need not be in serial order, volume two can be published before volume one.

Descriptive Element in Multivolume Books

The rules regarding choice of heading in case of multivolumes are the same as applicable to all other publications. The differences come in the case of descriptive element. The variations occur in the following three areas:

(i) Title

(ii) Pagination

(iii) Date of publication

Let us discuss the above elements in brief.

Title

In multivolume publications usually there are two types of titles.

(i) Common title or common title pages to all the volumes.

(ii) Separate title for each volume in addition to a common title.

The description for these two types vary as the first category consists of only one title for all the volumes and the second category consists of a generic title and a specific title for each volume.

When a set of volumes have different title, the information about each title is to be given in the notes area as content of the volumes.

Example of a common title

Hinumanth Rao

Indian history and culture/Hanumanth Rao and K. Basavesvara Rao.—Guntur : Sri Vigjnana Manjisha, 1970. 3 v.

In this set of three volumes, the title pages of three volumes are identical, the only exception being, in each volume the number of volumes has been written as Volume I, Volume 2 and Volume 3.

The second type of example is given below, also with three volumes but each volume has its own title in addition to the common title :

Naqvi, Shariful Hasan

Readings in Indian history, 3v

V1. Ancient India

V2. Medieval India

V3. Modern India

Pagination

In the physical description area when a printed monograph is in more than one volume, the number of the volumes has to be recorded as shown below :

3v.

4 v. etc.

There are also cases where the number of bibliographical volumes varies with the actual physical volumes in which case it is to be written as:

6 v. in 4

8 v. in 5

In the multiple sets of volumes there are several variations in pagination. Some volumes may have continuous numbering of pages and in many cases individual volumes get their own pagination. The AACR-2 has suggested the following method to show the pagination in the physical description area :

If a set of volumes is continuously paged, the pagination has to be given in parentheses after the number of volumes like

2 v. (xviii, 826p.)

3 v. (xxxi, 1017p.)

Preliminary pages that figure in the subsequent volumes are to be ignored. If there is separate pagination for each volume it can be given in two ways.

3 v.

3 v. (xii, 428; xix, 536; ix 620p.)

In this case, only the number of volumes first is given and alternatively the number of pages of the three volumes have been given.

Date of Publication

When several volumes of a set of monographs are released, they need not be published in a single year. They may be published during a specified period . In such cases we have to take the first publication of the volume that is published first and the last date if the publication is complete; like 1968-1976 which means the volumes were issued between 1968 and 1976. In case the publications of all the volumes are not yet completed the date should be kept open, like 1968— which means that some more volumes are likely to be published. The date should be closed when it is known that the set has been completed.

Sizes of volumes

In the physical description area the recording of sizes has to be done as follows :

If the volume in a multivolume set differ in height and the difference is two centimetres or less, the largest size is given. If the difference is more than two centimetres, both the smallest size and the largest size, are given, which are separated by a hyphen like.

Example:

21-25 cm.

Examples

Modern
Electrochemistry
An Introduction to an Interdisciplinary Area

John O'M Bockris
and
Amulya K.N. Reddy

A Plenum/Rosetta Edition

Other information

Call N.	541.37 BOC
Acc. No.	28156-28157
Date	1973
Size	22 cm

Published by Plenum Publishing Corporation, New York.

The book is in two volumes

The pages are : vl-xxxii, 622, lx

v2-xxvii, 623-1432, 1vi

The example has been worked out below.

Main entry

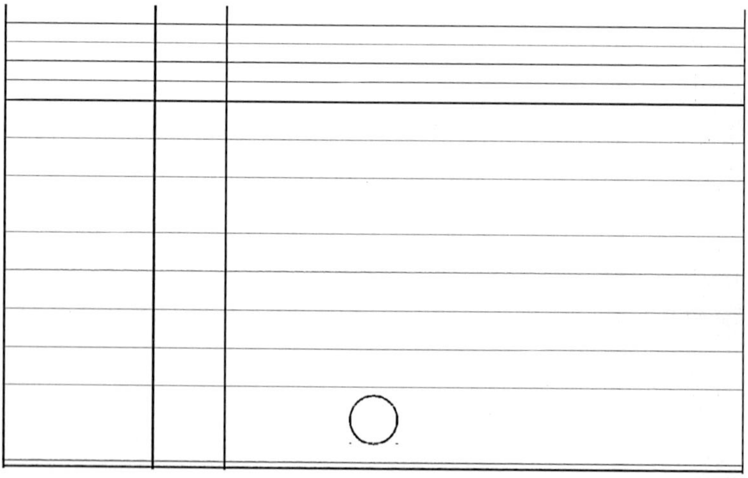

There is an edition statement in the title page. It is not clear what type of edition the publishers are referring to. In such cases Rule No. 1.2B3 states "in case of doubt whether a statement is an edition statement, take the presence of such words as edition, issue, version ... as evidence that such a statement is an edition statement, and record it as such".

The book is in two volumes and has continuous pagination. However, there are some other peculiarities in pagination. Both the volumes have preliminary pages numbered in Roman numerals and in addition, the index in both the volumes have been separately numbered, again in Roman numerals. Incidentally, the AACR-2 has not envisaged such a problem. Rule No.2.5B20 at best says "If a set of volumes is continuously paged, give the pagination in parentheses after the number of volumes. Ignore separately paged sequences of preliminary matter in volumes other than the first'.

Accordingly the volume number is given and the preliminary pages of the first volume followed by the total number of pages. There is no direction as to what action is to be taken for the end pages. We have given the end pages of the second volume only and ignored the end pages of the first volume. The alternative is to transcribe it as 2 v. only and ignore the pagination completely as stated in Rule No.2.5 B17.

Added Entry – Subject

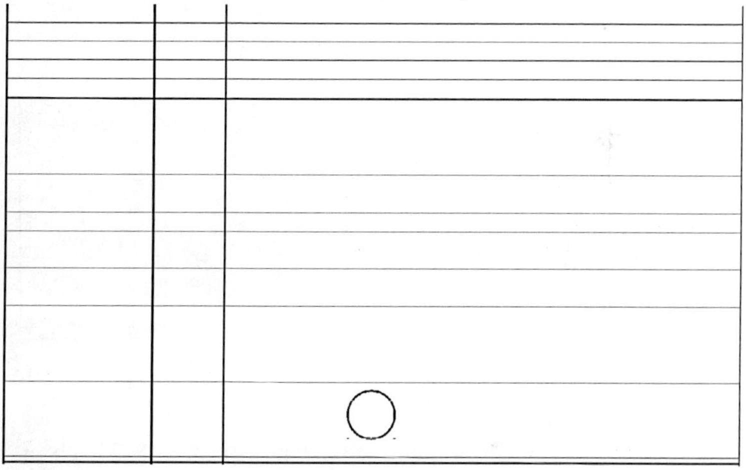

Added Entry – 2nd author

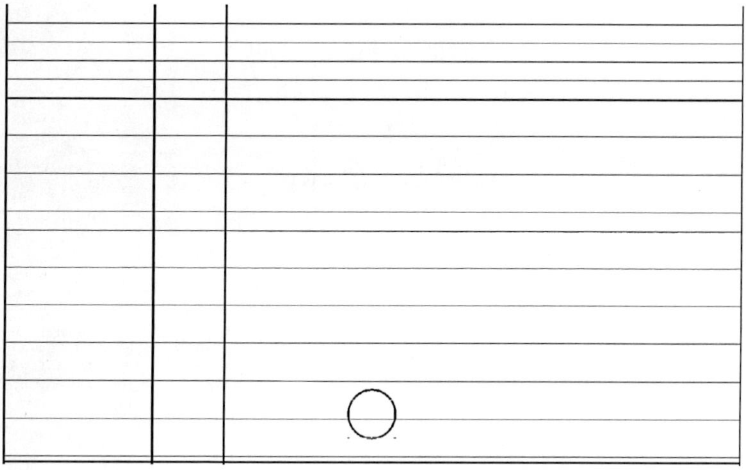

Added Entry – Title

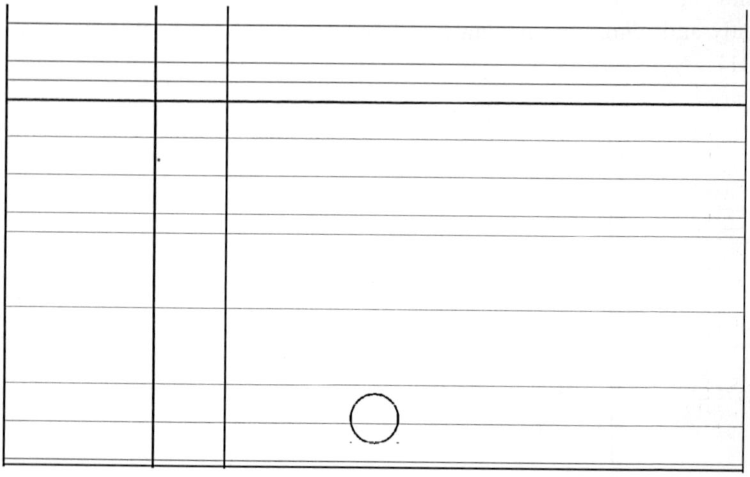

Example of 2nd type of multivolume books in AACR-2 is given below.

Dewey Decimal Classification

and

Relative Index

Edited under the Direction

of

Benjamin A. Cluster

1979

Forest Press, Albany, New York

Other Information

Call No. 025.43 DEW-D. 1-3

Acc. No. 23235-47

Note: Vol. 1. Introduction, Table

Vol. 2 Schedules

Vol. 3. Relative Index

Main Entry

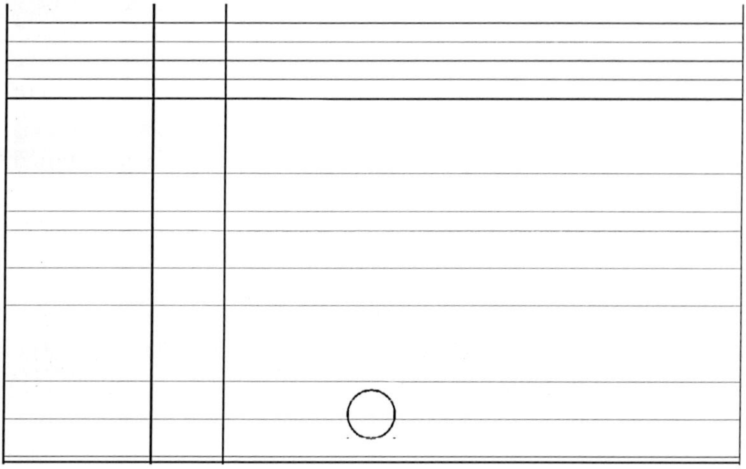

In this examples, the independent titles of each volume are shown in contents. Rest of the parts of the entry are same as of Ist kind of books.

Q. : Discuss briefly the treatment of multivolume books in CCC.

Ans. Classified Catalogue Code defines a multivolume book as a "Book in two or more volumes giving a continuous exposition, and for this or for any other reason in the distribution of thought among the volumes, compelling the treatment of all the volumes as an inseparable set i.e., as if they together formed a single volume". A set of books are to be treated as multivolume when they have the following specifications:

— the set possesses a common index,

— the sequence of pagination is continued throughout all the volumes of the set,

— the subject matter is so distributed among the set, that it is not helpful to treat each volume as a separate book.

CCC further states that there are two types of multivolume books (i) The constituent volumes do not have a special title or title of its own other than the common title of all the volumes. All the titles of all the volumes being the same, they do not create any problem in the title-position of a Main Entry. (ii) All other types of multivolumes fall under the second category.

The multivolume books stated under category (i) are to be catalogued like a simple book. The only extra element is the number of volumes that are to be recorded after the statement of title. Let us say, we have a set of seven volumes of the "Poetical works of William Wordsworth". The heading and title portion will be:

WORDSWORTH (William).

Poetical works. 7V.

After the title a full stop lies to be used in the title section and then the number of volumes and the alphabet "V" in capitals, should be written with a full stop.

If, any volumes of the above set are not available that information in a library should be supplied in square bracket, in the title section, e.g.

WORDSWORTH (William).

Poetical works. 7V. [*V6 not in library*].

Besides, there are the cases when all the volumes of a set are not published and they are received at different intervals as and when published. In such cases, the book number and the volume number should be kept open. This will be made clear with an example.

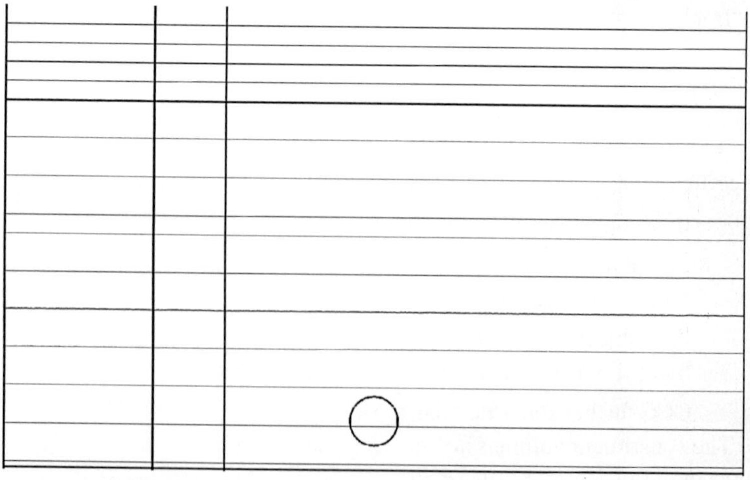

In the book number, M8 is 1988 and M8.1 stands for the 1st

volume and M8.3 stands for the 3rd volume and the book number has been kept open with a dash. In the title section also, V3 is an open number, indicating the volumes are not complete and some more volumes are likely to be received. V3 is to be written in pencil and when the set is completed, it should be erased and the new number of the complete set should be written. Same procedure should be followed in the case of book numbers.

When a set of volumes receive different accession numbers, the information should be recorded accordingly. If the accession number is continuous it should be written, say 1340-1342. The second type of multivolumes, where each volume has its own title, should be recorded in the note section.

Example :

Dewey Decimal Classification

and

Relative Index

Edited under the Direction

of

Benjamin A. Cluster

1979

Forest Press, Albany, New York

Other information

Call No. 025.43 DEW-D1-3

Acc. No. 23245-47

Note: Vol. 1. Introduction, Table

Vol. 2 Schedules

Vol. 3. Relative Index

Main Entry

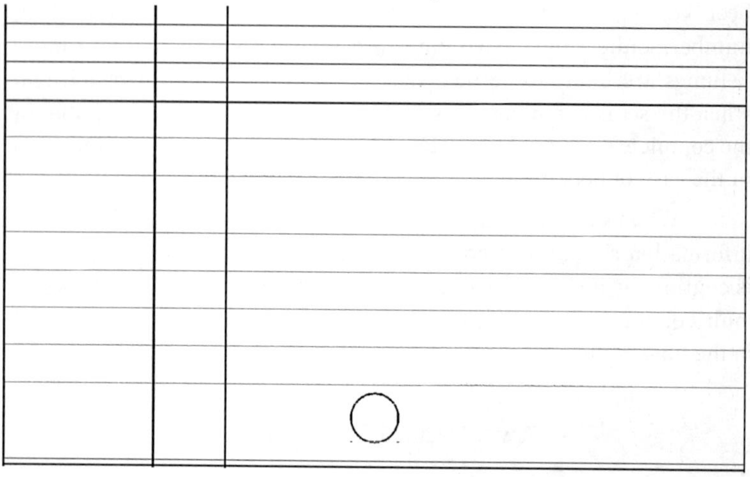

Q. : What do you understand by series ? How the series are treated in classified catalogue code ?

or

Discuss briefly pseudo-series treatment in CCC.

Ans. CCC describes a series, "as a set of books, not constituting a multi-volumed book''. It has several other characteristics and they are categorised in CCC as follows :

1. The books are issued, normally, successively by one publisher or by one sponsoring body or person, usually in a uniform style, and having some similarity of subject or standard of purpose;
2. Each book has normally a distinct and independent title and/or other features of its own;
3. Each book has normally a different author;
4. There is a collective name to denote the set, called Name of the Series and it is given in all or at least in one of the books of the set.

Some series become famous and readers ask for books published under the name of the series concerned. Hence it becomes necessary to provide Added Entries under the name of the series.

Rendering of Series

In the Main Entry, the name of the series is in be rendered in the note section in a separate paragraph. It also receives an Added Entry which is called the Book Index Entry. In rendering the name of the series either in the note section of the Main Entry or in the heading of the Book Index Entry, the initial article and honorific word, if any are to be omitted. The rest of the name of the series is to be written in the sequence in which they appear in the document. The rendering in the note section should be as follows:

1. The name of the Series;
2. A full stop;
3. The word "Ed by", followed successively by the name(s) of the Editor (s) of the Series, if the Series has Editor(s).
4. A full stop; and
5. The Serial number.

In case the series is edited by two editors, the names of both the editors are to be written in the sequence in which they occur in the source document with the conjunction "and'' connecting them. But if there are more than two editors, the name of the first editor alone is to be written and followed by the word "and others".

In several cases the series are numbered indicating the position of the publication in the series. The number, if shown in the publication, the same is to be given in the note section as stated above. CCC also recommends improvization of a series number, if the same is not shown in the publication. This can be given in the sequence of accessioning the book or in any other convenient manner which is to be decided by the library concerned. There are also cases in which instead of serial number, a year may be given. In such a case the year has to replace the serial number.

An example is given below to show how to write the series statement in the Main Entry.

Main Entry

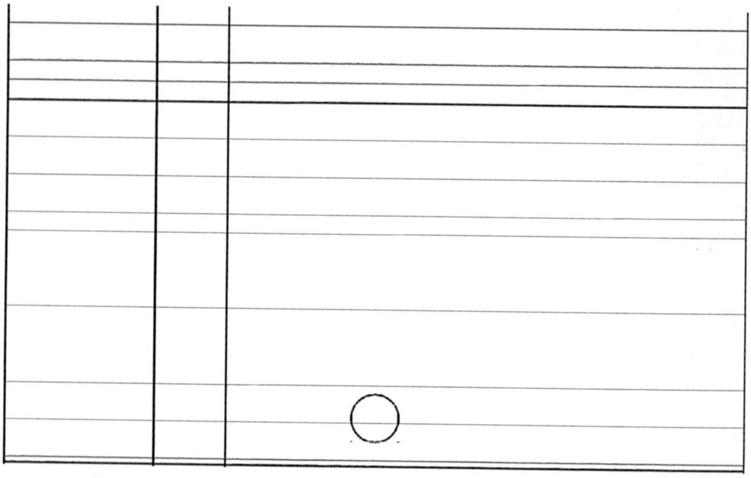

The statement, written in circular bracket, Wiley farm series, is the name of the series. There are two editors for the series which are shown accordingly. After the name of the series a full stop has been used. The names of the editors are shown by Ed for editors and again a full stop has been used after the names of the editors, before giving the series number.

The Added Entry for the name of the series is called Book Index Entry. The series name in the leading section is to be written in capital letters, as shown below :

Book Index Entry (Series)

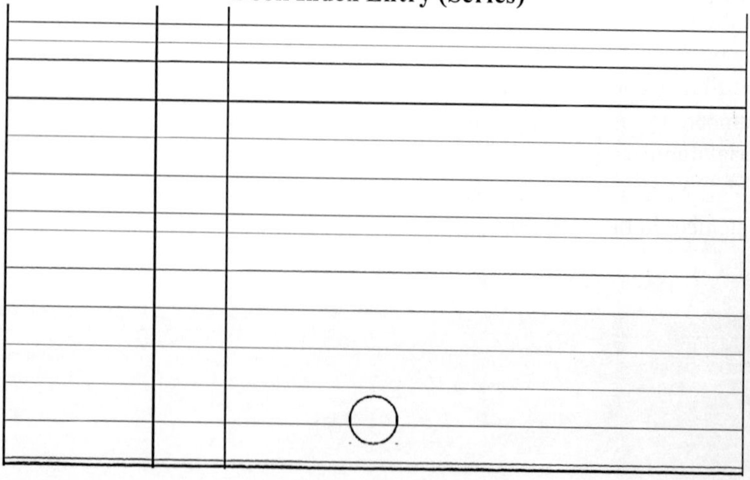

In the Added Entry for the series, the name of the series in the leading section has been written in capitals. The number of the series is to be shown in the column. If there are more books under this series there is no necessity of preparing another card. In the same card the other books also can be shown. This is called Consolidation of Series Index Entries.

An example for Consolidated Series Index Entry is shown below.

Consolidated Series Index Entry

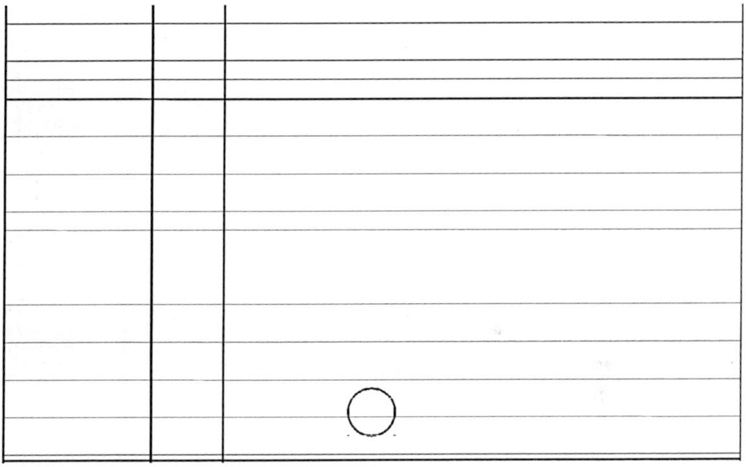

If there is a possibility of adding the other books in the series, gaps can be provided so that, they can be included in the card at a later date

Multiplicity of Series

There are rare cases when a single book may have two or more series. They can be independent or interdependent series. If a book belongs to two or more series, the notes corresponding to them are to be called:

1. Independent Series, if the individualization of the name of each series is independent of the names of other series;
2. Series with Alternative Names, if the same series has two or more names and the same serial number is mentioned in each for a particular book or volume included in it; and.
3. Dependent Series, if the individualization of the name of any series necessarily requires the name of another series.

When there are independent series, they are to be written in separate sections. An example given in CCC is reproduced below to show the rendering of independent series note in the Main Entry.

Main Entry

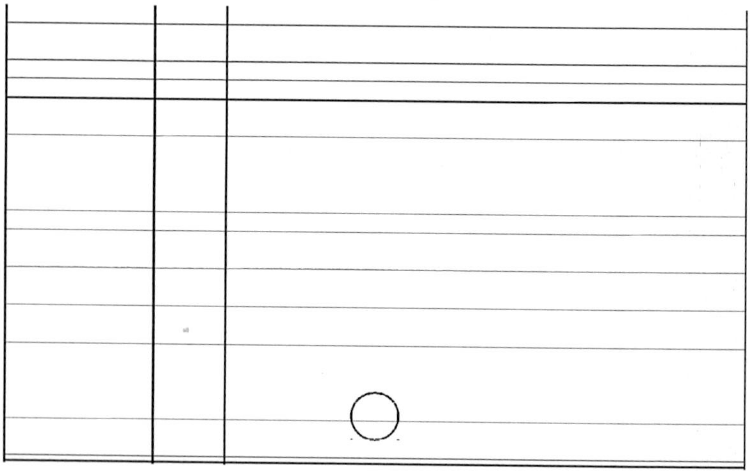

Besides, there may be interdependent series. You cannot render the name of a sub series without mentioning the main series. In case of interdependent series, the primary series of be written in the usual style of rendering. The interdependent series are to be written :

1. preceded by a semi-colon;
2. then the name of the second series;
3. a full stop;
4. the series number of the book in the secondary series;
5. a semi-colon;
6. the name of the next series;
7. a full stop;
8. the serial number of the series.

The example given in CCC on interdependent series is reproduced below:

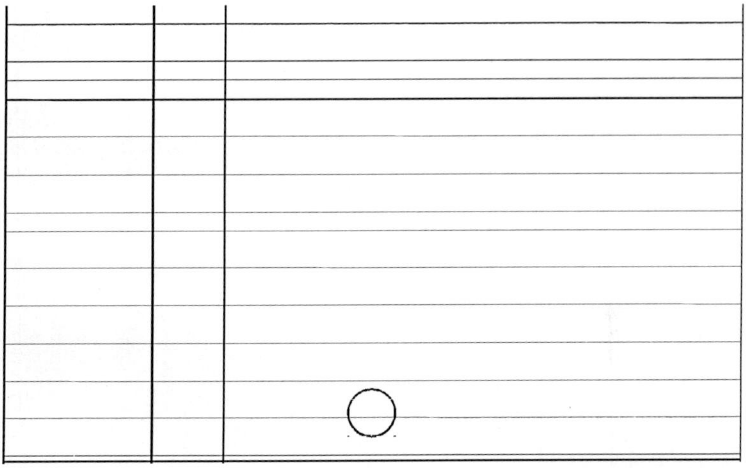

In the above case, there are three interdependent series notes forming a single sequence. The second and the third series statement cannot be rendered without mentioning the name of the first series.

In the case of series with alternative names the names of the series are to be written one after the other in the sequence in which they are mentioned in the source document with an intervening 'or'. Each alternative name of the series is to be rendered in the way the names of independent series are rendered.

The example on Series with Alternative Names is given below:

Main Entry

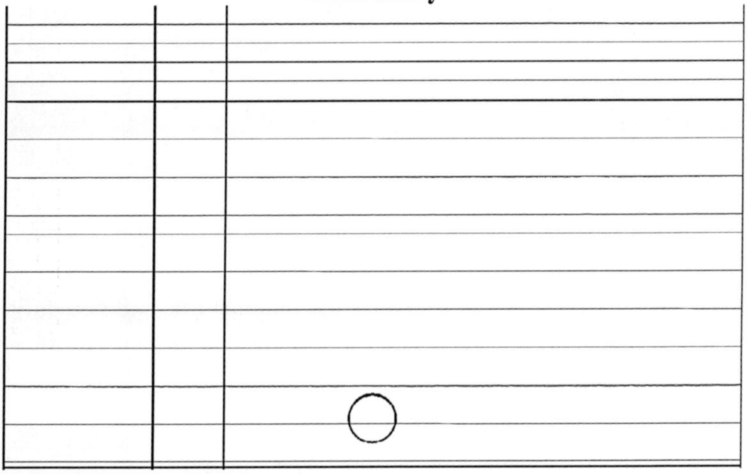

Book Index Entry (Series)

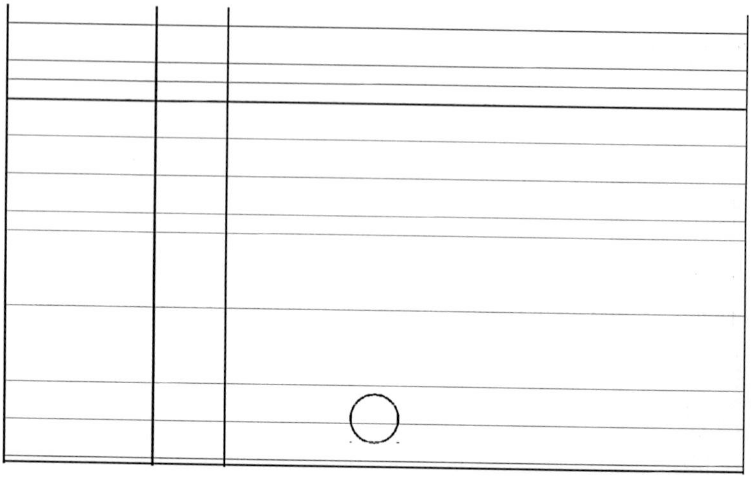

Book Index Entry (Series)

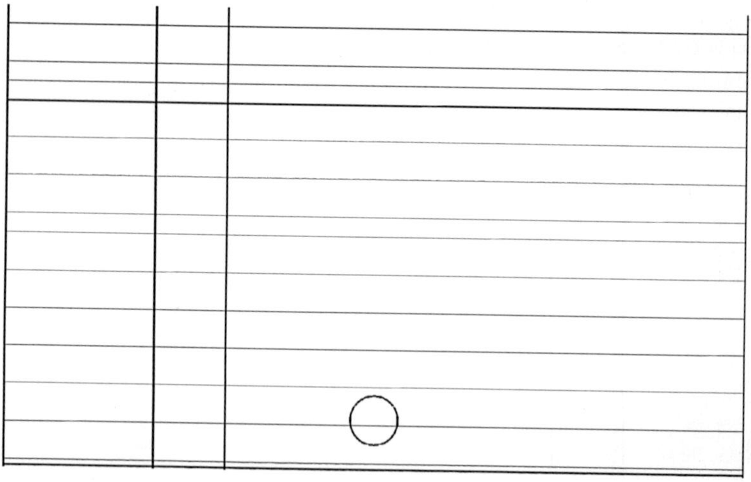

Pseudo-Series

There are publications which have a common title and still do not form a multi-volume set. Such titles also have their own title in addition to a common title. Readers some times ask for the books published under such category under their common title. To meet the requirements of readers who seek such information from the catalogue, CCC has introduced the concept of Pseudo-Series. This is a creation of the Cataloguing Code and not publishers' innovation. CCC has categorised Pseudo-Series of three different kinds. They are:

Pseudo-Series of kind 1: A set of books not constituting a multi-volumed book and with the following attributes:

1. All the books are of common authorship;
2. All the books belong to the same edition (the editions having a distinctive name);
3. The title of each book has a distinctive part in addition to the name of the edition;
4. Each book is or can be assigned a Serial Number belonging to a system or competes ordinal numbers; and
5. The name of the author, taken along with the name of the edition, is suitable to be used as if it were the Name of a Series.

An example of this kind has been worked out below. Only the Main and Series Entries have been shown below:

Main Entry

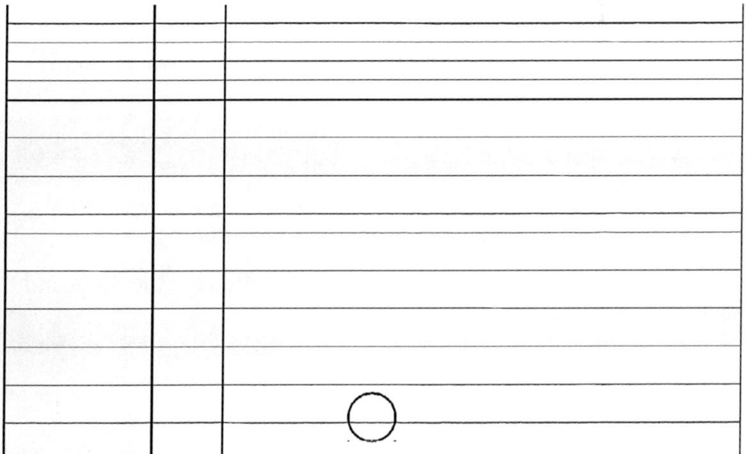

Book Index Entry (Pseudo-Series)

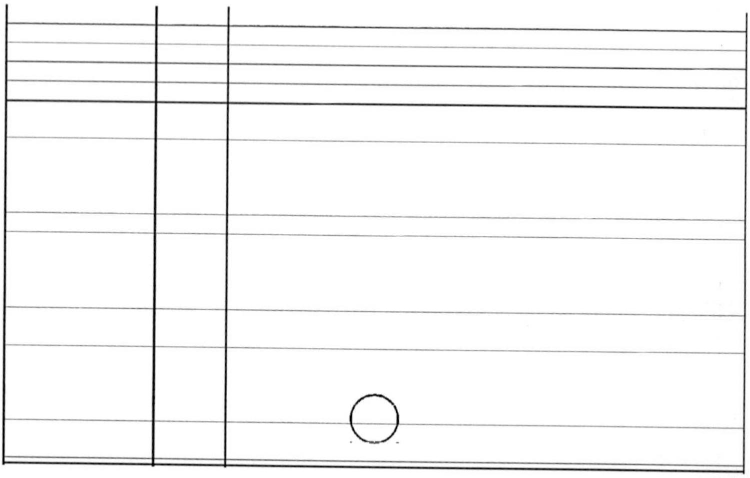

Pseudo-Series of kind 2 : It is a set of books, not constituting a multi-volumed book and having the following attributes:

1. All the books are of common authorship;
2. The titles of various books have a common part capable of being used as their common generic title;
3. The title of each book has a distinctive part of its own in addition to the generic part;
4. Each book is or can be assigned a Serial Number belonging to a system of simple of complex ordinal numbers; and
5. The name of the author taken along with the generic title is suitable to be used as if it were the Name of Series.

Below an example has been worked out, showing the Main and Pseudo-Series Entries.

Main Entry

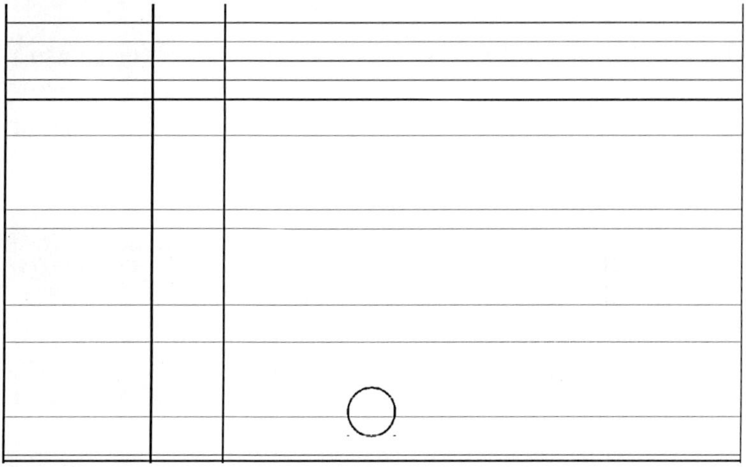

Book Index Entry (Pseudo-Series)

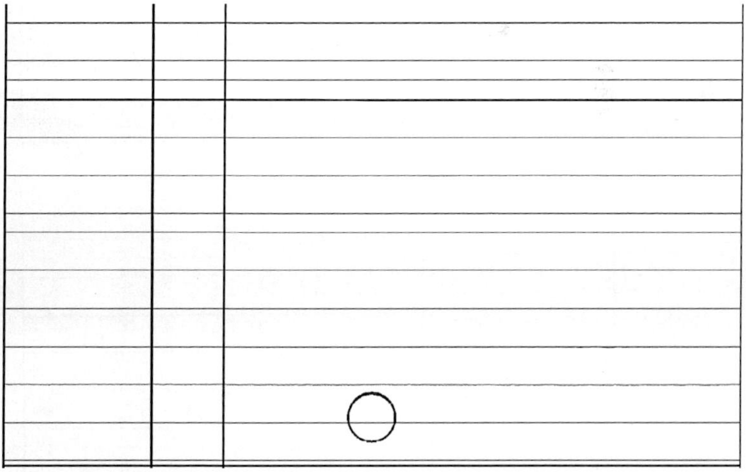

The third kind of Pseudo-Series as given in CCC is:

A set of books not constituting a multivolumed hook and with the following attributes:

1. All the books are not of a common authorship:
2. The title of various books have a common part capable of being used as a common generic title;

3. The title of each book has a distinctive part of its own in addition to the generic part ;
4. Each book is or can be assigned a serial number belonging to a system of simple or complex ordinal numbers, and
5. The generic title is suitable to be used as if it were the Name of the Series.

Below is given an example of Pseudo-Series of kind 3.

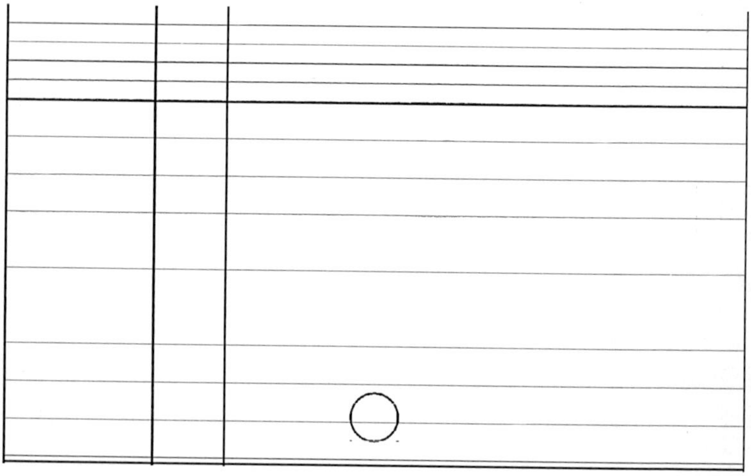

Book Index Entry (Pseudo-Series)

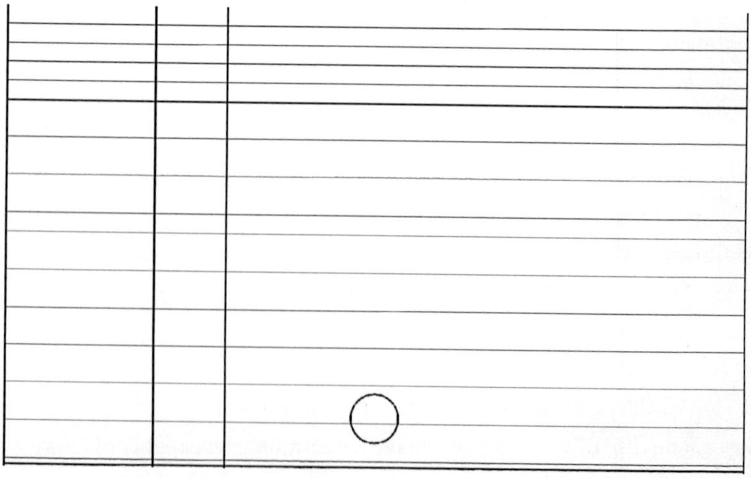

Q. : Discuss briefly the treatment of series in AACR-2 with examples.

Ans. A Series is defined as a group of separate items, usually related in subject or form, and issued successively. They are generally issued by the same publisher or distributor in a uniform style with a collective title. The AACR-2 has explained a series as "A group of separate items related to one another by the fact that each item bears, in addition to its own title proper a collective title to the group as a whole."

Statement of Responsibility

When an organisation starts a series, it usually entrusts it to one or more persons or bodies to oversee the work publication. They look after the editorial work involved in the publication of the series. Sometimes for identification of a series the editor's name may be required. The AACR-2 does not give much weightage for the editors of series unless the name of the editors appears in conjunction with the series and they are considered necessary for the identification of the series. The following examples given by AACR-2 makes it clear when the statement of responsibility for the series has to be given.

— Map supplement/Association of American Geographers

— Technical memorandum/Beach Erosion Board

— Research monographs/Institute of Economic Affairs

In all the above cases the statement of responsibility identities the series. Enquiries, if any are likely in regard to the names of the organisations shown above not the name of the series. It is only in such eases that AACR-2 recommends to make an added entry for the statement of responsibility. In case, an entry has been prepared for the statement of responsibility, it should be shown on the back of the series card.

Numbering of Series

In case of books, the importance of International Standard Book Number (ISBN) is noteworthy. For series also there is an international number called International Standard Serial Number (ISSN). If this appears, it is to be transcribed after giving the name of the series.

As stated eartier, that series are usually published on a particular theme in succession and they are also numbered. Numbering within the series again varies. They may be given just a number, or may be stated as a volume or only a year may be mentioned. For examples:

— American Mathematical Society Translation, Series 2: v .94

— Middle Eastern Languages and Linguistic; no. 2

— Surveys in Applied Mathematics; 3

There can be several series which do not give any numbers at all. In some cases specially when they are memorial lecture series, they give only the year of the delivery of lectures like.

Sakharam Ganesh Devsakar lectures on Indian History; 1980

Subseries

There are a few rare occasions when we find names of two series together. The second named series in such cases is called subseries. It is more like a series within a series. To transcribe the subseries we will have to give the name of the main series first. In some cases both may have different numbering. For example:

American universities studies series XI, Anthropology and Sociology; v. 10

There is a possibility of having two ISSN numbers when we come across subseries. One for the main series and the other for the subseries. The rule in such a case is to omit the ISSN number of the main series and to transcribe the number of only the subseries.

Transcribing Series Information

The sources of information about the series can be taken form anywhere in the Publication. Usually it figures on the fly-leaf or the page facing the title page. It may figure in the title page itself. If the information is taken from outside the publication to be enclosed in square brackets.

Series area in the main entry will be after the physical description. It is preceded with full stop, space, dash and space. The series statement itself is enclosed in parentheses. Statement of responsibility if any is given with a slash.

Example

EXPONENTIAL DIOPHANTINE EQUATIONS

T.N. Shorey

R. Tejdeman

There is a series : Cambridge tracts in mathematics: 87

The cataloguing of the book is by and large simple, the only extra element in this example is a series.

It has been worked out below:

Main entry

This is a book written by two authors and no principal responsibility indicated, hence it is entered under the first named author. The second author gets an added entry.

The only new element introduced in the example is the series statement. It is written after the physical description with a full stop, space and dash and space. Series statement should always be enclosed in circular brackets. The series number is given with a semicolon.

Q : What do you understand by a serial publication and a periodical ? How they are differ from each other ? Explain how they are treated in CCC?

Ans. Generally speaking, a serial or periodical publication is that publication which is regularly published periodically in sequence and in which articles, stories, book reviews etc on one or more subjects by various authors are published.

A serial is a "publication issued in successive parts and intended to be continued indefinitely". Serials include newspapers, periodicals, annuals, memoirs, proceedings, transactions of societies and monographies series. Classified Catalogue Code has given the following attributes to periodical publications:

(i) A volume, or a small group of volumes of it, is intended to be published or completed normally once a year (or at other regular intervals), though irregularity in interval is not ruled out.

(ii) Each successive volume, or periodical group of volumes, is usually distinguished by the year of publication and/or by a number belonging to a system of simple or complex ordinal numbers. Such a number is usually called a Volume Number.

(iii) The intention had been to continue the publication of the volume for ever, but in several cases the actual intention is not carried out.

(iv) The intention had been to continue the same title in all the volumes, though there are several cases of changes in name made after.

Whereas, a periodical publication is made up of volumes with distinct and independent contributions, not forming a continuous exposition. Contributions to periodical publications are made by diverse hands and the subjects falling within one and the same universe of knowledge. It is not usually released complete as a volume but only in parts. Serial publications embody more or less the same kind of information, usually in the same pattern, mainly relating to its year of coverage. Serials are usually released as a complete volume. It is not made of diverse contributions. Some examples of serial publications are:

- Manorama Year Book
- Delhi Telephone Directory
- Who's Who in India
- Statesman's Year Book.

Problems in Cataloguing Periodicals

Cataloguing of periodical publications poses several problems because of their complexity. CCC describes that "their vagaries may transcend all imagination and anticipation. It looks as if nothing relating to a periodical publication can escape the sport of caprice-sponsor, name, periodicity, format, pagination, excrescential attachments to all or stray volumes, and, as but not least, span of life and resurrection". Some of the common problems faced by the cataloguer are, change in the name of the publication, while volume numbers continue, irregularity in publication, irregularity in volume number, change of sponsor, amalgamation of two or more periodicals into one, splitting of a periodical into two or more periodicals, change in frequency of publications and so on.

Procedures of Cataloguing Periodicals

Some of the common elements which are applicable to catalogue the periodical publications are:

1. Leading Section : In the main entry the leading section will have only the Class Number . In case of books both the Class Number and Book Number are written. But for a periodical publication Book Number is not written in the leading section for the reason that the entry stands not for one volume but for all the volumes that are added to the library from time to time.

2. Heading Section : The heading in case of a periodical publication will be the title proper, omitting the name of its sponsor, if any, occurring in continuation of its titlc proper. The name of the sponsor is to be written after a comma, if the name is part of the title proper. The name of the sponsor is to be out in circular brackets if the sponsor is not the part of the title proper. The first two words of the title proper are to be written in block letters.

3. Periodicity Section : The periodicity of the periodical is to be shown in a separate section after the title. It should be written in square brackets. In this section, the statement of periodicity is recorded in the following way:

1. For the volume which completes in a year, the statement will contain:

    — 'I V per year'

    — a full stop

    — the term "V"

    — number of the first volume (but not in all cases)

    — a dash

    — some space and a semi colon

    — the year of commencement

    — a dash

2. For the volume which completes in less than one year, the statement will contain:
   - number of volumes per year
   - the term 'V per year'
   - a semi colon
   - number of bound parts in a volume, in case of more than one
   - the term 'parts per volume' if it is operative
   - a full stop
3. For the volume which completes in more than one year, the statement contains:
   - the term 'I V for'
   - the number indicating the number of years
   - the term 'years'
   - a semi colon
   - number of separately bound parts of the volume, if more than one
   - the term 'parts per volume'
   - and a full stop

For irregular periodicals the periodicity statement begins with 'Irregular'.

4. Series Note Section : If the periodical is having any series, it is to be enclosed in circular brackets. The rendering of a series note in the main entry for periodicals is same as in the case of books. At the end of the series note, the serial numbers of all the volumes are to be given in succession.

5. Holdings-in-Brief Section : The volumes of non-conference periodical publication which are available in the library are to be shown in holding section. The holdings of the periodicals should be shown as follows:

1. The term 'This library has'
2. The term' V'
3. The number of volumes available in the library. This statement contains the following information:

- The number of earliest volume;
- a dash;
- The number of latest volume;

4. A semi colon;
5. The years of the volumes (the years covered by the volumes, not the years of publication of the volumes). This statement contains the following information:
   - The year of the earliest volume;
   - A dash; and
   - The year of the latest volume

5.A. In cases where the periodical is currently subscribed by the library, the numbers of the latest volume and its years are to be written in pencil. This is called an open entry.

5.B. If the periodical is discontinued, the number of the last volume and its year are to be linked to show that the periodical is no more subscribed by the library. This is called a closed entry.

For conference periodical publication, the holdings section should be written in accordance with rules PB162 and PB163. For the proceedings of a conference, the information regarding each volume will be given in the left half side of the card. The place of conference is to be incorporated between Year Number and Book Number.

For Example:

1	1954	Delhi	N54	4051
2	1955	Bombay	N55	5034
Volume Number	Year Number	Place Name	Book Number	Accession Number

6. Tracing Section : Tracing for periodical publication is recorded at the back side of Main Entry Card. The back side of the Main Entry card is divided into two halves i.e., Right Half and Left Half. On the Left Half, we will record Cross Reference Entry (s) and Class Numbers.

On the Right Half of the card, the following information should be recorded:

1. Headings used for each Class Index Entry.

2. Headings used for each Class Index Entry arising out of Cross Reference Entry.

If the whole information can not be accommodated at the back side of the card, the information is to be continued in the front and back side of the fresh card.

Skeleton of Tracing Section

Cross Reference Entry (s) Class Numbers (s)	Class Index Entries Class Index Entries (arising out of Cross Reference Entries)

7. Holdings-in-Full Section : For this section, a continued card is to be used. In the leading line, the class number of the periodical publication is recorded. Each line of this section of periodical publication will contain the Volume Number, the Year Number. The Book Number and the Accession Number of one volume in tabular form. The successive lines of this section should be devoted to successive volumes. If the consecutive volumes has a set of consecutive Year Number, consecutive Book Numbers and consecutive Accession Numbers then the information of this set will be entered in one line with the help of inclusive notation. For example:

2-18	1962-78	N62-N68	5400-16
Volume Number	Year Number	Book Number	Accession Number

The holdings-in-full may be continued from the left half to the right half. When the full information can not be accommodated in front and back side of the card, the additional continued cards may be used.

Skeleton of the Holdings-in-full Section

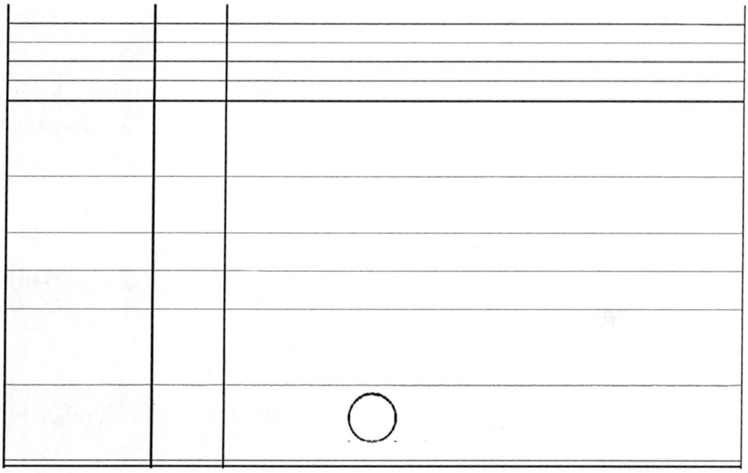

Class Index Entry for Periodical Publication

Class Index Entries are also made for periodicals. The last link of Class Number should be given the Class Index Entry and this will in reality be the same as that of its Main Entry. For periodical publication the directing words used in the case of books are to be omitted.

Additional Class Index Entries are to be given in case of the following:

1. Every alternative name of the periodical, including its contracted name, by which the periodical is popularly known.
2. In case of a periodical having sponsor, the heading is to obtain by interchanging the name of the sponsor and the title of the periodical.
3. Each variation is obtained by substituting alternative name of the sponsor in the heading referred in category (2).

For the heading discussed above a comma is to be inserted between the title and name of the sponsor.

Apart from the above situations, there are other Class Index Entries called Specific. Generic and Optional Class Index Entries.

Specific Class Index Entry : It is given for the title of the periodical with and without alternate title.

Generic Class Index Entry : It is given for the title of the periodical with and without alternate title. This entry is given under the heading Periodical' or Serial' as the case may be.

Optional Class Index Entry : This entry may be given for a periodical publication corresponding to the links of its Class Number ending with the Common Isolate Digit and Geographical Isolate Number. For example:

INDIA, PERIODICAL, SOCIOLOGY. Ym44

PERIODICAL, SOCIOLOGY. Ym

Example :

THE INDIAN ECONOMIC REVIEW

Vol XXIV January-June 1988 Number 1

Other Information :

Class No. Xm44 N65

Acc. No. 4856 4561; 5865-5878

Published biannually: One volume per year

Year of publication. 1965

Library holdings: Vols 8-13 and 16-29

and still being received in the library.

Main Entry

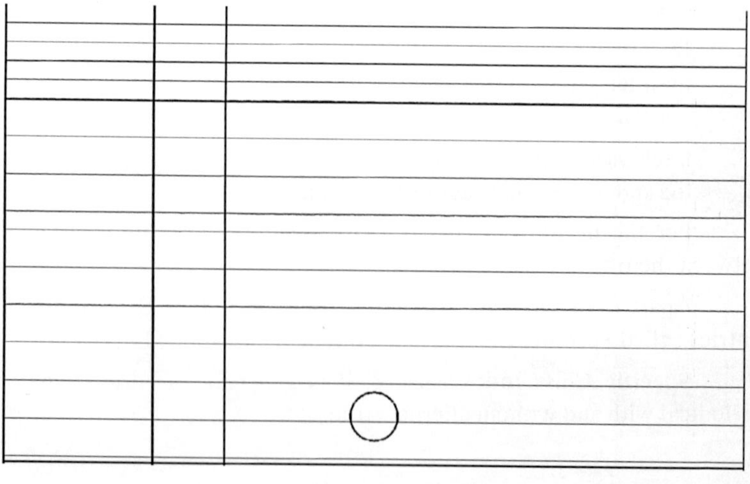

Holdings - in - Full Section

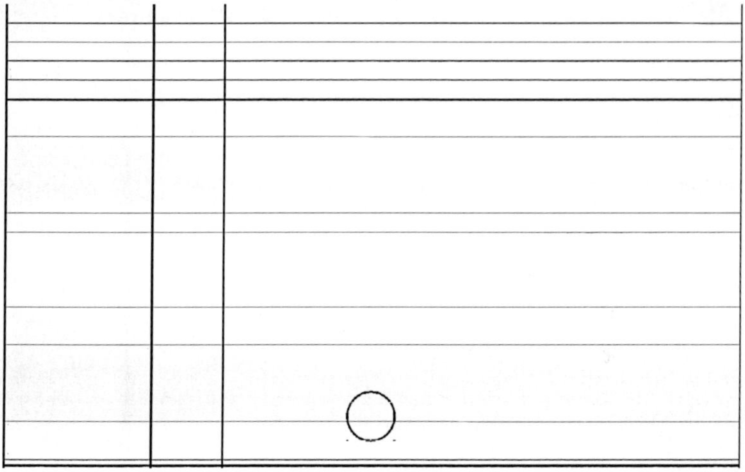

The first two words in the heading are to be written in block letters. The volume number 29 and the year 1993 of the volume are to be written in pencil to indicate that the periodical is still being received in the library.

Class Index Entry (Specific)

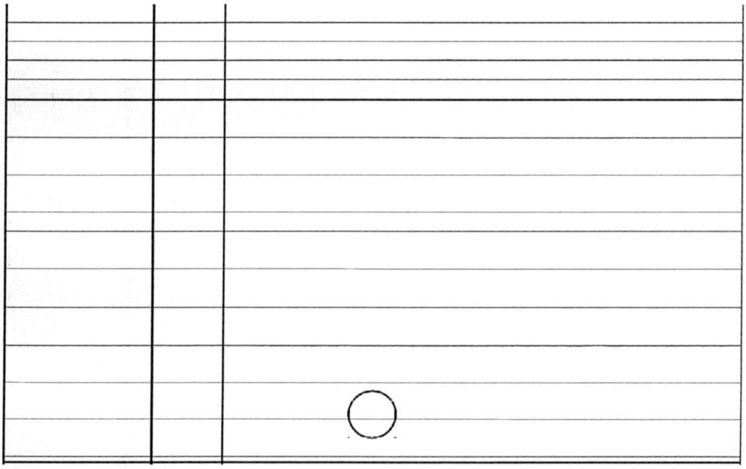

Q. : Defining serial or periodical publication according to AACR -2, discuss its treatment in AACR - 2 with examples.

Ans. According to AACR-2, a serial or periodical publication is a publication in any medium issued in successive parts bearing numerical or chronological designations and intended to be continued indefinitely". One may come across daily and probably read some popular magazines. Some of these serials are called periodicals, journals and magazines without much distinction. Periodicals and journals are synonymous, but a magazine refers to popular journal which does not have a lasting value. The AACR-2 includes under serials several other publications, such as newspapers, annuals (reports, yearbooks etc.), memoirs, proceedings, transactions etc. of societies. Cataloguing of reports, proceedings and transactions fall under corporate bodies, though they also can be catalogued as a serial.

Problems in Cataloguing of Serial Publications

Cataloguing of serial publications poses several problems. The physical characteristics associated with its bibliographic description such as title of the serial, its frequency, sponsor etc. change very often. Besides to this, sometimes a single periodical may split into two or more with different titles or two or more distinct periodicals may merge to constitute a single periodical with a different name. This necessitated that serial should be treated as a special class of material in so far as their cataloguing is concerned. This situation calls for special rules in cataloguing serial publications. The aim of those rules is to prepare catalogue entries that will stand the test of time and allow necessary changes as and when called for.

Normally bibliographical description for a main entry of a serial publication includes the following information:

1. Title and statement of responsibility area
2. Edition area
3. Numeric, alphabetical or chronological designation area
4. Publication/distribution area
5. Physical description area
6. Note area
7. Standard number
8. Terms of availability area

The chief source of information is the title page of the first issue. Some serial publications issue separate title pages which can be used for cataloguing purpose. In case the first issue is not available, the current issue may be utilized for the purpose.

The rules pertaining to cataloguing of serial publication are given in chapter 12 of the AACR-2. In case some of the rules are not stated a direction is given as to which rules are applicable.

Example

American
Journal of Mathematics
Founded by the Johns Hopkings University
Edited by
J.H. Sampson
(and several others)

Published under the Auspices of the Johns Hopkins University With the Editorial cooperation of American Mathematical Society.

Volume 110, Number 5
October 1988

The Johns Hopking University Press
Baltimore, Maryland
U. S. A.

Other Information	
Call No.	510.5/ AME
Size	26 cm.
Date of 1st issue	1878
Periodicity	Six issues a year
Library lacks Vols	1-68

Main entry

Added entry – Subject

Added Entry–Founder

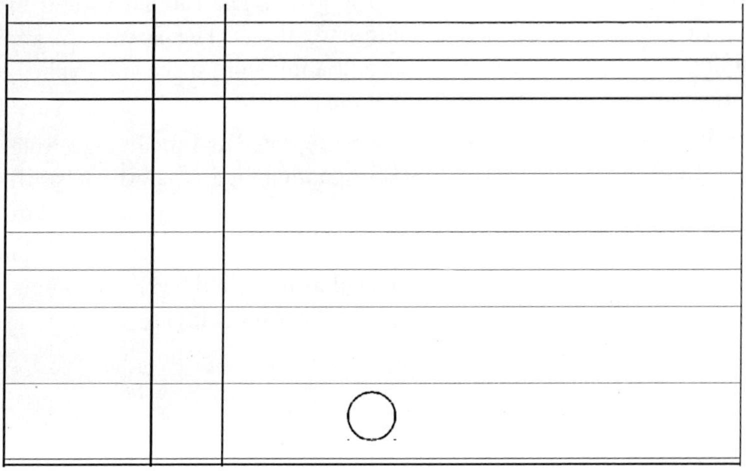

Added Entry - Founder

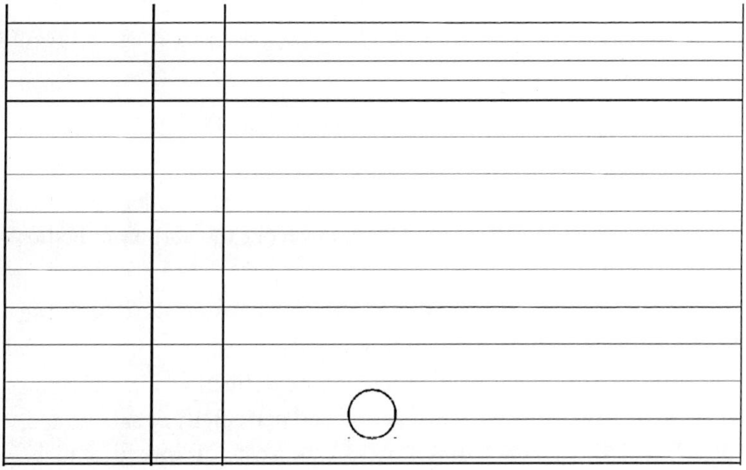

The rules governing the cataloguing of serial publications are given in chapter 12 of AACR-2. The main heading is made under the title, though the periodical is a publication of a corporate body. When the publication is of an administrative nature dealing with the corporate body itself, then the heading should be the name of the corporate body as per rule 21.1B2.

Rule No. 12.3B1 directs to give the numeric or alphabetical

designation of the first issue of the serial which is being catalogued. Accordingly, Vol. 1, No. 1 (1878) is given. The rule also states to transcribe the year of publication in parenthesis. The parenthesis are followed by a hyphen, four spaces and a full stop, space and hyphen, before giving the place and name of the publisher.

The year of publication is to be repeated as stated under Rule No. 12.4F 1. The specific material designation for a serial which is still in progress is "v". Other physical description is usually the height of the serial.

The periodicity of the periodical as done in the above example is also to be indicated. Some of the usual periodicities are :

Weekly

Issued twice a month

Monthly

Quarterly

Annual

Irregular

Frequency varies.

However, periodicity need not be mentioned if it is already part of the title of the serial.

Library holdings are to be shown as directed under Rule No. 12.7B20. The added entries are made, covering the corporate bodies associated with the publication.

Q. : Explain the rules with example for periodicals (i) Splitting and (ii) Amalgamation according to C.C.C.

Ans. A periodical publication can be defined as a publication that is published at undetermined period and periodicity or said period, which is generally more than once in an year, or intended to be published. Generally, different articles, stories and other works are compiled in its each issue.

The glossary of AACR II defines serial as " a publication in any medium issued in successive parts bearing numerical or chronological designations and intended to be continued indefinitely." Serials include periodicals; newspapers; annuals (reports, year books, etc.); the Journals, memories, proceedings, transactions, etc., of societies; and numbered monographic series.

Whereas, as per Classified Catalogue Code, such kind of periodic publication is called a magazine or periodical in whose every issue is generally formed of the contributions of two or more writers, in which there is no continuity of thought and the contributing authors of the specific subject in its issues are generally different, but all the subjects belong to the same stream of knowledge. It is generally not published as a complete volume, but it is said that this is published as fasciculus or numbers. It necessarily spreads knowledge. Moreover, similar type of information is not repeated by updating in the same pattern in its each volume.

Everything related to the periodicals is temporary i.e. its title, editor, promoter, periodicity, number of pages, shape and size, form and colour - nothing is permanent. Their supplements are published from time to time. These get amalgamated in some other periodical, otherwise one periodical is split into two or more publications. This type of temporary state gives rise to problems and difficulties in cataloguing. Following rules have been given in C.C.C. for cataloguing of periodicals that are amalgamated and split up.

Amalgamation

Generally, the periodical is amalgamated in some other periodical as per the following:

1. Two or more periodicals are amalgamated under one of the titles of amalgamated publications and whose volume number continues in the initial sequence itself.
2. Two or more periodic publications get amalgamated under one of the titles of amalgamated publications, but the sequence of the volume number changes.
3. Two or more periodic publications are amalgamated under a new title, whose class number is of one of the amalgamated periodic publications.
4. Two or more periodicals are amalgamated under a new title and their class number is also different from these amalgamated periodic publications.

PF-1 Continuation of Title and Volume Number : When the title and the volume number are amalgamated under the title of one of the amalgamated periodic publications, then this titles is continued in a new main card.

Rule Number PF 11 : Same class number shall be given in the new card, which is given in the previous card and these will be treated as continued cards.

Rule Number- PF12 : Entry of main cards of all the amalgamated publications are closed for publication and library ,as per the section PB135 and PB137.

Rule Number PF13 : An additional note will be added in inverted commas after the holding section in the new card.

1. Term "Amalgamates" and
2. Class number and the name of that periodic publication with which it is amalgamated, will be given on a separate line.

Rule Number PF14 : An additional note will be added after 'periodicity' language in the new card as given below:

1. Term "Amalgamation with" and
2. Class number and name of the publication that has been amalgamated.

PF-2 Continuation of title but not of volume number : When the title in a periodical is continued from the previous publications, but the sequence of the volume number changes, then it will be treated as per the provisions of rule number PF1:

For example:

1. Tm 73, M9

   EDUCATIONAL REVIEW (United States of America).

   (2V Per, year VI-76; 1891-1928)

   This Library has VI-76; 1891-1928

   "Amalgamation with

   Tm 73, NI SCHOOL AND SOCIETY"

2. Tm73, NI

   SCHOOL AND SOCIETY.

   (2V per year VI-27; 1915-28).

   This Library has VI-27; 1915-28

3. Tm73, NI

   SCHOOL AND SOCIETY

   (2V per year V28-; 1928-).

This Library has V28-33; 1928-33

"Amalgamates

Tm 73, M9 EDUCATIONAL REVIEW (United States of America)"

Rule Number PF3 - New Title and Old Class Number : When the periodic publications are amalgamated under a new title, then a new title is given in the new main card.

Rule Number PF31 : If the class number remains same as that with the earlier title, then that sequence of the volume is maintained with the new title. This is treated as per the rule number PF1 itself.

Rule Number PF4 : New Title and New Class Number: When the periodical is amalgamated under a new title and a new class number, then it is catalogued with the new title according to the following rule number:

Rule Number PF41 : An additional note is added in inverted commas:

1. Term "Amalgamates" and
2. The class number and the title of the periodical that has been amalgamated are written in another line.

Rule Number PF42 : Entry of main cards of all amalgamated publications are closed for publication and library as per the section PB135 and PB157.

Rule Number PF43 : An additional note is added with each amalgamated publication in inverted commas in the last main card.

1. Term "Amalgamated in" and
2. Class number and title of the amalgamated publication. For example:

1. Gm 73,N

   BIOLOGICAL ABSTRACTS

   (IV per year VI-; 1927)

   This Library has VI-7; 1927-33.

   "Amalgamates

   G91 m 73, N ABSTRACTS OF Biocteriolology; and

   I m 73, N BOTANICAL ABSTRACTS"

2. G91 m 73, N

   ABSTRACTS OF Bacteriology.

   (1 V per Year. VI-10; 1917-26)

   This Library has VI-10; 1917-26.

   "Amalgamated in

   Gm 73, N BIOLOGICAL ABSTRACTS."

3. I m 73, N

   BOTANICAL ABSTRACTS

   (1 V per year VI-7; 1920-26).

   This Library has VI-7; 1920-26.

   "Amalgamated in

   Gm 73, N BIOLOGICAL ABSTRACTS".

Splitting Up

Generally, a periodic publication is split up in two or more publications in the following manner:

1. Original class number is split up with a publication in two or more periodic publications.
2. Splitting in two or more periodic publications and the original class number does not exist with any publication.
3. The issue of multiple periodical is split in two or more periodicals with homogenous title or without it, but it is split as independent periodical.

1. Rule Number PG1: Class Number Continued by M/E

When a periodic publication is split into two or more periodic publications and one periodical regulates the original class number, then a new main card is prepared.

Rule Number PG11: Previous main card and the publication that continues the previous class number, that shall be treated as "continued cards".

Rule Number PG12 : Entry of the previous main card is closed for publication and the library as per the part PB135 and PB137.

PG13 : An additional note will be added in inverted commas in the previous main card:

1. Term "Split Partially into"; and
2. Class number and the title of each publication (except for the continued previous class number) in which it has been split. This information will be given in a separate line.

PG14 : Except for those class numbers that are continued from previous, a note will be added with these in inverted commas in each main card of the publication in which these have been split:

1. Term "Split Partially from" and
2. Class number and the title of the original publication.

Examples:

(l) Gm56, K, 1

PROCEEDING, SERIES B, Royal Society of London.

(Irregular V76; 1905).

This Library has V75 - 142; 1905 /06-1927/33;

"Split from

Am56, K, 1 PROCEEDING, Royal Society of London".

(2) Bm44, N

JOURNAL, Indian Mathematical Society.

(1V for two years. VI5-; 1923/24-)

This Library has VI5-19; 1923/24-1931/32

Each V from V16 has as supplement

Bm44, N Report, Indian Mathematical Conference".

''Split partially into

Bm 44, N, 1 MATHEMATICS STUDENT, Indian Mathematical Society)".

2. Class Number Continued by None

When a periodic publication is split into two or more periodic publications, and the previous class number is not continued by any periodical then, in such case, the periodical will be catalogued as per the rule number PG1 and its sections. However, the term "Split" shall be used in lieu of the term "Split Partially".

Example:

1. Am42, M

JOURNAL, College of Science, Imperial University of Tokyo

(Irregular V 1 -45; 1887-1925).

This library has VI-45; 1887-1925.

"Split into

BZm42, N2 JOURNAL, Faculty of Science, Imperial University of Tokyo, Section 1, etc.

HZm42, N2 JOURNAL, Faculty of Science, Imperial University of TOKYO, Section 2, etc.

Im42, N2 JOURNAL, Faculty of Science, Imperial University of TOKYO, Section 3, etc.

2. BZm42, N2

JOURNAL, Faculty of Science, Imperial University of Tokyo, Section

1. Mathematics, Astronomy, Physics, Chemistry.

(Irregular. V1-; 1925/29-).

This library has VI-; 1925/29-

"Split from

Am 42, M JOURNAL, College of Science, Imperial University of Tokyo".

In the same manner, main entry for other publications that are split, shall be formed.

3. Splitting into Independent Periodicals

When two or more multi-split periodical publications are split independently with homogenous titles then such publications will be catalogued as per the rule number PG2. However, 'Split on Completion of each Volume into' will be used instead of the word 'Split'.

Example:

On the Completion of a Volume, the Abgila (= Annals, bulletin, granthalaya, Indian Library Association), gets totally split up into

1. Annals, Indian Library Association
2. Bulletin, Indian Library Association
3. Granthalaya, (Indian Library Association).

The title page and the index are not issued so as to cover the whole of the Abgila. On the other hand, each of its constituents is provided with an independent title page and index.

Entry will be made in the following manner:

2m44, N4

LIBRARY BULLETIN (Indian Library Association)

(IV per year VI-5 N2; 1942 April-1946, July)

This library has VI-5 N2; 1942 April - 1948, July

2m44, N4, 1

(No V in 1946, August 1948, December)

"Continued as

2m44, N4, 1 ABGILA, etc. (Indian Library Association)"

ABGILA etc (Indian Library Association).

(IV in 2 years. VI-2; 1949-52)

2m44, N4, 1

ABGILA, etc. (Indian Library Association)

(1 V per year V3; 1953)

"Split on Completion of each volume into

2m44, N4, 2 ANNALS, Indian Library Association.

2m44, N4, 3 BULLETIN, Indian Library Association.

2m44, N4; GRANTHALAYA, (Indian Library Association)"

2m44, N4, 2

ANNALS, Indian Library Association.

(1 V in 2 Years VI-2; 1949-52)

This library has VI-2; 1949-52

2m44, N4, 2

ANNALS, Indian Library Association.

(1 V Per year V3-; 1953)

This library has V3; 1953

"Originally published as part of

2m44, N4, ABGILA (Indian Library Association)."

Entries for other split up publications will be formed in the similar manner.

Q. : What are the non-print materials? Briefly discussing the problems faced during their cataloguing also discuss the structure of their descriptions.

Ans. The non-print media are those on which printed words or visuals are not directly represented, such as magnetic tapes, digital recordings, etc. Wall (1985) has provided a threefold definition for non-print materials. According to him the non-print material should satisfy the following aspects;

(i) the item must appeal to the sight and/or hearing of the library user.

(ii) under normal conditions, the item must require additional equipment for usage.

(iii) the printed word must not represent the essence of the medium.

These three criteria sets the parameter for distinguishing non-print material in a library collection. On the basis of the above definition the materials that are grouped under non-print media will include: audio tapes, video tapes, films, slides, transparencies, CD-ROMs etc.

Types of non Print Media

The Non-Print Media can be broadly categorized into following four types :

(i) Films

(ii) Magnetic material

(iii) Plastic material

The following table shows the various type of Non-Print material coming under these three categories :

Films	Magnetic Material	Plastic Material
1. Film Strips	1. Tapes	1. Transparent plastic
2. Slides	(i) Sound tapes :	3. Vinyl Discs
3. Cine films	– Open reel	4. Optical Storage :
4. Microforms :	– Cassette	– Laser vision
– Microfilm	(ii) Video tape :	– CD audio
– Microfiche	– Open reel	– CD-ROM
– Micro-opaque	– Cassette	– CD-I
– Aperture Cards	2. Discs	– DV-I

(1) Film Media : Films have a layer of emulsion on the polyester base on which images are created by chemical response to light fixed by the processing of other chemicals. The holes along the edges are used to pull the film through the camera or projector. Transparent films are used in a variety of formats. The various types of media falling under this category are discussed below :

1. **Film Strips:** It is a collection of images available in two different formats:

   — Single or half frame

   — Double or full frame

   Single frame strips are passed through the viewer or projector vertically. The double frames on the other hand are passed horizontally.

   Filmstrips generally come in small circular gamester. Notes explaining the contents of the images in the individual strips are supplied along with it.

2. **Slides:** These are single frame photographic images mounted on cardboard or plastic frames. Glass is sometimes used to cover and protect the film within the mount. Slides are produced in formats of different dimensions, ranging from 35 mm to about 250 mm square. The larger ones are suitable for overhead projectors. The slides are placed in a box with sets numbered serially.

3. **Cine films:** These have sequence of images arranged vertically. When these images are projected on the screen at an appropriate speed, they give the appearance of a continuous movement. The various formats of cine films are : 35 mm and 16 mm, with sound track; 16 mm without sound track; and 8 mm which is now obsolete. Cine films are usually stored on open reels.

4. **Microforms:** It is a generic term indicating any form of micro record, on flat or roll film, paper or other material.

   The various configuration of microforms are discussed below:

   (a) Microfilm is available in both 35 mm and 16 mm formats. The films are available either with or without sprocket holes, with or without self threading cartridges and in colour or black and white.

   (b) Microfiche is a single piece of film about the size of a post card. It consists of a number of rows of reduced images of documents produced on a transparent sheet of film, using a special stop and repeat camera. The top of the fiche contains information about the contents in eye legible format. Microfiches are available both in colour and black and white. The prevalent sizes available are 3 × 5 inches and 4 × 6 inches.

(c) Micro-opaque cards are similar to microfiches. The difference is that the information is reproduced on a white opaque cards and not on films. The Micro-Opaque Cards are available in 3 × 5, 4 × 6, 5 × 8 and 6 × 8 inch formats. Micro opaques are not very popular and gradually they are becoming obsolete.

(d) Aperture card is an opaque card of approximately 7 × 3 inches, which contains a window for inserting the microfilm. One can insert a single 35 mm film or several 16 mm films on the aperture card. The card contains information about the image. This helps in mechanical sorting, storing and retrieval.

Apart from the above 4 major varieties, the other formats of microforms in the market arc: Ultra fiche, Micro-card, Micro-Print and Microlex.

(II) Magnetic Media : Magnetic media can be broadly divided into two formats: tapes and discs. Magnetic tapes are further divided into two categories Sound tapes or Audio tapes and Video tapes.

1. Magnetic tapes are made of a polyester base over which oxides of iron and Chromium are coated. By magnetization and rearrangement of the magnetic fields borne by the oxides, a message is recorded on the tape. This message (whether sound or video) can be 'read' by a device in the play back machine.

Sound tapes (Audio tapes) are available in two formats: Open reel and Cassette, Open reels are gradually becoming obsolete and no more used for dissemination of copies of recordings. However, these are still used for preparation and storage of masters or originals.

Audio cassettes have standard dimension of 10.2 x 6 cm and the tape is 3.8 mm used. The varying lengths of recording are: 30, 60, 90 and 120 minutes. The tapes for computers, i.e., Digital Audio Tapes (DAT) are generally shorter and of lower quality. The common lengths are 10, 12 and 15 minutes.

Video tapes are also available in two formats: Open reels and Cassettes. Open reels are strictly used for production purposes. The Cassettes are available in three varieties:

(a) U-Matic

(b) VHS (Video Home System)

(c) 8 mm Video

U-matic cassettes are generally used for industrial and educational purposes. These are of 3/4 inch having varying lengths of recording 10,15,20,30,40,50 and 60 minutes. VHS are 12.65 mm tapes having tape speed of 2.34 cm. The varying lengths of recording time available are: 30,60,90,120,180 and 240 minutes. 8 mm video cassettes are not very common. The playback of these cassettes are either through a television set directly attached to the camera or through a dubbing mechanism in which picture and sound is transferred through a cable.

2. Magnetic Discs are used with computers as the backing store for recording information or data and programmes. Mainframe computers use disc packs, which are stored in the computer service area. More commonly used and relatively inexpensive are Hard discs and Winchester discs which are kept with a reading head enclosed in dust free containers. The 'mini' or 'floppy' discs are used with microcomputers and are stored and filed separately. The commonly used format for floppy discs are 3, 1/4 inch size. Earlier, 8 inch and 5, 1/2 inch floppy discs were used, these are obsolete now.

(III) Plastic Materials : Materials under this category can be divided into three sections:

- Transparent plastic
- Vinyl discs
- Optical Storage System

1. **Transparent plastic** refers to the transparencies, which are used with overhead projectors. The information is either written with special quick drying ink or through photocopying process and computer printers. The thickness varies form 0.05 mm to 0.25 mm. Special transparencies are used for colour photocopying and computer printing.
2. **Vinyl discs** are marketed in 17.8 cm, 25.4 cm and 30.5 cm diameter sizes. The disc has a central hole which fits with the spindle of the turn-table. The inter-table provides for 33 1/3, 45

and 78 revolutions per minute (RPM). These are used for audio recording. The technology is now obsolete.

3. **Optical Storage System** is becoming increasingly important mechanism for storage of information, data, etc. The discs are made of plastic material. The plastic surface contains spiral of pits backed by an aluminized reflective surface. The surface is protected by a transparent lacquer. The presence or shape of a pit is read by a laser beam reflected from the mirror-like surface. Various configuration of optical storage systems are:

   (i) *Laser vision* : These are available in two formats — one having facility for one hour continuous moving picture on both sides without still pictures and the second one with 36 minutes duration on both sides having facility of controlling each frames. Both the varieties are available with Sound Channels. An extension of laser vision principle known as AIV (Advanced Interactive Video) is also available now.

   (ii) *CD Audio* : These are becoming very popular formal for distributing music recordings. The recordings are done on one side in digital form.

   (iii) *CD-ROM* : (Compact Disc Read Only Memory) are increasingly used to store information for retrieving through the computer. Apart from the text, sound and graphic tan be also recorded. The other version of CD-ROM is WORM discs (Write Once and Read Many times) where the user can store data directly from the computer using CD writer devices. Re-writable discs are also available in the market.

   (iv) *CD-V* : V stands for Video. The discs are coloured gold to differentiate them form the CD discs. The discs carry audio in digital format and video in analogue form.

   (v) *CD-I* : I stand for Interactiveness. It can carry combination of text, graphics, audio and still and moving pictures.

   (vi) *DV-I* : It is Digital Video Interactive. These discs contain video, audio, graphics and text. The recording is done in the similar manner as on CDs. To accommodate more information the recording is done in compressed format.

Problems in cataloguing of Non-print Materials

The main problem in non-print material cataloguing is with their diverse nature and physical characteristics. With rapid growth in new formats and techniques of storing information is a difficult job to standardize cataloguing procedure for non-print media in the library. The major problems faced in cataloguing non-print media are:

— the characteristics of the materials;

— the diverse nature of non print collections;

— the characteristics and needs of users; and

— cataloguing practices and procedures.

Cataloguing of non-print media requires cataloguers to have familiarity with a variety of information such as the General Material Designation (GMD), specific physical characteristics of individual formats and the software and hardware associated with the uses of the item. To establish cataloguing procedures for non-print media, the library/information centre must take decision on the following aspects.

— the classification scheme to be adopted.

— the numbering system for the call number.

— subject heading system to be followed.

— the extent and detail of descriptive cataloguing and added entries.

For descriptive cataloguing the following decisions need to be taken:

(i) Cataloguing of Materials as Individual Item or Sets : In the case of sets of media collection, decision needs to be taken whether to group them together and have a single catalogue card or to treat them as individual items and link them through series added entry. If the set deals with one subject then it may be catalogued together. If the individual item in a set deals with different subjects then the items may be separated by different class numbers and subject heading. In such cases series added entry should be prepared to link all the material together.

(ii) Added Entries : The number of added entries will depend upon the level of description adopted for cataloguing the material and users approach to the material. It is essential that atleast, title, names and series added entries may be prepared. Other added entries may be as per the requirement of the user.

The information given in a catalogue entry for a document may be divided into three parts:

— the heading section

— the description section, and the

— Subject description section

Structure of Non-print Media Descriptions

The bibliographic description of non-print media follows the similar norms as for books and other materials. The main structure of the bibliographic entry comprises the heading, the description area and the subject description.

The structure of bibliographic description as per the AACR 2R rules is given below:

First Level of Description : Title proper/ 1st statement of responsibility .— Edition Statement. — Material or type of publication specific details. — 1st publisher, distributor, etc., date of publication, etc.

Extent of item

Note

Note

Standard number.

Second Level of Description : Title proper (general material designation) = parallel title: other title information/ 1st statement of responsibility; each subsequent statement of responsibility. — Edition statement/ 1st Statement of responsibility — Material or type of publication specific details. — 1st place of publication, distribution etc. 1st publisher, distributor, etc., date of publication, etc.

Extent of item other physical details; dimensions — (Title proper of series/ statement of responsibility relating to series, ISSN of series; numbering within the series. Title of subseries, ISSN of subseries; numbering within subseries)

Notes

Notes

Standard Number.

Third Level of Description : All elements that are required by rule are to be included. Apart from that the optional elements may also be included for the purpose. Third level of description in generally required by National Libraries and Research libraries. The National Bibliographies usually follow the third level of description.

The difference between level one and level two for non-print material is the expanded physical description in level two. The General Material Description (GMD) and artistic content of the material is included in the body of the entry rather than giving in the note section in the second level. The only drawback in the second level is that it does not provide for the accompanying materials statement.

The problems peculiar to non-print materials are the physical structures and access modes. The filing of the material will depend on the access mode. The following access modes are possible:

— Author/title

— Form

— Subject

The structure of the catalogue card for non-print material depends on the access modes of the users. Therefore all these three access points should be included in the card.

Source of Descriptions

In the case of non-print media the information about title, author, etc., does not exist in one place rather they may be scattered all over the material content. Information for the catalogue entry can be found from the following sources:

1. The material itself, including the container if it is the integral part of the non-print media; for instance covers of audio/video cassettes.
2. Accompanying material such as manuals, pamphlets etc. in paper format.
3. Outside sources such as bibliographies, producer brochures, catalogues etc.

AACR 2R prescribes the following sources of information for different types of non-print materials.

Types of Material	*Chief Source of Information*
Music	Title page
Sound Recordings	Label

Disc	Reel and Label
Tape (open Reel to Reel)	Cassette and Label
Tape Cassette	Catridge and Label
Tape Catridge	Label
Roll	Container and Label
Sound Recording or Film	Film itself and its container, if it is integral part of item.
Motion Picture Video Recording and Graphic Materials	Item itself including any labels and the container.
Machine readable Datafield	Internal user Label
Microform	Title Frame

The information is taken from above sources.

7

Subject Heading, Chain Procedure and Subject Indexing

Q. : "Chain procedure is a versatile system of deriving subject heading." Explain.

or

Discuss the need for a subject catalogue. Explain with examples, the procedure to derive subject heading by using 'Sears List of Subject Headings.'

or

Discuss the importance of subject headings in a library catalogue. How does chain procedure help in this context ?

or

Write an essay on chain procedure method of assigning subject headings.

or

Write as essay on chain procedure method of assigning subject headings.

or

What are the methods prevalent for deriving 'Subject Headings'? Describe the method you will prefer for preparing 'Subject Heading'.

Ans. Subject cataloguing is that specific procedure of cataloguing by which the cataloguer chooses the appropriate subject heading for the subject discussed in the catalogued books. Thereafter, he presents a subject-wise list of the books on the basis of the alphabetical order of these headings. The main objective of the subject cataloguing is to fulfil the subject related needs of the readers.

Subject heading is that element which gives complete indication of the subject covered in the book, including all of its various aspects and forms. In short, subject heading should be a synonym and indication of the specific subject of a book.

Selection of the subject heading is very important in formation of the subject entry. The headings of the subjects remain uniform, ordered and specific by it. The need for the for the formation of subject heading arises for providing information of a specific subject and all its aspects, for complete readings material available in the library under the subject catalogue. According to *M.E. Sears*, "the subject catalogue tries to list under one form of heading all books on a given subject that the library possesses".

Method of Deriving Subject Headings

The following are the two main methods of deriving subject heading.

1. Printed List of Subject Headings, and the
2. Chain Procedure.

(1) List of Subject Headings

The meaning of the list of subject headings is to present a prior list of indicative headings of cross-references of subject-wise lists by which these can be prepared. The cataloguer determines the subject headings on the basis of these lists of subject headings only. Subject headings lists are required for determining the cross references and to maintain uniformity and standardization in the subject headings.

Following are the standard subject heading lists used for determining the subject headings in English language:

(i) Sears List of Subject headings, (SLSH)

(ii) A.L.A. List of Subject Headings for Use in Dictionary Catalogues,

(iii) Library of Congress Subject Headings (LCSH)

Utility of Subject Heading Lists : The cataloguer receives pre-prepared headings from the subject heading lists. These lists act as a dictionary for collection of subject headings. These lists provide guidelines to the cataloguer in formation of the subject headings. In other words, the cataloguer gets the benefit of the experience of many other cataloguers from these lists.

The pre-prepared subject headings in these lists are according to the needs of the users. Use of these lists can establish co-ordination and uniformity in the library catalogue.

Limitations of Subject Heading Lists : Enough time and effort is required in collection and printing of these lists. Moreover, separate lists have to be prepared for each language. This procedure of forming subject headings is not very practical as the work of preparing subject headings from these lists involves too much effort and time.

The subject heading lists are never complete and up-to-date because new subjects are introduced every days. Hence, it is necessary to include these subjects in the list also.

Besides, general subject headings lists are not useful for the specialized libraries. This is the reason for which separate subject heading lists are prepared for these libraries.

Sears List of Subject Heading (SLSH)

Sears list for use information of subject headings was first printed in the year 1923. This list was initially prepared for use in small libraries and later its scope was extended to small as well as medium sized libraries. This list satisfies the requirements of small libraries. Improvements have been made in this list form time to time on the basis of the experience of the various libraries. The latest edition of this list is 18th edition.

The objective of this list is to keep the documents of a specific subject under a uniform subject heading. Other than this those headings are also given in this list after X&XX that are used for the formation of 'see' and 'see also subject directions.

Formation of Subject Headings in SLSH

SLSH is an enumerated list of subject headings. In providing subject headings, the subject cataloguer has only to choose from SLSH the appropriate heading that matches the contents of documents being indexed.

The structure of the headings is on similar patterns of LCSH, with some modifications to serve the needs of small public libraries and school libraries. SLSH is guided by the general principles such as "Specific and Direct Entry", "Common Usage", "Uniformity" in the formations of its subject headings. Subject headings are constructed in SLSH in a variety of ways ranging from lists of single word headings and descriptive phrases of single concepts in two or more words to complex and compound subjects.

Single Word Heading

The simplest form of subject heading consists of a single noun, which is the most ideal type when it is possible to represent the thought contents of a document by a single term.

Examples : Art

Agriculture

Education

Religion

There are many identical words with different meanings (i.e., homographs) that might cause ambiguity. Such words are identified by providing a scope word giving the contextual meaning of the word.

Examples: Seals (Animals)

Seals (Numismatics)

Seals (Christmas, etc.)

Seals (Law)

A choice must be made between the singular and plural forms of single words. Abstract ideas, concepts or actions are usually stated in the singular, whereas objects and things are rendered in their plural forms.

Credit	–	Singular
Beauty	–	-Do-
Books	–	Plural
Flowers	–	-Do-

Sometimes both the singular and plural forms of a noun are used as headings. In such cases, they carry different meanings. As for example:

Essay	:	refers to the technique
Essays	:	refers to the works
Symphony	:	refers to the musical form
Symphonies	:	refers to the musical scores

Phrase Heading

A phrase heading consists of two or more words representing the subject of a document. The different types of phrase headings as recognized in SLSH are discussed below :

(a) Compound Headings : Compound headings consist of two nouns or noun phrases joined by the word "and" to connect topics or concepts or opposite subject, or to express a relationship between two concepts or things, which are usually treated together in documents. As for example :

Bow and Arrow

Cities and Towns

Religions and Science

Belief and Doubt

Joy and Sorrow

(b) Objectively Headings : Often a specific concept is best expressed by qualifying the noun an adjective. As for example :

American literature

Electrical engineering

Tropical fish

In the past the expression was frequently inverted (e.g. Psychology, Religious; Art, Municipal). The noun was placed first in order to keep all aspects of a broad subject together. In recent years these arguments have been abandoned in favour of the direct order of natural language with few exceptions, such as the names of battles and massacres, and the State. When inverted headings have been inverted, a reference from the older inverted form to the direct form is usually added.

(c) Prepositional Phrase Headings : Some concepts are expressed by nouns or nouns phrases connected by prepositions that express their relationships. As for example :

Freedom of Information

Electricity in Agriculture

Complex Subject : Dealing with complex subjects. i.e., documents that deal with more than one concept in a particular relation, the main and subdivisions are stated together.

For example :

Birds – Eggs and nests

Birds – Migration

Birds – Protection

Education – Curricula

Education – Finance

Examples of form headings :

Chemists – Directories

Bible – Pictorial works

Geology – Maps

Examples of headings presented form a particular point of view:

Education – History

Religion – Philosophy

Mathematics – Study and teaching

Examples of headings with chronological subdivisions :

Unites States – History – 1775-1783, Revolution

United States – History – 1945-1953

Examples of geographic names : Subject divided by place :

Agriculture – India

Theatre – Paris

Examples of geographic names : Names of places divided by subject :

United States – Census

China – Boundaries

Tibet – Climate

In summary, the formation of subject headings in SLSH is less complicated and more straightforward.

Entry Format

With the fifteenth edition, the SLSH has adopted the thesaurus format to help the cataloguer to distinguish relationships among terms and of establishing appropriate references in the catalogue based upon these relationships. The SLSH has also adopted the symbols generally used in most thesauri to label the terms associated with a headings.

Subject entries in SLSH are printed in boldface and the cross reference terms appear in light faces. In the list, the right half of each page is kept blank. All entries, references and instructions are confined to the left columns and the blank space is provided for the local cataloguer to add any new headings and references made for the, and thus converting the volume into an authority file. The general format of entry in SLSH is as follows :

Subject Entry in bold face followed by Dewey Decimal Classification number	:	Card games 795.4
Scope Note	:	(in this entry, there is no scope note)
USE references	:	UF Cards, Playing Playing cards
General references	:	SA names of card games, to be added as needed
Broader Topic (BT)	:	BT Games
Narrower Topic (NT) references	:	NT Bridge (Game) Canasta (Game) Card tricks Solitaire (Game) Tarot
Related topic (RT) references	:	RT Gambling

Note : SA – See Also, BT – Broader Topic, NT – Narrower Topic, RT – Related Topic

Cross References

With the fifteenth edition of SLSH in 1994 "*see*" and "*see also*" references and the complementary "x" and "xx" were replaced by the thesaurus symbols UF/USE, BT, NT, RT and SA. There are three types of cross references used in SLSH and these are discussed below :

(i) Specific "See" References : The UF symbol stands for "*Used for*", and it designates those preferred terms or phrases from which "*see*" references are to be made. Such words or phrases might include the following :

(a) Synonyms or near synonyms; e.g. Playing cards *see* Card games.

(b) Inverted headings to normal order; e.g. Psychology, Religious *see* Religious psychology.

(c) Conjunctive i.e., terms connected by "and"; e.g. Religion and Science *see* Science and Religion.

(d) Variant spellings; e.g. colour *see* Color.

(e) Opposite of a term; e.g. Intemperance *see* Temperance.

(f) Singular to plural; e.g. Mouse *see* Mice.

The two terms following the UF symbol in the example indicate that the reference exists in the SLSH as follows :

Cards, playing	Playing cards
Playing Cards	USE Card game

In the catalogue these become specific "*see*" references, as follows :

Cards, playing	*see*	Card games
Playing Cards	*see*	Card games

(ii) Specific "*see also*" References: A "*See also*" reference connects a headings to related headings or headings if the library has material listed under both headings. Following the BT symbol is a term "Games" that is broader in application than the subject heading "Card games" as demonstrated in example. Similarly, following the NT symbol are terms that are narrower than "Card games". A "*See also*" reference is made from a broader term to a narrower term. Accordingly, the cross references will be as given below:

Games
see also
Card games

Cards games
see also
Bridge (Game)

Card games
see also
Cansta (Game)

Card games
see also
Card tricks

Card Games
see also
Solitaire (Game)

Card games
see also
Tarot

Following RT symbols are terms related to the main term, on similar or associated subjects. Related terms are of more or less equal specificity, neither broader nor narrower. In the example, the term "Card games" is related to "Gambling" because not all cards games involve gambling and not all gambling involves card games. In the catalogue, references between related terms are reciprocal. Hence, the reference entries in the catalogue will be

Games	Card games
see also	*see also*
Card games	Gambling

(iii) General References : The symbol "SA" stands of "*see also*" and introduces a general reference, which refers from one heading to an entire category or class of headings rather than an individual heading. A general explanation or direction is given instead of a long list of individual headings. In the example of "Card games", the symbol "SA" introduces the general reference to "names of card games, to be added as needed". This instruction provides reminder to the cataloguer not to be limited to the names of card games given in the example. There happened to be three card games appearing in the NT field under "Card games". If the library acquires a work devoted to the card game Rummy, a reference entry is to be made as follows :

Card games
see also
Rummy (Game)

Standard Vocabulary

All SLSH is not backed by any library collection, so updating and revision of subject headings cannot keep pace with changing current terminology and growth of new subjects. While revisions are taken care of by publishing new editions of SLSH at periodic intervals, tools that can help libraries to keep the subject headings current and updated are the "Readers' Guide to Periodical Literature", "Applied Science and Technology Index", etc. which are also published by Wilson Company. These bibliographic tools provide acceptable current subject headings, using the principles of LCSH and SLSH. If these headings also are found inadequate, the subject cataloguer is advised to construct the headings on the basis of the principles of subject headings of SLSH.

Filing Order

Filing of entries of SLSH follows the ALA Filing Rules (1980). All headings are interfiled disregarding all punctuations. Headings with modifiers given in round brackets and phrase headings appear intermingled with those with dashes and commas. Although this straightforward alphabetical arrangement may appear to be less logical than the one used with punctuations, but the increasing use of computers in libraries and the wish to adhere to standard rules have prompted the practices to adhere to standard rules which have prompted the editors of SLSH to adopt the ALA Rules for Filing.

Merits and Demerits

SLSH is comparatively simpler to use. The rules and principles are fairly explicit in their directions, containing scope notes and specific instructions for their use. If followed consistently, SLSH will provide useful reference guide for the user and also to the library reference staff.

Its disadvantage is that this is a American procedure. Hence, the words that are used in it are the words that are popular in America and which are not suitable to Indian conditions. Many discrepancies regarding the subject headings can also be seen in it.

The subject headings that are important and suitable to the needs or tastes of American conditions are elaborately covered in it. In this manner, this list is inadequate for Indian libraries form the view point of subjects of specific interest.

(2) Chain Procedure

Dr. S. R. Ranganathan has devised of this method of forming subject heading. He first mentioned this method in his book 'Theory of Library Catalogue'.

Chain procedure is an almost mechanical method of deriving subject headings from class numbers. In other words, this is a semi-mechanical method of deriving subject headings, which is received from the chain of sub-division of class numbers. This method is considered to be semi-mechanical as it helps the cataloguer to determine the need of the reader. As a result, it puts a limit on the personal opinion of the cataloguer in formation of subject headings.

Dr. S. R. Ranganathan has considered the main entry as the

specific subject entry in his book 'Classified Catalogue Code', but the reader is unable to understand the call number entry in the language of cataloguing. Hence, subject word entry is required to help the readers in receiving the reading material according to their specific subject. The chain procedure was developed to this need of the reader.

Various scholars of library science have defined the chain procedure in following manner:

E.J. Koats has defined the chain procedure as "A method, first propounded by Dr. Ranganathan for constructing subject index entries, without permutation of components by citing terms contained in particular chains."

According to *Encyclopaedia of Librarianship,* "It is semi-mechanical method of producing the requisite subject index entries for a classified catalogue based on analysis of the classification symbol of each subject".

In the view of *H.D. Sharma* "It is procedure of deriving subject word entry from a class number, in a more or less mechanical way."

Thus, it is clear from above definitions that the chain procedure is a method of forming subject word entries, where each class number is analysed, one by one, from its main subject to its specific subject to form the subject word entry.

It is Dr. Ranganathan's theory that the class number, of each book is tied up as different links that form a chain. Each link is analysed in order to form the subject word entry from the class number. According to him, following are the different types of links:

1. False Link : This is a link that has no meaning i.e., it ends up in the following manner:

(a) As connecting symbol;

(b) Numbers representing phase relation;

(c) Numbers representing intra-facet relation;

(d) Numbers representing intra-array phase relations;

(e) Time isolate.

2. Unsought Link : This is the type of link which ends with a part of isolate focus of a class number. Otherwise, it represents such subjects on which there is no reading material available or there is no possibility for the readers to find it.

3. Sought Link : This is the link, which is neither false link nor unsought but which provides every possibility for the readers to find the reading material through it.

Method

The complete class number is first written in the from of a chain in order to obtain the subject heading from it. Next, the meaning of these numbers is written in natural language.

For example :

234: 7.44' N9 t: A report on reference service in University libraries in India during 1990s. The representation of this class number in the form of a chain would be as follows :

2	↧	Library Science (Sought Link)
234	↧	University Library (Sought Link)
234 :	↧	(False Link)
234;7	↧	Reference Service in University Library (Sought Link)
234:7.	↧	(False Link)
234:7.4	↧	Reference Service in University Library in Asia (Sought Link)
234:7.44	↧	Reference Service in University Library in India (Sought Link)
234:7.44'	↧	(False Link)
234:7.44'N	↧	20th Century (False Link)
234:7.44'N9	↧	Reference Service in University Library in India during 1990s (False Link)
234:7.44'N9t	=	A Report on Reference Service in University Library in India during 1990s (Sought Link)

In the above example, the different kinds of link are determined on the basis of the Canon of Sought Heading and they are indicated within parentheses for each link. This is a principle, which regulates the inclusion or exclusion of a particular component of the heading on the basis of the users' approach.

Specific Subject Headings and Subject References derived from the chain of the given class number as under:

Subject Report, India, Reference Service, University Library, Library Science.

(i) India, Reference Service, University Library, Library Science.

(ii) References Service, University Library, Library Science.

(iii) University Library, Library Science.

(iv) Library Science.

The above mentioned Specific Subject Heading and Subject References, as drawn by chain procedure, (known as Class Index Entries) are arranged in a single alphabetical sequence in the subject index part of the Classified Catalogue. Subject Index part may be referred to classified part by the class number.

INDIA REFERENCE SERVICE,
UNIVERSITY LIBRARY,
LIBRARY SCIENCE. 214:7.44

LIBRARY SCIENCE 2

REFERENCE SERVICE, UNIVERSITY LIBRARY,
LIBRARY SCIENCE 234:7

REPORT, INDIA, REFERENCE SERVICE,
UNIVERSITY LIBRARY,
LIBRARY SCIENCE 2.14:7.44 'N9t

UNIVERSITY LIBRARY,
LIBRARY SCIENCE. 234

In Dictionary index or catalogue, bibliographical details of the documents (s) dealing with the subject represented in the specific subject heading are provided under that specific subject heading. Cross reference entries are prepared for subject references. They are linked to their specific "subject heading by the *"See also"* references:

INDIA REFERENCE SERVICE, UNIVERSITY LIBRARY. LIBRARY SCIENCE.

See also

REPORT, INDIA, REFERENCE SERVICE, UNIVERSITY LIBRARY, LIBRARY SCIENCE

LIBRARY SCIENCE

See also

REPORT, INDIA, REFERENCE SERVICE, UNIVERSITY LIBRARY, LIBRARY SCIENCE

REFERENCE SERVICE, UNIVERSITY LIBRARY, LIBRARY SCIENCE

See also

REPORT, INDIA, REFERENCE SERVICE, UNIVERSITY LIBRARY, LIBRARY SCIENCE

REPORT, INDIA, REFERENCE SERVICE, UNIVERSITY LIBRARY, LIBRARY SCIENCE

Bibliographical Details/Citation of the document (s) dealing with the subject

UNIVERSITY LIBRARY. LIBRARY SCIENCE.

See also

REPORT, INDIA, REFERENCE SERVICE, UNIVERSITY LIBRARY

It has been found that those who use dictionary catalogue would like to retain some kind of entries they had been accustomed to, when they depend on List of Subject Headings. Accordingly, the rules of chain procedure used for classified index did not prove equally helpful if used for Dictionary index. In 1964, Ranganathan suggested certain modifications in the rules of chain procedure in respect of the process of derivation of specific subject headings and subject references in a Dictionary Catalogue. These modifications reflect changes in the sequence of component terms in a subject heading. Ranganathan suggested to break the chain into different parts at the point(s) where the digit denoting common isolates such as Space, Time, Form, etc. and indicating phase relation occur. The specific subject heading is to be derived from last SL of each part in reverse rendering process, starting from the first part and continuing to further parts, if any, one after another. Then, the components of derived subject heading should be arranged in the sequence of their derivation from each part of chain of the class number. Applying this rule to the above example, we get the following components of specific subject heading in the sequence of their derivation from each part:

1st Part	:	Reference Service, University Library
2nd Part	:	India
3rd Part	:	No Sought Link is available since the time concept has been considered as False Link
4th part	:	Report

The specific subject heading would consist of arranging the component terms in the sequence of their derivation from each part :

REFERENCE SERVICE, UNIVERSITY LIBRARY. INDIA, REPORT.

According to Ranganathan's modifications, the subject reference headings are to be derived for each of the SL of the whole class number starting from the last SL and ignoring different parts of the class number. Subject reference headings are to be constructed with necessary and sufficient upper Sought Link terms to make them meaningful and individualized. Applying this rule, we get the following-subject reference headings for the above example :

Report, India, Reference Service, University Library.

India, Reference Service, University Library.

Reference Service, University Library.

University Libraries.

Library Science.

Subject Reference Headings are to be linked to the Specific Subject heading by means of *"See also* " references.

In this manner, the subject heading is derived by this method and the class index entry of the classified catalogue is formed, while the specific subject entry in the dictionary catalogue is formed by the last required link. The remaining links are used for forming 'see also' entries.

Merits of Chain Procedure

Following are the merits of chain procedure:

1. Easy and Convenient : Chain procedure of finding subject heading is an easy, convenient and semi-mechanical method in comparison to other methods. The cataloguer has to use his personal knowledge and judgmental abilities to form the subject headings from the subject heading lists. On the other hand, the subject heading is automatically received upon reaching the appropriate link by using chain procedure. Hence, even a person with little knowledge about the classification system can derive the subject heading quite easily by using this procedure.

2. Pure and Uniform : As this is a semi-mechanical procedure based on definite rules, its resulted headings are correct and free from any defects. Thus, if the chain procedure is adopted in the whole library for forming the specific subject entries, it will bring uniformity in the subject entries.

3. Economical : This method of deriving subject headings is more economical than other methods because expensive and large subject heading lists are not required in this procedure. This saves nation's wealth. At the same time, as this procedure is semi-mechanical, it saves a lot of time and effort of the cataloguer. Moreover, the number of entries in the catalogue also remain limited by this procedure.

4. Chain Procedure and Alphabetical Order : The class index entries gathered in the alphabetical part of the classified catalogue fulfil those needs that are not fulfilled by the entries of the classified part. For example, subjects like Indian Libraries, Indian History, Indian Philosophy etc. are scattered in the classified part of the catalogue and also in the shelves. However, these subjects come together in one place in the alphabetical part. This is because an order, which is opposite to the chain procedure, is presented in it.

5. Symbiosis between Cataloguing and Classification : This procedure establishes a live-relationship between cataloguing and classification. This is because the cataloguer forms the subject heading from the class number given by the classifier. In this manner, if the classifier has formed incorrect class number by mistake, the cataloguer will detect this mistake and bring it in the notice of the classifier.

6. Quick Formation of Headings : During the formation headings by this procedure for the British National Bibliography, A. Wells especially noted that the work of forming headings by using this self-regulated and semi-mechanical procedure can be done by the assistants more quickly.

Limitations or Demerits

This procedure suffers from following limitations along with the merits mentioned above:

1. The quality and success of the subject headings derived by this procedure is dependent on the quality of the classification system because this procedure is completely based on the classification system.
2. The cataloguers were benefited by going through many volumes of subject heading lists and other such collections during the process of forming subject headings before the chain procedure. The cataloguer is deprived of this benefit when this procedure is used for forming the subject headings.
3. Only those words are used for forming subject headings in the chain procedure, which are provided in the lists of the classification system. Thus, the work of the cataloguer not only depends on the work of the classifier, but the independence, knowledge etc. of the cataloguer also become limited.
4. As the work of forming subject headings is based on the classification system, the work of the cataloguer becomes dependent on the work of the classifier. If the class number formed by the classifier is incorrect, many wrong entries will be formed if the cataloguer does not rectify the mistake in the class number.
5. The arrangement of the elements in the subject headings formed by the chain procedure is not according to the tastes and liking of the public. The sequence in these headings is such that the less important element is mentioned first and the more important facts are written later. According to E.J. Koats, "Readers see the subject list under that element of the subject heading, which is more realistic than others." The less realistic element comes before the more important element of the subject heading in the dual-point classification system.

   For example:

   Class number of *Tulsidas ka Jeevan Charitra'* is 0152, 1J34w According to this, the heading of the first class index entry will be :

   Jeevan Charitra, Tulsidas,

   However, the readers will prefer to lookup this heading in the following manner and also expect this from a catalogue:

   Tulsidas, Jeevan Charitra.

   Concluding, it can be said, though chain procedure was intended initially to provide class index entries to a classified catalogue, rules and procedures were formulated for deriving subject headings for a dictionary catalogue also. In fact this method can be extended to formulate subject entries to bibliographies, documentation lists, abstract bulletins and also query analysis to formulate search strategies to retrieve documents from any bibliographic file.

Q. : What do you understand by Indexing Languages? Discuss with examples.

or

What do you understand by Indexing System' ? Differentiate between Pre and Post- Coordinate Indexing Systems.

Ans. Indexing Language is the language which is used to describe a subject or other aspects of information in an index or in a library catalogue. The generally accepted difference between a library catalogue and an index is that an index entry merely locates a subject a concept, whereas a catalogue entry includes some descriptive specification of a document containing the subject. But the line of demarcation is not, in practice, hard and fast. The indexing language can be an alphabetical language or may be a classification scheme. But, our emphasis would be on alphabetical indexing languages. There are three main categories of indexing languages. They are: (a) natural indexing languages; (b) free indexing languages, and (c) controlled indexing languages.

1. Natural Indexing Language

One of the greatest hurdles in discussing natural indexing language is that it is not easy to identify or know as to what exactly constitutes a natural indexing language. We do not generally come across lists of natural indexing languages. Obviously, a natural indexing language is the language of the documents that are indexed or catalogued for a library. Hence, it could be static as long as the document collection remains static. As soon as a new batch of documents is added to the library, the terms of the indexing language are changed to accommodate the new terms contained in the new set of documents. Each system will have a different indexing language even if the documents cover the same subject area. Also, since the indexing language is derived from the documents, added to the library or input into the system of different records, even if they represent the same documents, they generate a different indexing language. These variations affect the consistency associated with the library catalogue and so, present many problems. Most of the natural indexing languages are based upon the language of title, abstract and other text of documents.

There is a debate going on as to the effective use of natural languages for indexing and subject cataloguing purposes. One school of thought believes that full exploitation of the opportunities offered by computer systems could only be done by taking recourse to natural indexing language, whereas the other school holds the view that controlled indexing language is the only proper way to index documents. However it may be mentioned that controlled indexing language is, extremely time consuming, costly and uneconomic. One of the applications of natural language indexing is the production of indexes based on words in titles of documents such as, Key Word In Context (PWIC) indexes.

2. Free Indexing Language

It is the nature of free indexing that any word or term that suits the subject may signed as at subject heading in catalogue or as an indexing term. The terms may be human or computer assigned although free language indexing is commonly used in the computer produced subject catalogues or indexes. The computer generates the list by indexing every word which is provided, unless it is instructed not to do so.

3. Controlled Indexing Language

Control is necessary in respect of terms used as subject identifiers in a catalogue or index, because of the variety of natural languages. Such control may involve barring of certain terms from use as headings or access points in a library catalogue or an index. The term which are to be used are specified and the synonyms recognised and as far as possible are eliminated. Preferred word forms are noted. The list of terms, thus, prepared constitutes what is called controlled indexing language. One of the methods by which such a language is formed, is to list or store the acceptable terms in a vocabulary. Such lists contain specific decisions relating to the preferred words, and also decisions regarding the form of words to be used; for example, singular or plural, nouns or adjectives. There are mainly two types of controlled indexing languages in verbal plane. They are: subject beading lists and thesauri. These two types of controlled indexing languages have the following functions:

(i) to control the terminology used in subject catalogues and indexes; and

(ii) to control the display of relationships in catalogues and indexes.

Subject heading lists are lists of index terms normally arranged in alphabetical order, which can be used to determine the terms to be used in a catalogue for describing subjects (i.e., as subject headings) by cataloguers. These lists attempt to solve some of the problems concerning alphabetical subject approach. They serve as guides to the cataloguer and aid him in the task of subject cataloguing. The basic functions of a subject headings list may be stated in the following terms:

(i) The list records terms which shall be used in a catalogue or database, and also indicates the form in which they shall be shown. It acts as an authority list for index terms and their form.

(ii) The list makes recommendations about the use of references for the display of relationships in a catalogue in order to guide the users to distinguish associated terms.

Sear's List of Subject Headings' and 'Library of Congress List of Subject Headings' are examples of popular list of subject headings.

Indexing system

An indexing system is a set of prescribed procedures for organizing the contents of records of knowledge or documents for the purposes of retrieval and dissemination. Another definition reads that "an indexing system is the means whereby an indexing language can be applied to make an index." It appears that both these definitions have common roots. The only difference is that the first definition is somewhat broader in scope. It may be stated that the need for an indexing system stems out of the work of devising index headings. These index headings mainly relate to documents dealing with compound or multi-concept subjects although, elementary one-concept subjects are not excluded from the purview of an indexing system. For convenience, indexing systems could be divided into two basic groups: the *pre-coordinate systems* and *post-coordinate systems.* On the basis of experience, it may be stated that not every index necessarily exhibits all the features of either of these two types of Indexing systems, and in fact it has been observed that some indexes do possess characteristics of both types of indexing systems. However, this division is useful in understanding these two categories of indexing systems.

Types of Indexing System

An indexing system may be of following two types –

- Pre-coordinate Indexing system
- Post – coordinate Indexing system

1. Pre-Coordinate Indexing Systems

Pre-coordinate indexing systems are conventional systems mostly found in printed indexes. In this type of system, a document is represented in the index by a heading or headings comprising of a chain or string of terms. These terms taken together are expected to define the subject content of the document. The leading term determines the position of the entry in the catalogue or index, while the other i.e., qualifying terms are subordinated to it. For example consider the title of document, "Use of Computers in Library and Information Activities". It might be represented by headings such as:

LIBRARY ACTIVITIES : Use of Computers

COMPUTERS : Use in Library Activities

Since the coordination of terms in the index description is decided before any particular request is made, the index is known as pre-coordinate index. One of the characteristics associated with pre-coordinate index is that the headings in the index are relatively specific compared to one-concept headings such as LIBRARIES or COMPUTERS. Pre-coordinate indexes are mostly prevalent as printed indexes. For example, the indexes to abstracting and indexing journals, national bibliographies and subject indexes to library catalogues apply principles of pre-coordinate indexing in varying measures. Such indexes arc compiled both manually as well as with the help of a computer.

There are two aspects of great significance in relation to pre-coordinate indexes. The first aspect concerns with the consistent description of subjects. In case all subject headings describing many concepts, consistency should be introduced in to the terms used to represent individual concepts that constitute the multiple-concept heading. Also, the order in which the individual terms representing the unit concepts of a multiple-concept stated must be consistent. Some basic principles have to be evolved and followed regarding an acceptable citation order of the terms. There must be a theoretical basis by which consistent citation orders could he achieved. Use of such theoretical principles may result in the derivation of a structured system of headings with consistent citation order between similar, yet distinct subjects. The citation order is less likely to be over looked if some rationale determines such citation order which is to he followed.

The second aspect is the need to provide access for those users who approach the subject under consideration from one of the secondary concepts. Since only one term can appear in the primary position in the prescribed citation order, the preferred citation order should be the one, which caters to a majority of users. In this context, it may be stated that the same citation order, however well founded it is, will not prove suitable to every searcher. To obviate this problem, references or added entries should be provided in the catalogue or index. At least, one added entry is usually provided or each of the secondary concepts contained in the preferred citation order. Generally, there is some pattern by which such references could be generated to an acceptable level.

Both these aspects arise because of the fact that pre-coordinate indexing systems are basically one-place-systems. In other words, these systems normally provide one main entry for each document and are mostly suitable for catalogues and bibliographies. These are very helpful to the searcher since a number of searches can he conducted simultaneously by tracing entries under similar headings.

All pre-coordinate indexing models are based on classificatory principles such as, facet analysis and synthesis. The functions performed by a pre-coordinate indexing models are:

(*i*) *Its collocating function* brings together in the file document surrogates on the same similar subjects. Most subjects are to be dealt with would be multi-conceptual (e.g., Survey of bank credits to industrial estates). Rules are necessary for the ordering of terms in an index headings, so that indexers represent the same or similar subjects consistently, there by helping the indexer to perform the collocating function effectively.

(*ii*) *Its retrieval function* recalls references to documents in response to generic and specific enquiries. This is aided by providing entries under each significant term as well as reference entries *'see' and 'see also'* in the index. The reference entries help in bringing together narrower and related subjects together Another way of aiding the retrieval function is to subject each enquiry to conceptual analysis and translation before the index is searched. Once the search strategy is formulated and the index is ready to be searched, the actual retrieval itself is aided by the proper collocation of entries in the index.

In a pre-coordinate index, each significant term in a stung becomes the lead term or filing element. Associated with the need to provide multiple entries is also the need to see that each of these entries is intelligible and unambiguous in covering the intended meaning.

(iii) It supports searches with varying precision and recall requirements.

(iv) It enables the searcher to interact with the system in obtaining satisfactory results.

(v) It establishes syntactical relationships between the terms of a subject statement in retrieval file. This relationship connects the components of a subject statement into a coherent whole and so determine its overall meaning. Besides, this relationship exists between a specific concept and the family of interconnected ideas with which it is generally associated. These two relationships are important for retrieval file to enable generic as well as specific searches.

2. Post-Coordinate Indexing Systems

These systems are also called coordinate indexing systems. As in the pre coordinate systems, the starting point, here too, is the identification of multi-concept subjects and then compound concepts from the documents to be indexed. Once the multi-concept subject is analysed into its elementary compound concepts, entries are prepared under terms, which represent elementary concepts. In other words, by this method only simple subject concepts are indexed. These concepts are not coordinated at the time of preparation of catalogue or index. Since the coordination of concepts does not take place till such time a request is made by user for information about a particular compound subject, this method of indexing is called post-coordinate or sometimes simply coordinate indexing. In its early stages, post-coordinate indexing employed subject concepts as they were expressed in the document for index description of the document. Although, indexing can thus be done in 'natural language', i.e., by using significant words taken directly from the document but in many cases, post-coordinate indexing language employes terms which mostly represent isolate concepts and are not in the form of compound subject headings. For example, if we have a document dealing with the compound subject "Computer Cataloguing in Libraries", the subject analysis of the document may consist of three simple concepts namely,

Computers

Cataloguing and

Libraries

The document is indexed under each of these simple concepts and index entries are prepared. Thus, the compound subject of the document receives an index description consisting of their concepts entered individually in the index. If a user is interested only in documents dealing with the compound subject then he has to coordinate all these terms at the search stage and retrieve the documents dealing with the compound subject. This is accomplished by retrieving documents containing common document numbers under individual component concepts. Coming to another document representing the subject 'Torsion in the Reinforced Concrete in Service Cores in Tall Buildings'. This multi-concept subject may be analysed into the following unit or elementary concepts:

Torsion

Reinforced Concrete

Service Cores

Tall Buildings

If it is intended to prepare post-coordinate index for this example, we may have to prepare entries under the following index headings:

Buildings, Tall

Concrete, Reinforced

Service Cores

Torsion

Most important features of the post-coordinate indexing system are :

(a) No sequence of terms or citation order is necessary. Every term gets equal weight;

(b) constituent concepts of a composite subject are kept separately uncoordinated by the indexer and the coordination of concepts is done by the searcher at the search stage;

(c) The searcher has wide options of the free manipulation of the classes at the time of searching. As a result, the searcher has the complete freedom to coordinate the index terms in any combination or order required;

(d) Multidimensionality in relationships of concepts can be retained.

Besides there also exist other two indexing models, which are key - word Indexing and non-conventional model i.e., Citation indexing model. These are briefly discussed below:

3. Key Word Indexing Models

Computers began to be used to aid information retrieval system in the 1950s. The first use of computers in information retrieval was the production of indexes. The Central Intelligence Agency (CIA) of the USA is said to be the first organization to use the machine produced Key Words from Title Index since 1952. H P Luhn and his associates produced permuted title indexes in the International Conference of Scientific Information held at Washington in 1958. Luhn named his index as, "Key Word-in-Context". (KWIC) index and reported its method of generation in a paper in 1959. The success of KWIC was established after its adoption by American Chemical Society in 1961 in its publication "Chemical Titles".

"Keyword" means subject denoting words, chosen mainly from the titles and/or sometimes from abstract or text of the document for the purpose of indexing. The words chosen may be single words, multi-words or even phrases that convey content information of the document. However, the system developed by Luhn was from the words in the title of a document. Several keywords may be chosen for a document to provide access form different approaches of the user. Since the keyword indexing is based on natural language terminology of the documents, this system is also known as "Natural Language Indexing System".

The KWIC index, developed by H P Luhn, is said to be one of the earliest and successful computer-generated keyword indexes. In his method, he suggested the selection of words from the title excepting the unwanted or insignificant words. While the words will form index term, other words in the title, what he said as "will be wrapped around it". These words will serve as the context. KWIC indexing system is based on usage of natural language terminology to generate the index entries. All of the words in the titles of a batch of documents for which an index is required, are matched, by a computer against a stop-list. This stop-list or stop-wordlist is a record of words which are insignificant in an index. They include words like articles, auxiliary verbs together with such general words as "aspect", "different", "method", "very", etc. Depending upon the subject orientation of each major search system has defined their own list of "stop words". Some words which might be feasible access points in a general index prove worthless in index devoted to a special subject area. Indiscriminate marking articles, prepositions, etc. may create problems because of important scientific and technical terms such as "Vitamin A", "On line", etc. In view of this, words to be included in the list of "stop-words" are required to be selected in the light of the subject orientation of the index. Stop-words do not appear as entry words but they are displayed in the titles in the index in order to provide the context of the document. No controlled vocabulary is required for keyword indexing. Indexing terms are selected from the natural language of documents. In addition to KWIC index, there are a number of varieties of keyword indexes that have been developed over the years. Two most important versions are Key Word Out of Context (KWOC) and Key Word And Context (KWAC). They differ only in terms of their formats but indexing principles/techniques remain more or less same.

The principal merit of keyword indexing is the speed with which it can be produced. The production of keyword index does not involve costly indexing staff. It requires minimum of intellectual effort compared to those of other indexing models. The keyword index reflects current terminology in a particular subject field since words used as access points are those used by the author in his title. As far as an author can be expected to be an expert in his field, the words used to describe the document seem be both current and accurate. The commulation of entries in keyword index is straightforward. The computer interfiles the entries from a number of batches of input and prints the commutative index.

Despite their advantages, keyword indexes suffer from some severe limitations. The efficiency of keyword indexing is invariably the question of reliability of expressive titles of documents as most of such indexes are based on titles. If the titles are not meaningful the system becomes ineffective. For example, what conclusion about subject content can be drawn from the conclusion about subject content from the title; "New rules old games?" Some titles are misleading or eye catching, rather than informative. For example, the subject content of document entitled "Asian Drama" deals with the economic conditions on Asia, rather than the drama of Asia. Some subjects simply cannot adequately be precisely specified by a short title. Most of the terms used in Science and Technology are standardized, but the situation is different in humanities and social sciences. Since no controlled vocabulary is used, keyword indexing appears to be unsatisfactory in respect of control of synonyms and homonyms particularly in the subject areas of the humanities and Social sciences.

(4) Non Conventional Indexing Model or Citation Indexing

Another unique indexing model was developed by Eugene Garfield in early 1960's. The model is non-conventional in the sense that it does not use subject terms in indexing. Instead, the indexing is done by the name of author - cited and citing references to sources. Here, the name of the author, the source document where a particular paper is published is taken into consideration. The author and the source document cited are considered for indexing. This indexing named as 'Citation Indexing' and developed on the same idea of Shepherd's Citation Index and it is a unique example of a non-conventional model. Here, the problems of citation order, semantics, change of terminologies of a subject are automatically solved, as it is not based on terminologies. It works quite well in providing subject approach to information. The Science Citation Index, Social Science Citation Index and Arts and Humanities Citation Index are the examples of this model.

Q. : What types of subject indexing models are in vogue? Listing them, discuss some of the important indexing system.

or

Write briefly about :

- **PRECIS**
- **POPSI**
- **KWIC**

Ans. Subject Indexing is that element which gives complete indication of the subject covered in the documents, including all of its various aspects and forms.

There are many factors that govern the design of subject heading systems. Some of the more important ones are:

- content analysis of documents to select the right key words that represent their specific subject;
- rendering the selected key words in a logical sequence according to prescribed principles and postulates;
- establishing main and added entries in standard formats;
- provision of cross references to subject concepts to obtain as many relevant documents as are available in the library through catalogue or index file; and
- arrangement of entries.

Types of Subject Indexing Models

A number of subject indexing models have been designed and developed in the past hundred years or so, many of which are in use in libraries and other bibliographical publications all over the world. We can classify them in to following four kinds:

(a) Authority lists based Subject Indexing Models, e.g., Library of Congress Subject Headings (LCSH), Sears List of Subject Headings (SLSH), etc.

(b) Pre-coordinate Indexing Models, e.g., Chain procedure, PRECIS, COMPASS, POPSI, etc.

(c) Post-coordinate Indexing Models, e.g., Uniterm Indexing.

(d) Keyword-based Indexing Models, e.g., KWIC, KWAC, KWOC, etc.

Some of the important Indexing models are discussed below –

1. Preserved Context Index System (PRECIS)

PRECIS (Preserved Context Index System) was designed and developed by Derek Austin in about 1970 as an alternative procedure for deriving the subject headings and subject index entries for British National Bibliography (BNB). Since 1952, for nearly 20 years, BNB followed chain procedure for deriving subject index entries. Two most important factors worked for the development of PRECIS: (i) idea of replacing chain indexing technique of BNB; and (ii) the decision of the British Library to generate computer produced BNB with all the indexes in view of launching the UKMARC project. Accordingly, a research project for a suitable alternative or generating subject indexes directly from the machine readable records were undertaken by the British Library with the following objectives, which ultimately resulted in the development of PRECIS:

1. The computer, not the indexer, should produce all index entries. The indexer's responsibility would be only to prepare the input strings and to give necessary instructions to the computer to generate indexes according to a definite format;
2. Each of the sought terms should find index entries and each entry should express the complete thought content/full context of the document unlike the chain indexing where only one entry is fully coextensive with the subject and others are cross references describing only one aspect of the complete content of the document;
3. Each of the entries should be expressive;
4. The system should be based on a single set of logical rules to make it consistent; and
5. The system must have references for semantically related terms.

The steps in these processes are :

- Content analysis of documents to determine their specific subject;
- Selecting appropriate indexing terms;
- Determining the role or status of each indexing term and putting the terms into the input string to fall into a sequence, based upon the application of Role operators of PRECIS;
- Generation of index entries; and
- Alphabetical arrangement of entries.

The content analysis of documents is an activity independent of any indexing technique. The most important aspect of PRECIS is the preparation of input string by the human indexer. Where each term is prefixed by a notation or the Role Operators that indicates how each term has to function, either as a lead term or lead-in term.

Precis-Scheme of Role Operators

Primary operators

Environment of core concepts	0	Location
Core concepts	1	Key system Thing when action not present, Thing towards which an action is directed, e.g. object of transitive action, performer of intransitive action.
	2	Action; Effect of action
	3	Performer of transitive action (agent, instrument); Intake; Factor
Extra-core concepts	4	Viewpoint as form
	5	Selected instance; study region, study example, sample population
	6	Form of document; Target user

Secondary operators

Coordinate concepts	f	'Bound' coordinate concept
	g	Standard coordinate concept
Dependent elements	p	Part; Property
	q	Member of quasi-generic group
	r	Assembly
Special classes of action	s	Role definer; Directional property
	t	Author-attributed association
	u	Two-way interaction

Codes Used In Precis Strings

Primary codes

Theme interlinks	$x	1st concept in coordinate theme
	$y	2nd subsequent concept in theme
	$z	Common concept
Term codes	$a	Common noun
	$c	Proper name (class of one)
	$d	Place name

Secondary codes

Differences		
Preceding differences		1st and 2nd characters :
	$0	Non-lead, space generating
	$1	Non-lead, close-up
	$2	Lead, space generating
	$3	Lead, close-up
		3rd character = number in the range 1 to 9 indicating level of difference
Date as a difference	$d	
Parenthetical differences	$n	Non-lead parenthetical difference
	$o	Lead parenthetical difference
Connectives	$v	Downward-reading connective
	$w	Upward-reading connective

Typographic codes

$e	Non-filling part in italic preceded by comma
$f	Filling part in italic preceded by comma
$g	Filling part in roman, no preceding punctuation
$h	Filling part in italic preceded by full point
$i	Filling part in italic, no preceding punctuation

The following document title for the purpose of demonstrating the stages of concept analysis and assigning the appropriate role operators to prepare an input string is explained:

DOCUMENT TITLE : *Reference Services in University Libraries in India*

(i) Identify the concept signifying an action (if there be any). In the above example, the action concept is denoted by the term "Reference Services" and this term should be prefixed by the operator (2).

(ii) Identify the kind of action represented by the term. i.e., whether transitive action or intransitive action. "Reference services" is clearly a transitive action since it is capable of taking an object. The object of transitive action is considered as the key system and is coded by the operator (1). In the present example, it is the "University libraries" which' represents the object of action, so the input siring would be

1. University libraries
2. Reference services

(iii) The term "India" signifies the environment (i.e. geographical location) in which the whole thing takes place. Accordingly, the operator (0) is to be prefixed to this concept and the resulting input string would be:

0. India
1. university libraries
2. reference services

According to PRECIS, an input string must contain any one of Primary Operators 0 to 3 or combination of them.

(iv) The next step is to identify whether there is any other concepts which may be denoted by any of the operators from 4 to 6 or by secondary operators. Here the term "libraries" is the part of "Universities". Consequently, the above string is to be revised by coding "universities" with the operator (1) and "libraries" with (p). As a result, we will get the following input string ?

✓

(0) India

✓

1. universities

✓

(p) libraries

✓

2. reference services

It is to be pointed out here that the primary operators have ordinal filing values and the terms in the above input string are sequenced accordingly. The secondary operator (p) is preceded by primary operator to which it is part or property. Certain conditions must be satisfied while writing the input string and these will be checked by the computer at the time of input:

(a) Every string must/begin with-a concept coded with an operator (0) to (3).

(b) Every string must contains the operator (1) and/or (2).

The terms, except proper names (i.e. India), are written in lower case initials. An upper case initial may be needed in the index entries, but this is left to the computer. The terms which should come as access points are to he marked with a tick (✓) mark.

Entry Format

In order to achieve the principle of "Context dependency", a "Two-Line-Three-Part" entry format is followed. This entry format allows to indicate the simultaneous relationship of the terms listed in the string and sets every term in its context. The three parts of the entries are given below:

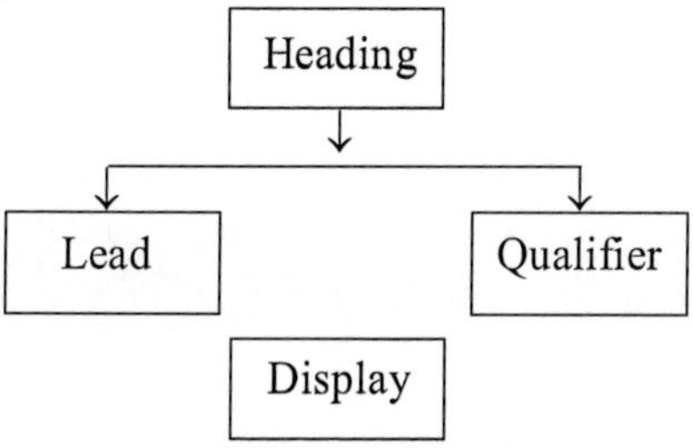

(a) "Lead" is occupied by approach term or filing term and is offered as the user's access point in the index. This is printed in bold face to emphasize its significance as the primary filing element.

(b) "Qualifier" position is occupied by the term(s) that sets the "Lead" into its wider context.

The "Lead" and the "Qualifier" together is called "Heading".

(c) "Display" position is occupied by the term(s) of narrower context.

The "Qualifier" and "Display" positions are not necessarily occupied in all index entries.

Index entries in the standard format are generated with the primary operators (0), (1), and (2) through a process, known as "Shunting", by the computer. The first index entry will be generated by the computer by pushing the first term of the input string into the lead position:

INDIA

Universities. Libraries. Reference services

The second index entry will be generated by pushing the second term into the lead position and thereby shifting the existing lead term into the qualifier position, leaving the rest of input string in Display position. This process continues till the last string marked (✓) comes into Lead position such as :

UNIVERSITIES. India

Libraries. Reference services

LIBRARIES. Universities. India

Reference services

REFERENCE SERVICES. Libraries. Universities India

This is termed as Standard Format of PRECIS. Apart from the standard format, index entries in PRECIS may also be generated by other two formats named Inverted Format and Predicate Transformation.

Index entries in the inverted format are generated whenever a term coded by an operator in the range from (4) to (6) or its dependent elements appears in the lead.

If a concept is coded (3) which is immediately preceded by a concept coded either by (2) or (s) or, (t) - each of which introduces an action of one kind or another - the predicate transformation takes place when the concept coded by 3 comes into the lead position.

The role operators and codes provide full scope for handling complex and compound subjects and also multiworded single concepts. The PRECIS manual gives guidance to every aspect of string formation applying every role operators.

Standard Vocabulary and Reference Structure

The standard vocabulary used in PRECIS incorporates the following aspects:

It is a structured vocabulary that includes the types of semantic relationship of equivalence, hierarchical and associative terms.

In PRECIS, the syntax and semantics are treated as separate components, and are handled by different procedures. The semantic aspects of PRECIS, i.e. establishing inter-relationships between the terms such as synonyms, BT, NT, and other related terms in a machine-held thesaurus serves as the source of "see" and "see also" references in the index. The following figure exemplifies these types of cross references.

Relationship	*Method of Display*	*Example*
Equivalence (Synonyms, Near-synonyms, etc.)	"*See*" References	Fauna *see* Animals Pisces *see* Fish
Hierarchical (Genus/Species, Whole/Part)	"*See also*" References	Animals *see also* Vertebrates Vertebrates *see also* Fish
Associative (Non-hierarchical)	"*See also*" References	Zoology *see also* Animals Ichthyology *see also* Fish

In PRECIS, it is considered that two terms are linked by the associative relationship if they share an obvious semantic connection; they are not displaying either equivalence or hierarchical relationships. They are related in the sense if one thinks of one of the terms, the other term automatically strikes the mind. If "ichthyology" is the term rearing to the name of a Discipline, "Fish" is its' object of study, which strikes the mind automatically. An information retrieval thesaurus displays these types of relationships between concepts in an organised manner.

Merits : PRECIS is one of the most successful, system. It has been in active use for the last twenty years. One of the reasons for its outstanding success is the support it got from the British National

Bibliography. The experience it obtained from indexing a large number of documents for BNB, gave it a unique opportunity to assess its performance and introduce many refinements to improve its quality. It now forms part of the MARC records generated in Australian National Bibliography as well as those from BNB, and has been used successfully in the indexing of films. Its theoretical foundation, initiated and supported by the Classification Research Group of Great Britain, is one of the highlights of its success. Besides, the experience it acquired at BNB, ANB and other bibliographical publications, and also in non-English indexing systems, the PRECIS Manual contributed over considerably to its application in many situations.

Demerits : It is certainly inefficient if used manually, as the generation of the appropriate entries from a string of terms is very time consuming. The application of the 'Role Operators' for the formation of the string may not produce the same results when different indexers interpret the operators with reference to the difference in interpretation. For example, there are a number of instance where the primary concept is coded (1) or (2) and there are some concepts which might legitimately fall into either category.

2. Postulate-Based Permuted Subject Indexing (POPSI)

Postulate-based Permuted Subject Index (POPSI), designed by Ganesh Bhattacharyya at the Documentation Research and Training Centre (DRTC), Bangalore, is another indigenous indexing model besides Ranganathan's Chain Procedure. It is now about fifteen years since it has been designed and is in the process of further development, particularly in its application. POPSI can be applied to micro and macro level documents available in the form of non-print/non-book forms. As the system is comparatively new, its use in subject files is rather limited.

POPSI is built around a set of fundamental theoretical ideas on classification both in the analysis of subjects as well as in the structuring of the names of subjects. The deep structure of POPSI arises from the General Theory of Subject Indexing Language, which should form the basic framework for any system of subject indexing.

All ideas, concrete or conceptual could be regarded as a manifestation of one or the other of a set of postulated Elementary Categories of POPSI. These Elementary Categories are: Discipline (D);

Entity (E); Action (A); Property (P) and Modifier (M). These Elementary Categories are explained below:

Discipline (D) includes conventional fields of study, or any aggregate of such fields; e.g. Physical Sciences, Physics, Chemistry, etc. Entity (E) includes manifestations of ideas that are concrete or conceptual, as contrasted with their properties and actions performed by them or on them; e.g. Energy, Light, Plants, Place, Time, Environment, etc. Action (A) includes manifestations denoting the concept of 'doing'. Action may manifest as Self Action or External Action; e.g. Function, Migration, Selection, Organization, Education, etc. Property (P) includes ideas denoting the concept of 'attributes' — qualitative or quantitative; e.g. Property, Effect, Power, Capacity, Efficiency, Utility, Form etc. Modifier (M) relates to the manifestations of any of the Elementary Categories D, B, A, and P. Modifier refers to an idea that qualifies the ideas of the Elementary Categories, without disturbing the conceptual wholeness of them.

The following diagram is a schematic presentation of the deep structure of a Subject Indexing Language (SIL) :

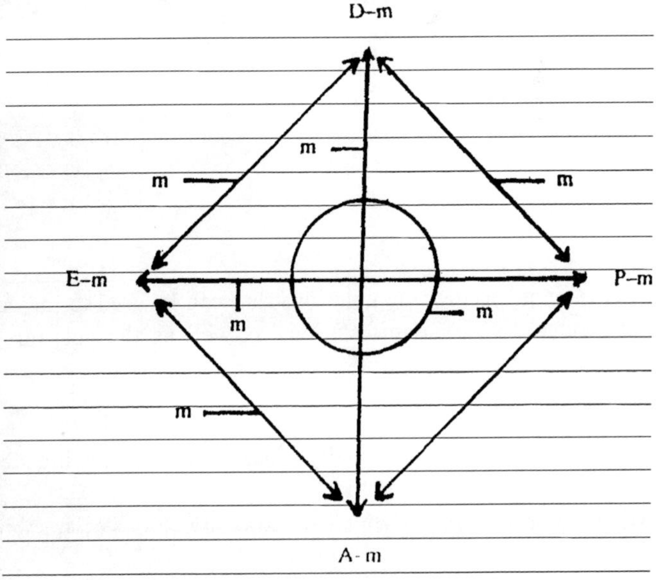

The arrows indicate the multi-relationships between the elementary categories.

POPSI Procedure

POPSI as a process for preparing subject-index consists primarily of (a) analysis; (b) synthesis; and (c) permutation. The task of analysis and synthesis is mainly guided by the following POPSI table of notations.

0 Form modifier	6 Entity, 7 Discipline → 1 Action, 2 Property → Part, Species/Type, Special modifier
1 General Treatment	
2 Phase relation 2.1 General 2.2 Bias 2.3 Comparison 2.4 Similarity 2.5 Difference 2.6 Application 2.7 Influence	Note: As . 1 and .2 are dependent ECs, these are to be preceded by the notations for the ECs to which these are dependent.
Common modifier 3 Time 4 Environment 5 Place	8 Core, 9 Base → Feature analogous to 6/7/. 1/.2

The table prescribes the notations that can be used to indicate mostly the categories of manifestations as well as the position of manifestations in subject-propositions.

Steps in POPSI

The POPSI procedure normally consists of the following steps which is illustrated with an example:

(0) Title of the document : Use of microcomputers for indexing the non-print media in the university libraries in India.

1. Content Analysis : It involves the identification of different component ideas associated with the subject content of the document and analysis of the same in terms of ECs and modifiers.

Library & Information Science	= D (implicit)
University library	= E (explicit)
Non-print media	= P of E (explicit)
Indexing	= A on P of E (explicit)
Use	= Application phase relation (explicit)
Microcomputers	= E-based m (explicit)
India	= Common m of place (explicit)

2. Formalization : It involves the arrangement of component terms according to the principles of sequence of components indicating the status of each component term.

Library and information Science (D), University Library (E), Non-print media (P of E), Indexing (A on P of E), Use (Application PR), Microcomputers (E-based m), India (Common m of place)

3. Modulation : Each of the component terms in the analysed and formalised subject proposition is modulated by augmenting it with interpolating and/or extrapolating the successive superordinates of each manifestation.

Library and Information Science (D), Library Academic library, University library (E:), Information sources, Documentary source, Non-print media (P of E), Indexing (A on P of E), Use (Application PR), Computers, and Microcomputers (E-based m), Asia, India (common m).

4. Standardization : It consists of deciding the standard term especially the manifestations having synonyms for preparing cross-reference entries. In steps 3 and 4, Classaurus has been suggested to be used to ensure consistency in practice.

Here, the term, "Non-print media" is replaced by the Standard term "Non-book materials".

5. Preparation of the Entry for Organizing Classification (Preparation of EOC) : It consists of preparing the entry for generating organising classification by inserting appropriate notations from the POPSI-table.

Library and Information science 6 Library. Academic library. University library, Information sources. Documentary source. Non-book material 6.1 Indexing 2.6 (Using) Computer. Microcomputer (5) (in) Asia, India

6. Approach-term Selection : It consists of deciding the approach terms for generating associative classification for its effect; and of controlling synonyms. e.g.,

Non-print media *see* Non-book materials

7. Preparation of Entries for Associative Classification (Preparation of EAC) : It consists of preparing entries under each approach-term, either individually, or in association with other terms, by cyclic permutation of sought terms for generating associative classification effect in alphabetical arrangement.

LIBRARY and information science 6 Library. Academic library. University library, Information sources. Documentary source. Non-book material 6.1 Indexing 2.6 (Using) Computer. Microcomputer 5 (in) Asia, India.

The same EOC will have to be repeated under each of the following approach terms:

Academic Library

University Library

Information Science

Information Sources

Documentary Source

Non-book material

Indexing

Computer

Microcomputer

Alternatively, the heading of an entry for associative classification can be made more specific by making it multifaceted by using term from the superordinate links in the chain, e.g.

Information sources, University Library

Documentary source, University Library

Non-book material, University Library

Indexing (Using) computer, Non-book material, University Library

Indexing (using) Microcomputer. Non-book material, University Library

Computer (used in) Indexing, Non-book material, University Library

India. Computer (used in) Indexing. Non-book material, University Library etc.

8. Alphabetization : It involves in arranging all the entries in a single alphabetical file. Word-by -word arrangement of entries has to be done.

It may be noted that in Steps 1 to 5, the special interest at each step is to arrive at an organising classification. The foundation of these steps is predominantly the postulates about the different structures of different subjects. Therefore, this part of the procedure is postulate based. On the other hand, in steps 6 to 8, the special interest is to arrive at various associative classifications. The foundation of these steps is predominantly the technique of Permutation. The 'Permutation' in this context refers to 'transformation' or the process of changing the linear order in a definite sequence. Therefore this part of the procedure is referred to by using the term 'Permutation'. Hence the entire system is known as Postulate-based Permuted Subject Indexing (POPSI).

Entry Format : In POPSI, a subject index entry consists of three distinct sections:

(i) Approach-term section consisting of approach-term, with or without upper links. This permits the location of entries for the subject.

(ii) Organising classification section consisting of entry(ies) for organising classification. This section provides data for comprehension of the entries to permit relevance prediction.

(iii) Location/Address Section consisting of the serial number(s) of the record(s) to aid the location of bibliographic information for the document(s) representing the subject relating to the one being sought.

3. Key-Word-In-Context (KWIC) Indexing

It was in 1958 that H.P. Luhn tried to exploit potentialities of computer to derive a solution to the problem of speedy dissemination of information. This resulted in the KWIC index based on titles of documents. Each entry in KWIC index consists of three parts :

(i) *Keyword* : Significant words of the title which serve as approach/ access terms.

(ii) *Context* : The rest of the terms of the title provided along with the keywords specifics the context of the document.

(iii) *Identification or Location Code* : A code (usually the serial number of the entry) which provides address of the document where its full bibliographical details will be available.

The preparation of KWIC index consists of the following steps

(a) The keywords are selected from the title of the document.

(b) In case of computerised system, a "Stop list" is prepared and is kept in the computer. The "Stop list" is a list of words which are considered to have no value for indexing and no index entries are generated for the terms included in the list. The list includes insignificant words such as articles (a, an, the), prepositions, conjunctions, pronouns, auxiliary verbs together with such general words as "very", "viewpoint" "aspect", etc.

(c) The KWIC routine serves to rotate the title to make it accessible from each significant term. Accordingly, the index is generated under each significant term by placing it in the searchable position (beginning or in the middle) by rotation and other words in the title are what is known as, "Wrapped around it". The other words in the title serve as context.

(d) The last word and first word of the title are separated by using a separating symbol.

(e) The identification or location codes are printed at the right end of each entry.

(f) The index entries are then arranged alphabetically by keywords.

Now take an example of the title "Indexing of films by using computers" to demonstrate the index entries generated through KWIC principle :

COMPUTERS/Indexing of films by using	338
FILMS by using computers/Indexing of	338
INDEXING of films by using computers	338

Alternatively, filing keywords are placed in the middle of the page :

Indexing of films by COMPUTERS/		338
Indexing of FILMS	by Computers/	338
INDEXING	of films by computers/	338

Varieties of keyword indexes are evident in the literature and they differ only in their formats, but indexing techniques remain more or less same. Key-Word Out of Context (KWOC) Indexing, Key Word And Context (KWAC), Key-Word-Augmented in Context KWAC etc. are some of the examples.

In many cases, title do not always represent the subject of the document co-extensively. Also KWIC and KWOC could not solve the problem of retrieval of irrelevant documents. To solve the problem of false retrieval, the methodology of enrichment of the keywords of the title with additional keywords taken either from the abstract or the original text of the document and then inserting into the title or adding at the end to give further index entries was developed. The CBAC (Chemical Biological Activities) uses this techniques where title is enriched by another title like phrases formulated by the indexer.

8
Centralized and Cooperative Cataloguing

Q. : What do you understand by centralized cataloguing? Discuss the advantages and disadvantages of centralized cataloguing.

Ans. Due to the problems of growth in volume of published materials, the emphasis on rapid transfer of documents and bibliographic records from producer to consumer, and the resultant need for more and better library service, traditional patterns of cataloguing and processing are changing significantly. Most libraries and library systems of any size have either centralized their technical services or entered into cooperative arrangements with other libraries.

Centralized Cataloguing is defined as the "cataloguing of documents by some central organization" for the benefit of other libraries. It provides a varying degree of cataloguing services to its clientele from a central point. This form of cataloguing can take place within one library system or within a number of library systems. Sometimes, the centralized cataloguing may be done by another agency.

Objectives of Centralized Cataloguing

There are several readily identifiable objectives to be sought when setting up a centralized cataloging unit. These are as follows:

1. Elimination of duplicative work.
2. Effective employment of specialization.
3. Higher quality of cataloguing output.
4. Better service levels of member libraries.
5. Lower per-unit cataloging cost.

1. Elimination of Duplicative Work : The first objective is the most obvious, and has been the subject of a great deal of discussion in the past. The benefits that accrue from the elimination of duplicative work are direct; the cataloguers may process ten books in a given time rather than processing the same book ten times at ten different locations in the same time period. The saving of time is reduced by the need to duplicate the output, distribute it to the client, and alter the output at the destination to fit the client's collection. Obviously, the less alteration and adaptation needed, the greater the savings that accrue from non-duplicative premise enables cataloguing for other to be a commercially viable proposition. Mass production of unit cards is the basis of the activities of several commercial cataloguing firms.

2. Effectiveness of Specialization : The second objective, more effective use of cataloguers, closely follows the first, in the same way, freeing them both to process more books and to process books with a greater degree of precision. With the centralization of cataloguers handle the books in the same way, freeing them both to process more books and to process books with a greater degree of precision.

With the centralization of cataloguers come several personnel advantages. The specialist cataloguer has more scope for his activities, and the central organization may be able to afford more specialist cataloguers. In this manner, scarce specialties and competencies may be provided by a system where an individual member is either unable to afford specialists, has too little scope for them, or, regardless of monetary considerations, is simply unable to obtain them. Although independent libraries may have to forego specialist treatment of certain resources, the system can provide that treatment by amalgamating the resources needing it into a mass large enough to justify the service of the specialist.

3. High quality of Output : Higher quality of output like greater efficiency of personnel utilization, is not guaranteed by simple size alone. It is a possibility realized only by skillful management and rational planning. Management can ensure quality by assigning personnel where they are most suited to work, carefully training them, providing them with the kind of resources they need to do the job properly such as manuals and relevant reference tools in adequate quantities, and then setting up rational and effective quality-control procedures. Planning is essential because foresight is needed to set up a quality-control system that will do its job without degenerating into a sloughs of mutual distrust of everybody work and an exhaustive checking of every detail by several people. Aside from the organizational and management considerations, quality also depends upon the caliber of personnel hired and the ground rules under which they do their cataloguing.

4. Better Service for Member Libraries : Better service for member libraries, the fourth goal, is of central importance to those systems composed of small-town libraries. To small libraries, a central processing unit can mean a quantum jump in service to their readers, the difference between the minimal and the quietly excellent. For them, the problem of standardization is vastly outweighed by the benefits to be gotten by affiliation with a system. A typical example of the quantum jump is the Public Library System through a scheme of centralized technical services and a rotating collection circulated from the processing center, the resources of the member libraries are increased tremendously, up to ten times the number of books as are complete centralization of the technical service function, coupled with a distribution and rotation system for a central collection of books.

5. Lower per unit Cataloguing Cost : Lower cost per capita in cataloguing is the sum of the careful planning and supervision that made possible the benefits mentioned above. It should be noted that overall cost may seldom decline, because the central unit is used to extend and improve library service rather than simply to make cheaper that service which already exists, with no thought to improvement. Nevertheless, in a well-planned system, the rising overall cost, when divided by the volumes processed, should not produce figures per capita that are more expensive than those which earlier obtained. This per-capita cost saving can be negated by the same factors that negate other objectives, namely the failure to adequately standardize the job at hand. When custom cataloguing is the end result of centralization, the saving will disappear quickly.

Steps for Centralized Cataloguing

A planning of Centralized Cataloguing may include several steps:

1. Identification of system members and their needs.
2. Identification of degree of common resources and objectives.
3. Determination of feasibility of the proposed central unit.
4. Coordination of standardization between member, and the

5. Planning of the centre.

Before any centre is actually planned, prospective members should be known and their needs and problems studied, so that the centre when set up will address itself to those needs. Identification of commonality between members goes hand in hand with a feasibility study; if the members have little hope of achieving its objectives. When commonality has been determined, coordination between members should take place in order to insure that the centre will have a standard base upon which to achieve the saving that centralization offers. A detail of its activities should be matched with the practices of all the members.

Advantages

1. Duplication of work can be avoided.
2. Cost of cataloguing can be minimized.
3. Uniform and standard cataloguing practices can be adopted.
4. Cataloguing can be qualitatively improved.
5. Some of the professional staff who are relieved of cataloguing work can be utilized for other useful professional service.
6. Preparation of union catalogues will become easy.

Disadvantages

1. Pooling up the necessary funds to opt for centralized cataloguing may be difficult for some libraries.
2. Because of local variations it may be difficult to go in for centralized cataloguing.
3. Centralized cataloguing system may cause delay. A library with a lower number of accessions can complete the job of cataloguing much earlier.
4. Similarly such libraries may not need all the catalogue cards prepared by the central organization. It may not buy all the books because of its limited funds and requirements. Excess cards will be a waste then.

Q. : Describe some of the important forms of centralized cataloguing.

or

Write short notes on :

— **Cataloguing-in-publication**

— **MARC Service**

— **Pre-natal cataloguing**

Ans. In simple terms, centralized cataloguing is defined as "the cataloguing of documents by some central organization". The main purpose of centralized cataloguing is to save duplication of effort in the cataloguing department of several libraries.

In centralized cataloguing we observe that there are several forms of centralization like:

1. Card (or Sheaf) Service
2. MARC (Machine-Readable Catalogue) service
3. Information service
4. Cataloguing-in-Source

1. Card (or Sheaf) Service : This is the type of centralized cataloguing where the unit entries are prepared by a central organization. The individual libraries can buy these cards in multiple numbers. An individual library can file them in their catalogues after adding suitable headings. BNB card/ sheaf service, printed catalogue cards distributed by Library of Congress and H.W. Wilson and Company belong to this category. In a number of countries, printed card services have been started. Mention may be made of Micro-graphic Catalog Retrieval System (USA) which is a microfiche service. From this, one can produce cards by means of readers/printers. Library of Congress also distributes proof sheets, one each of all its cards. With the help of proof sheets, a typist can type out single cards and prepare other cards without much problem.

2. MARC Service : In this service, cataloguing data are prepared for documents in machine readable form on magnetic tapes, etc. by a central organization. In actual practice, it means that the central organization catalogues the documents, records the data on magnetic tape and supplies libraries with copies of the tapes. By using a computer, from the magnetic tape they can then produce printed catalogues of their collection or entries on cards and various kinds of bibliographies. The MARC service is receiving increasing acceptance all over the world. The magnetic tape itself can be used to replace the card catalogue. For instance at National Aeronautics and Space Administration (NASA), the card catalogue was actually a magnetic tape. This requires permanent access at computer, that is online operations.

Following the King Report on Automation in the Library of Congress, a programme to produce cataloguing data in machine-readable form called MARC (Machine-Readable Cataloguing) was established. The Library of Congress launched a pilot project in 1966 for machine-readable cataloguing data. Test tapes and appropriate computer programmes on punched cards were distributed to 16 participating libraries in October 1966. The number of these libraries was later increased substantially. The pilot project called MARC I ended in 1968. This was followed by a permanent subscription service called MARC II. By subscribing to MARC II service, a library can acquire in machine-readable form cataloguing data for American publications as well as foreign publications acquired under Shared Cataloguing Program (An acquisition programme of the Library of Congress on a worldwide basis). The data provided under MARCII contains headings (author/title, LC subject), descriptive data, class numbers (Library of Congress, Dewey Decimal Classification, National Library of Medicine, National Agriculture Library) and identification numbers. In last few years MARC has expanded its scope from English-language records to all roman-alphabet language. Besides, the conversion system has changed from paper tape input device to on-line terminals.

Library of Congress MARC service began with US imprints in 1969 and it was followed by national MARC services in many countries of the world. MARC provides a standard format for the transmission of bibliographic data. It had a powerful influence on the handling of bibliographic records in machine-readable form.

3. Information Service : In this type of centralized service, a central organization produces a bibliography from which libraries can prepare their own catalogues. These catalogues can be prepared either by using the catalogue information from the bibliography for the books they have to catalogue or by cutting and pasting on cards the appropriate entries from the bibliography. The British National Bibliography (BNB) and the Indian National Bibliography (INB) are such types of tools.

4. Cataloguing-in-Source : The idea behind this is, a publisher of a book, if he can provide the catalogue entry in the book itself, will be helping the purchasing libraries. Their processing work is reduced to a large extent. What is needed in such service is that the catalogue code followed should be the one which is universally acceptable. The entry should also carry class number according to a popular and acceptable scheme of classification. Such a service is known as Cataloguing-In-Source (CIS).

Ranganathan made a plea from such cataloguing of a book even before its release. He termed it as 'Prenatal Cataloguing'. There is yet another term for similar service; namely, Cataloguing-in-Publication (CIP).

(i) Cataloguing-in-publication : CIP began in July 1971 at the Library of Congress. This programme processed over 28,598 titles during 1978. At present, there are many American publishers, who send material to the Library or Congress in advance of publication. This makes it possible to print the main elements that appear on a catalogue card in the book itself, usually on the verso of the title page. This programme covered about 73 per cent of total USA publications of book titles. The entries are prepared at LC from galley proofs and data returned to publishers within ten working days. Subtitle, imprint, and collation are omitted, but a complete record, with the exception of collation is entered in MARC. The Machine-readable catalog is made available four to six months before the book's publication. Final CIP cataloguing is undertaken from folded/gathered sheets or pre-publication bound copies by LC Library technicians who verify the cataloguing and add collation.

Form of CIP Entries : Cataloguing-in-publication program provide the catalogue entries in three forms:

(a) **LC Cards :** LC Cards which are made available before the publication data of the book. These cards can be subscribed by any Library of Congress. All the participating libraries received these cards from the Library of Congress as a member of CIP Programme.

(b) **Cataloguing Data printed in the book itself :** A catalogue entry in the form of a more or less accurate facsimile of Library of Congress card appeared on the verso of the title page of the book itself. The catalogue entry contain all the major information required in a Library Catalogue. Catalogue card can be prepared by copying the catalogue entry from the book and be filed in the Library Catalogues under different sequences by a Semi-Professional or Clerical Staff.

(c) **MARC Tape :** The CIP entry record is also made available on the MARC Tape before the appearance of the MARC Tape of final cataloguing copy. The Machine-Readable form of Catalogue Entry is made available four to six months before the publication of the book.

An example is given below to illustrate the kind of cataloguing data by the Library of Congress Cataloguing-in-Publication.

Wynar, Bohdhan S

Introduction to cataloguing and classification.

(Library science text series)

Bibliography : P. 597.

Includes indexes.

1. Cataloguing. 2. Anglo-American cataloguing rules 3. Classification – Books. I. Taylor,

Arlene G, 1941-II Title

z693.W94 1985 025.3 85-23147

ISBN 0-87287-521-1

ISBN 0-87287-485-0(Pbk)

The success of CIP depends on the cooperation extended by the publishers. If CIP were to be adopted throughout the world then building up national and universal bibliographies and preparing union catalogues will become easy.

(ii) **Pre-natal cataloguing :** Ranganathan mooted the idea of cataloguing and classification of a book prior to its release by the publisher. Since the cataloguing is to be done before it is delivered (released) for sale or use, he called the process 'Pre-natal Cataloguing'. In fact, he was suggesting pre-natal technical work. That is to say cataloguing and classification of a book before the publication is released by the publisher.

Pre-natal technical work is to be undertaken by the National Central Library of each country. The publisher is obliged to send a copy of the form proof of the book to the National Central Library under a legal provision. The National Central Library then prepares a master stencil of the catalogue cards for the book before its release. The catalogue cards are later made available for distribution to various libraries which acquire the book. Ranganathan suggested even providing the call number for the book before it is published and released. The class number can be printed in the back of the title page.

Ranganathan had said there would be a saving of 79 per cent if such centralized cataloguing is done. He pleaded international and national cooperation for implementing pre-natal cataloguing. He also pleaded for State Central Cataloguing Body for each constituent state and a National Central Cataloguing Body for effectively implementing Pre-natal Cataloguing in the country.

Concluding, it can be said that the outlook of centralized cataloging is bright. The Library of Congress, with its MARC programe, is moving rapidly toward the automated provision of cataloging on a real – time basis. Systems of centralized cataloging, through Library of Congress activities, become voluntary subsystems of an emerging national centralized cataloging unit. The layering of systems will increase until the whole nation has access to cataloging of the highest possible quality, of the widest possible variety, in the shortest possible time.

Q. : What do you mean by Co-operative Cataloguing and Union Catalogue? Compare centralized and co-operative cataloguing.

Ans. The term 'Centralized Cataloguing' may be broadly defined as any consolidated effort to bring under one control the technical operations necessary to prepare library materials for access and used at different service points.

Centralized cataloguing is a provision of a varying degree of cataloguing service to several clients from a central point. This point may be commercial or noncommercial, and it may provide service ranging from simple cataloguing to complete book-and-card sets that are completely processed and ready to insert into the client's collection and catalogues. Centralized cataloguing units may exist in almost any environment in which the need for cataloguing and technical service exists. Centers may supply clusters of tiny public libraries or groups of gigantic research libraries. Examples of centralized cataloging and processing may be found everywhere in the world, and the prospect is for more centralization in the years ahead.

Where as, Cooperative cataloguing refers to "a situation where a number of independent libraries share the work of producing a catalogue for their mutual benefit". It is done in two or more libraries for the benefit of each participant and results may or may not be made available to other libraries.

Forms of Cooperative Cataloguing

1. The Library of Congress is running a cooperative programme in which other libraries are expected to contribute catalogue card copies for printing. The Library of Congress edits each copy so as to correlate it with other entries provided on Library of Congress cards. These edited copies are printed and distributed to subscribers.
2. Under the Higher Education Act of 1965, Library of Congress was given the responsibility of acquiring all materials of value to scholarship currently published throughout the world, of cataloguing them promptly and distributing bibliographic information. In January 1966, a conference of national libraries and producers of current national bibliographies of England, France, West Germany, Norway and Austria was held in London. It was agreed that the description of books listed in the national bibliography of each country would be used by Library of Congress for cataloguing purposes. It was decided that producers of national bibliographies would supply to Library of Congress a copy of their publication in advance. This programme was named National Program for Acquisitions and Cataloging (NPAC). It is also called shared cataloging programme.

To implement NPAC, Library of Congress has established a global network of national and regional offices for international cooperation. Each office is responsible for the selection, acquisition and dispatch of materials published locally. These offices work in conjunction with the national sources of bibliographic data. These acquire a copy of the catalogue entries as early as possible. The entries are converted by the offices so that these conform to LC practice with regard to heading and some other details. Then these catalogue cards are sent to the Shared Cataloging Division of LC. In many cases, LC accepts cataloging undertaken for the national bibliographies in the countries concerned, adding only supplementary information necessary for the special requirements of LC. For instance, Library of Congress subject headings, Library of Congress classification number, Dewey Decimal classification, etc., may be added. The final catalogue cards are printed at the earliest.

Up to June 1974, NPAC covered 40 countries, offering all the advantages of international library cooperation in the field of cataloguing. NPAC is a good example of shared cataloguing. Shared cataloguing is a form of cooperative cataloguing. In this case, it also involves centralized cataloguing service. NPAC is a great achievement, a major step towards UBC, the Universal Bibliographic Control.

3. Creation of union catalogue on the basis of data supplied by individual libraries is a good example of cooperative cataloguing.

Aims and objectives

The aims and objective of cooperative cataloguing are virtually the same as that of centralized cataloguing. Just as in the case of centralized cataloguing through cooperative cataloguing we can gain the following:

1. Better use of resources;
2. Standardization of cataloguing practices;
3. Economy in expense;
4. Improving the quality of library service; and
5. Preparation of union catalogues with relative ease.

Union Catalogue : The term union catalogue needs some explanation. Larson defines it as "a catalogue listing in one sequence the holdings or part of the holdings of two or more libraries,". It is an important tool for a librarian. Ranganathan defines a union catalogue as a "List of all the documents in two or more libraries giving the names of all the libraries where copies of each document can be found. A union catalogue may cover all kinds of documents or any restricted kind of them". Union catalogue is a very good example of cooperative cataloguing where two or more libraries cooperate with each other in listing their holdings partially or fully. Union catalogues can be prepared at local, regional, national and international levels.

Union catalogue, once prepared efficiently, serves several purposes. A union catalogue:

1. Serves as a tool which can reveal the document resources available in libraries in a geographical region.
2. Reveals the strength and weaknesses of library collections.
3. Indicates the probable areas of collection specialization and cooperation.
4. Helps in coordination of collection development activities of the libraries.
5. Serves as a tool for bibliographical information.
6. Provides useful information for document selection.

Pre-requisites for a Union Catalogue :

Compilation of a union catalogue is possible only through library cooperation. Any such compilation should be very clear in the beginning itself about the:

1. Purpose of the Union catalogue to be compiled.
2. Region to be covered,
3. Materials to be covered; (decision as to the type of reading materials, language, period, subject, etc.).
4. Physical form of the catalogue.
5. Catalogue code to be followed.
6. Type of entries.
7. Level of description.
8. Arrangement of entries, and
9. The method of compilation and revision.

For a union catalogue of books, two entries consisting of author entry, and title entry are prepared. Author entry is the main entry, and title entry is an added entry. Title entry is a brief entry which refers to the main entry for maximum information. After each main entry is added the holdings section, indicating the names of libraries having the document.

For a union catalogue of periodicals, main entry is provided under the class number and, in addition, there should be class index entries and sponsoring body entry. Their reference to main entries should be through serial numbers.

In compiling union catalogue, if the library is large, then library circulates its catalogue of holdings amongst other cooperating libraries, then each may be able to indicate items available with them and also and further titles if not listed therein. This is certainly a time-consuming method.

A second possibility is that instead of one copy, a number of copies of the basic catalogue are circulated and a final catalogue would be a unified one.

A third possibility is that each library may make a catalogue of its holding and these catalogues may be cumulated.

A fourth possibility is that one or more persons may go from one library to another to collect information.

It is to be noted that photography has been made use of successfully in the compilation of union catalogues. Here, catalogues of cooperating libraries are photographed and catalogue entries made from the film by some suitable method of reproduction. It is to be kept in mind that problems of compilation depend a great deal upon the uniformity of cataloguing practices.

Now-a-days, the development of computer-based union catalogues has been achieved successfully even in developing countries. This is neither expensive nor difficult.

There must also be an adequate provision for continuous revision. Somebody or some agency must be regularly notified about the additions and withdrawals. A file of those should be maintained so that at the time of bringing out the new edition, the work would become easier.

Some of the union catalogues of periodicals are listed below:

Ranganathan, S.R. etc., Comp.

Union catalogue of learned periodical publications in South Asia, v. 1 physical and biological sciences. Indian Library Association, 1953.

Union list of learned American serials in Indian libraries, Delhi, Indian Council for Library Development, 1966.

Regional union catalogue of scientific serials: Kerala, Delhi, Union Catalogue Division, National Science Library, Indian National Scientific Documentation Centre, 1969. (A series of such union catalogues are being compiled by INSDOC. The above one represents just a sample).

The National Union Catalog: a cumulative author list (The author catalogs of the Library of Congress – National Union Catalog series vary in title, form, and coverage. These are complemented by the subject catalog of the Library of Congress).

Union list of serials in libraries of the United States and Canada. 3rd edn., edited by Edna Brown Titus, New York, Wilson 1965, 5 v.

Cooperative and Centralized Cataloguing

Centralized units aim to provide a complete job at one place and distribute the results to others, where as, cooperative cataloguing aims to complete a job by sharing the work involved, and then trading the results from one unit to another. Thus, the site and organization of the effort are the distinguishing points. Centralization gathers the work in one site and organizes the work force as a unit; cooperation divides the job among several sites and seeks not to control but to coordinate the scattered work force. The cataloguing of a large library system is often centralized, but it is not cooperative, except in a very insular sense. One simple form of cooperative cataloguing may be said of providing and maintaining a centralized cataloguing bureau, and reap the benefits accruing from it, by being freed from the necessity of having to provide entries for such books as are catalogued by the central bureau.

Some regard cooperative cataloguing as a part of centralized cataloguing, provided centralized cataloguing is coordinated by a central agency and the product is distributed from a single site. But in practice, the lines of demarcation break down. However, we can make a functional distinction. Centralized cataloguing reduces cataloguing effort by providing centralized services, and cooperative cataloguing makes it possible to put existing library resources to better use.

There also seems to be general agreement that centralized cataloguing is to be preferred to cooperative cataloguing for reasons of increased uniformity, more prompt availability of cards, and economy of operation.

In spite of many similarities in objectives and purposes of cooperative and centralized cataloguing, there are many differences also. These are shown in tabular form below:

Cooperative Cataloguing	*Centralized Cataloguing*
1. Services are not expected other to go-beyond the cooperating libraries.	1. In some cases services can be used by go-beyond the cooperating libraries by other libraries also.
2. Job is completed by the participating libraries through the sharing of the work.	2. Central agency does the work through the behalf of the libraries.
3. The work places for cataloguing are different.	3. A central work place performs the job.
4. Cataloguing work is coordinated.	4. Cataloguing work is centralized and controlled.
5. Participating libraries continue to perform their own technical service work.	5. Libraries taking advantage of centralized cataloguing have nominal, and technical service work.
6. It is not a commercial proposition and expenses are shared by the participating libraries.	6. Can be a commercial proposition also and other libraries can get services by paying specified costs.

9
Filing Rules for Entries

Q. : Explain the rules for filing of catalogue entries.

or

Write short notes on:

(i) Alphabetization

(ii) Rules for Filing Entries

or

What do you understand by 'Alphabetization'? Explain the rules for filing system in dictionary catalogue.

Ans. It is not enough to form the entries, but it is also very important to arrange these entries in a logical manner in view of the convenience of the readers. A good system of filing of entries in a catalogue will:

- Save the time of filing of the people who use it;
- Bring together related entries at one place;
- Expose the items about which the user may not know till the time of the search; and
- Facilitate manipulation and handling of the catalogue with ease, once the logic behind the arrangement is known.

Further, an entry misfiled is an entry lost. The user may miss the entry and thereby the details of the document for which the entry is misfiled. The user may think that the particular document is not available in the library.

The history of filing systems can be traced back to the history of libraries because basically man prefers order and early librarians, therefore, would have thought of orderly arrangement. Orderly arrangement of a library collection, however, laid the foundations for the schemes of library classification.

Filing systems for catalogue entries evolved over a period of time, such entries were prepared for a large library collection. When the number of documents is limited, filing of entries is not much of a problem. Only when the number of documents increases, the need for a good and effective filing system becomes necessary.

Some of the catalogue codes like Cutter's *Rules for a Dictionary Catalogue* and the *'Vatican Code'* have included filing rules also in their cataloguing rules. A few filing systems that have evolved over time are discussed below:

(i) Berghoeffer System

Towards the end of the 19th century Christian W. Berghoeffer introduced an interesting filing system for the Frankfurter Sammelkatalog. This system suggests the division of the catalogue into three sections as-a personal section, a geographical section, and a title section. In the personal section, only the surnames of the authors are taken into consideration ignoring forenames and initials. Titles are arranged in alphabetical sequence under each surname. This system is very useful for union catalogues.

(ii) ALA Filing Rules

The American Library Association published in 1942, the *A.L.A Rules for Filing Catalogue Cards.* This code for filing entries is based on a comparative study of filing rules which have appeared in printed codes and in manuals of library science, and also of the practices in a number of large and medium-sized public and university libraries. The revised version of the code appeared as a new set of rules under the title *ALA Filing Rules* in 1968. These Rules appeared in two formats – a full text, and an abridged paperback edition.

The 1968 rule is related to the provision of AACR-2. The Committees responsible for AACR-2 and for 1968 rule on Filing Rules worked in co-operation. The structured uniform titles recommended by AACR-2 is an effort towards a better scheme of filing the entries in some cases.

(iii) Library of Congress Filing Rules

For the Library of Congress the rules that were in practice, namely; *Filing Rules for the Dictionary Catalogues in the Library of Congress* (1956) and the subsequent provisional *Filing Arrangement in the Library of Congress Catalogs* by John C Rather (1971) were replaced by the *Library of Congress Filing Rules* published in 1980. These rules are more elaborate than the *ALA Filing Rules.* Emphasis in these rules is on the practical adaptability of the rules for computer processing of the entries.

(iv) Computer Filing

Computers can relieve the burden of laborious filing of entries. They can do the job quickly and automatically. Computers are now being used in library operations and in bibliographic control. But there are certain drawbacks in computer filing also because they cannot think like human beings. Suppose you give the instruction to a computer saying ignore the initial articles like "A", "An", "The" while filing. Then for a title like *ABC of Atomic Physics,* the computer will file the title as BC of Atomic Physics, which is rather unhelpful filing. However, with proper programming instructions some of the problems can be solved. The first code to deal specifically with computer filing was published in 1966 by Theodore C. Hines and Jessica L. Harris under the title *Computer Filing of Index, Bibliographic and Catalogue Records.*

(v) BLAISE Filing Rules

Automated information service provided by the British Library is known under acronym BLAISE (British Library Automated Information Service). "The BLAISE filing rules had their origins in the report of a Working Party on Computer Filing set up by the Library Association Cataloguing and Indexing Group". These rules for computer filing were prepared on the basis of the principles developed by the International Organization for Standardization (ISO).

(vi) Ranganathan's Principles

Ranganathan's Classified Catalogue has its two parts for catalougue i.e., classified part and the alphabetical part. In the Classified part we come across Class Numbers or Call Numbers as entries to be filed. A class number or call number includes numerals, letters, punctuation marks and symbols or characters like '->' <-' etc. Ranganathan uses the word 'digits' for these characters used by him as notation. In his *Colon Classification* he has assigned values for these digits which guide us in filing entries in classified part. Further his *Classified Catalogue Code Ed.* 5 Chapter EG and EH deal with the filing of entries in Classified Part and in Alphabetical Part respectively.

ALA System and Ranganathan's system of filing of entries are two important systems. Each of them is briefly discussed below:-

Filing of Entries according to C.C.C.

There are two parts of rules for filing of cards in C.C.C.:

1. Classified Part, and
2. Alphabetical Part.

1. Classified Part : The entries in this part are filed according to the class number. The class number is given in the leading section of the entry. This filing is done on the basis of the ordinal values under the system of classification. Following numbers are presented as per the ascending value of the ordinals in the colon classification:

) ← → 0 . : ; , - a b .... z ..... 9 A ..... Z (

Many times the class number in the leading section of the entries is same. Additional provisions have been made in the rules of C.C.C. for such situations.

According to *Rule Number EG21*, if same class number exists in the leading section of the system, then those entries will be placed first in which one or more book numbers are entered.

For example:

Bw M87 N51	Bw M87
KRISHNAMURTI (JS)	See also
Biography of Ramanujan	BxM87 N27
5680	Ramanujan
	Collected Papers P.xi-xix

In the above entry, that entry shall be placed first in which the book number is entered.

According to rule number *EG22*, those entries in which book number is given in the leading section, shall be placed according to the book number.

According to rule number *EG31*, those entries in which only one type of class numbers are given and there is no book number, then these will be filed according to the book number given in the third section.

For example:

(i) BwM87

See also

BxM87 N27

Ramanujan

Collected papers. Pxi-xix.

(ii) Bw M87

See also

B N19

Ram prasad

Mathematics P150-159.

The class number in both of the above entries is same and the book number is not given. Hence, filing will be done according to the book number given in the third section.

In this manner, cross reference entries of specific subject will be collected according to the languages of each direction and the filing of the material of each language shall also be in chronological order.

According to rule number *EG32*, if the book number in third section under the rule number EG31 is similar then it will be filed on the basis of the class number given in the third section.

2. Alphabetical Part:

Following two principles are popular for alphabetization:

1. **Letter by letter arrangement :** This is known as 'All through alphabetization'. In this, only the letter is considered as a unit for filing.

   Words, sentences or the space between the sections, difference in script, letters, or the type of letters is ignored in all through alphabetization. However, special rules are given for different forms of conventional symbols.

2. **World by word arrangement :** In this type of arrangement, the complete word is considered as a unit for filing.

Dr. Ranganathan adopted an approach between the 'Gastault alphabetization' and 'All through alphabetization'. In Gastault alphabetization, the word space, sentence space and the section space are given sequential values i.e., the positional values. Different positional values are given to the capital letters, small letters and letters in italics of English language.

Provisions have been made in following rules for the filing of entries in the alphabetical part:

According to rule number *EH1,* the filing of entries in the alphabetical part should fully alphabetized, just as in a dictionary.

According to rule number *EH2,* initial articles are ignored in alphabetical filing.

According to rule number *EH31,* vowels of the German language should be filed according to the position these hold in German alphabets.

According to rule number *EH4,* the prefixes such as 'Mac' or its abbreviation 'Mc' or 'M' that are used in Scottish names, should be filed according to the alphabetical order only.

According to rule number *EH70,* the sequence of positional values given below should be followed in ascending order for filing of entries in the alphabetical part:

1. Section space,
2. Full Stop,
3. Comma,
4. Numeral in their natural sequence,
5. Bracket,
6. Roman letters,
7. Underlined words,
8. 'and' or its substitute, semicolon,
9. etc.

For example:

CAMBRIDGE

Three hundred year 'Progress.

CAMBRIDGE

See also

CAMBRIDGE, INCOME TAX (Department of-)

CAMBRIDGE, BIBLIOGRAPHY.

CAMBRIDGE 1.

CAMBRIDGE 2.

CAMBRIDGE (City)

CAMBRIDGE ARCHAEOLOGICAL SOCIETY.

CAMBRIDGE ARCHAEOLOGICAL SOCIETY.
EDITORIAL (Department).

CAMBRIDGE ARCHAEOLOGICAL SOCIETY.
Ed.

CAMBRIDGE ARCHAEOLOGICAL SOCIETY.
and GLASGOW ARCHAEOLOGICAL SOCIETY.

ALA Filing Rules

ALA rules for filing Catalog Cards published by American Library Association, Chicago, is one of the codes for filing cards in an alphabetical sequence. This code is in two parts, Part one, alphabetical arrangement and Part two, order of entries. Its Part one contains four basic rules for alphabetization and special rules for the alphabetization of abbreviated forms, variant forms, and names. Part two deals with the problems relating to particular sequences (authors, subjects, titles, etc.). The number of rules provided in the above code is quite large; therefore, only selected rules are given here.

1. Basic Rule

A Alphabet "Arrange all entries, both English and foreign, alphabetically according to the order of the English alphabet'

B Word by Word" Arrange word by word, alphabeting letter by letter within the word. Begin with the first word on the first line, then go to the next word, etc. Apply the principle of 'nothing before something'. Considering the space between words as 'nothing'.

4. Articles

A. Initial articles "Disregard an initial article in all languages and file by the word following it…An exception to this rule is certain foreign proper names beginning with an article…"

B. Articles within the entry "Every word in the entry, including articles and prepositions, is generally regarded".

5. Initials

A "Arrange initials, single or in combination, as one-letter words"

B "Arrange initials standing for names of organizations as initials, not as abbreviations, i.e. not as if spelled in full".

E ''Arrange acronyms as words, unless written all in capitals with a space or period between the letters."

Examples:

W.M.O.

Wanderer Speaks

Where Eagles Dare

WHO

World in Crisis

6. Abbreviations

A "Arrange abbreviations as if spelled in full in the language of the entry except 'Mrs.', which is filed as written."

B "Arrange initials and other abbreviations for geographical names... as if written in full".

C "If subject subdivisions are abbreviated in subject headings as they commonly are in the tracing, arrange them as if written in full".

7. Signs and symbols

A "Disregard signs such as ... or ..., at the beginning of or within titles."

B "Arrange the ampersand (&) as 'and', 'et', ' 'and', according to the language in which it is used".

C "Arrange signs and symbols that are ordinarily spoken as words as if they were written out".

Examples:

Art and animation

Art & artists

Art and culture

Rs. 500 per month (Five hundred rupees per month)

Rs. And Ps. (Rupees and Paise)

8. Numerals

A "Arrange numerals ... as if spelled out in the language of the entry. Spell numerals and dates as they are spoken...".

9. Order of Entries under Same Word

A "When the same word, or combination of words is used as the heading of different kinds of entry, arrange the entries in two main groups as follows:

1. Single surname entries, arranged alphabetically by forenames.
2. All other entries, arranged alphabetically word by word, disregarding kind of entry, form of heading, and punctuation".

B "Arrange subject entries under a person or corporate name immediately after the author entries for the same name".

C "Interfile title added entries and subject entries that are identical and sub-arrange alphabetically by their main entries"

26. Author Arrangement

A "Under an author heading arrange different kinds of entries in groups in the following order".

1. Works by the author, sub-arranged alphabetically by their titles.
2. Works about the author:
   - (a) Without sub-division, sub-arranged alphabetically by their main entries.
   - (b) With sub-divisions, sub-arranged alphabetically by the subdivisions.

32. Subject Arrangement

A "Subject entries follow the same word used as a single surname".

B "Arrange entries with the same subject heading alphabetically by their main entries' then by title".

Similarly, rules are provided for filing title entries and references. Rule 33 of 1968 edition provides for problems like identical title added entries, arrangement of different editions of the same title etc., Details of sub arrangement under title main entries are also given in this rule.

For cross references Rule 35 is as follows:

35. Cross References

A "A reference or explanatory note precedes all other entries under the same word or words".

B "File *see* references in their alphabetical places.

C "File a *see also* reference before a first entry under the same word or words. If *see also* references are made for headings under which there are no entries in the catalogue, file there reference where the heading itself would be filed".

Concluding, it can be said that the classified arrangement does not present much of a problem. The arrangement is merely based on the ordinal values allotted to the digits by the scheme of classification concerned. Alphabetization can be done in a number of ways depending upon the set of rules followed. CCC follows the midway position between Gestalt alphabetization and all through alphabetization. *ALA rules* follow word by word arrangement and are more detailed. It needs to be investigated to find out, which can give better results. However, it may be said that alphabetization is not as easy as it might appear to be.

10
Recent Developments in Cataloguing

Q. : State the new trends in cataloguing.

or

Write an essay on the recent developments in cataloguing with emphasis on International Standard Bibliographic Description.

or

Write short note on I.S.B.D.

Ans. There has been a very fast growth in the area of cataloguing in the field of library science in modern times. This development has been so fast that the cataloguers are themselves finding it difficult to keep up with the latest trends. After 1950, efforts are being made to bring about an international consensus in the rules of cataloguing. International Federation of Library Association (IFLA) has made important contribution towards this end. The efforts of this federation were directed towards establishing uniformity in the techniques of cataloguing at an international level.

In 1967, the 'Anglo American Cataloguing Rules' was published by the joint efforts of American Library Association, Library of Congress, Library Association (Great Britain) and Canadian Library Association. All the large libraries around the world adopted this catalogue code. In addition to this, A.A.C.R.-2 is another great achievement. This catalogue code can be used for cataloguing of printed material as well as non-printed material.

The work of cataloguing was made computerised under the MARC project. Use of computer brought about uniformity in the equipment related with the books and has made the work short and more logical. It is for this reason that effort has been made for establishing book-related standards at an international level.

The efforts of International Standard Bibliographic Description (I.S.B.D.) have made the maximum contribution in establishing uniformity in the field of cataloguing. Besides, 'POPSI' and 'PRECIS' techniques have been propounded for fulfilling the subject-related needs of the readers.

International Standard Bibliographic Description

Efforts were made in the decade of 1950 for bringing about an international consensus on the rules of cataloguing. Many organizations and institutions worked to achieve this and are still making efforts towards this end. An international conference was organised by IFLA in Paris in 1961 for the principles of cataloguing. Ground was prepared for the International Standard Bibliographic Description in this conference and some principles were also propounded. The rules of the 'Anglo American Cataloguing Rules' were also envisaged on the basis of these principles. High level of uniformity in the main entry and the structure of name headings resulted from this.

An international meet of cataloguing specialists was held in Copenhagen in the year 1969. The proposals of Michael Goreman were discussed in this meet and an executive body was formed for detailed study of this proposal.

This executive body presented its final suggestions in 1971 and published the International Standard Bibliographic Description. The I.S.B.D. was published without keeping in view the future needs related to the specific subject, hence a need was soon felt for another specific I.S.B.D. In 1973, a meet was organized in Gajanabel in which thought was given to I.S.B.D. (Monograph). In 1974, the International Standard Bibliographic Description (Monograph) was published.

Aims of ISBD

1. **International Exchange :** Its aim is to prepare the record of the various eligible sources of exchange, so that the documents published in one country can be accepted in the libraries, catalogues or bibliographical lists of other countries. In other words, it facilitates international exchange of written or machine readable bibliographic information.
2. **Language Barriers :** Its second aim is to remove the language barrier in use of the documents so that the documents presented for use by the readers or users of one language can be used by

the readers of other languages.

3. **Conversion in Machine Readable Form :** Its third aim is to facilitate the conversion of bibliographic documents in machine readable form.

Scope of ISBD

ISBD determines the types, sequence and arrangement of all types of reading material. Accession point, used classification and some methods of control determined on the catalogue cards of national and local cataloguing institutions are beyond its scope. In addition to this, the number of type, formation of subject headings, single card entry and additional entries are also not controlled by this. Some of the features of the bibliographic description, that were earlier related with the form and nature of single card entry, has now been separated by it. The choice of classification system and the provisions of cataloguing are also left with the cataloguing institutions. The acquisition of the subject headings is also kept beyond its scope. Hence, ISBD is completely free from those features of bibliographic techniques in which there is a lack of ideological unity. The structure of entry, description of pages etc., notes and the issue of international bibliographies etc., are only covered in this.

Structure of ISBD

The ISBD (G) lists within its frame all bibliographic elements, which are required to describe and identify all types of materials, which are likely to appear in library collections. It assigns an order to these elements and prescribes a distinct punctuation system to differentiate them form each other. The eight areas of data elements provided in the ISBD (G) is shown below:

Area	*Prescribed Punctuation Proceeding (or enclosing) For Elements*	*Element*
1. Title and statement of responsibility area		1.1 Title proper
	[ ]	1.2 General material designation
	=	1.3 Parallel Title
	:	1.4 Other title information
	/	1.5 Statement of responsibility First statement; Subsequent

Area	Punctuation	Element
		statement
	=	2.1 Edition statement
2. Edition area		2.2 Parallel edition statement
		2.3 Statement of responsibility relating to the edition
	/	First statement
	:	Subsequent statement
	,	2.4 Additional edition statement
		2.5 Statement of responsibility following an additional edition statement
	/	First statement
	;	Subsequent statement
3. Material (or type of publication) Specific Area		
4. Publication, Distribution, etc. Area		4.1 Place of publication, distribution, etc.
		First place
	;	Subsequent place
	:	4.2 Name of publisher, distributor, etc.
	[ ]	4.3 Statement of function of publisher, distributor etc.
	,	4.4 Date of publication, distribution, etc.
	(	4.5 Place of manufacture
	:	4.6 Name of manufacturer
	)	4.7 Date of manufacture
5. Physical Description Area		5.1 Specific material designation and extent of item
	:	5.2 Other physical details
	;	5.3 Dimensions of item
	+	5.4 Accompanying material statement
6. Series Area	(	6.1 Title proper of Series
Note: A series statement is	=	6.2 Parallel title of series
enclosed by parentheses.	:	6.3 Other title information of series
When there are two or more series statements,		6.4 Statement of responsibility

	each is enclosed by parentheses.		relating to the series
		/	First statement
		;	Subsequent statement
			6.5 International standard series number of series
		;	6.6 Numbering within the series
		.	6.7 Enumeration and/or title of sub-series
		=	6.8 Parallel title of sub-series
		,	6.9 Other title information of sub-series
			6.10 Statement of responsibility relating to the sub-series
		/	First statement
		;	Subsequent statement
			6.11 International standard serial number of sub-series
		:	6.12 Numbering within sub-series
7.	**Note Area**		
8.	**Standard Number (or alternative) and terms of Availability Area**		8.1 Standard number (or alternative)
		=	8.2 Key title
		:	8.3 Terms of availability and/or price
		( )	8.4 Qualifications (in varying position)

General notes on the ISBD (G) framework

(i) In the above framework, the terms "first statement", subsequent statement" and the like, denote the order in which these statements are given in the description and have no other connotation.

(ii) In the above framework no indication is given of which area or elements may be repeated or may be considered optional. The specialized ISBDs give detailed guidance on these matters.

(iii) Wherever information ordinarily associated with one area or element is presented in the item as a grammatically integral part of another element, it is transcribed as such.

ISBD (G) provides a standard format within which all materials can be described and is of prime importance to cataloguers of non-print material. The rules in AACR 2R follows the ISBD (G) in two important aspects: the order of elements and the prescribed punctuation.

Following table shows the changes made in ISBD (G) structure as per the AACR II (revised rules).

Area	*Prescribed Punctuation Proceeding (or enclosing) For Elements*		Element
Note: Each area, other than the first area in a paragraph, is preceded by a period, space, dash, space (.–.)			
1. Title and Statement of Responsibility Area		.IB	Title proper
	[ ]	.1G	General material designation
	=	.ID	Parallel Title :
	:	.IE	Other title information
		.IF	Statement of responsibility
	/		[First statement]
	;		[Each Subsequent statement]
2. Edition Area		.2B	Edition statement
	=	.2B5	[Parallel edition statement]
		.2C	Statement of responsibility relating to the edition
	/		[First statement]
	;		[Each Subsequent statement]
	.	.2D	Subsequent edition statement .
		2E	Statements of responsibility related to each subsequent edition statement.
	/		[First statement]
	;		[Each Subsequent statement]
3. Material (or Type of Publication) Specific Details Area			
4. Publication, Distribution, etc.		4C	Place of publication.

Area	Punctuation	Rule	Element
Area			distribution, etc.
			[First place]
	;		[Each Subsequent place]
	:	.4D	Name of publisher, distributor, etc.
	[ ]	.4E	Statement of function of publisher, distributor, etc.
	,	4F	Date of publication, distribution, etc.
		.4G	Place of manufacture, name of manufacturer, date of manufacture
	(		Place of manufacture
	:		Name of manufacturer
	,)		Date of manufacture
5. **Physical Description Area**		,5B	Extent of item (including specific material designation)
	:	5C	Other physical details ;
	;	5D	Dimensions
	+	5E	[Each] Accompanying material
6. **Series Area**	(	6B	Title proper of series
Note: A series statement is enclosed by parentheses. When there are two or more series statements, each is enclosed by Parentheses.	=	.6C	Parallel title of series
	;	6D	Other title information of series
		6E	Statement of responsibility relating to the series
	/		[First statement]
	;		[Each Subsequent statement]
		6F	ISSN of series .
	;	6G	Numbering within the series
	.	6H	Subseries
	=		(Parallel title of subseries]
	,		(Other title information of subseries] [Statement of responsibility relating to the sub-series]
			[First statement]

[Each Subsequent statement]

[ISSN os subseries]

[Numbering within subseries]

7. **Note area**

Note : The punctuation used for date in the note area follows the ISBD style for the reporting of those data in the other areas of description except that a period ends each area rather than a period, space, dash, space (Rule 1.77A3).

8. **Standard Number and Terms of Availability Area**

	.8B	Standard number
=	.8C	Key title
:	.8D	Terms of availability
( )	.8E	Qualifications

Q. : What do you understand by a bibliographic record and bibliographic record format? Stating the types of format, briefly discuss some of the formats.

or

Write short notes on

— MARC format

— CCF

Ans. A bibliographic record is defined as-a collection of information which pertains to a single document and which is stored in machine readable form as a self contained and unique logical structure.

A machine-readable bibliographic record is arranged according to a particular format. Format conveys the notion of a formalized framework or structure, which will hold records of varying content according to certain set of rules or conventions controlling the representation of the data. These rules may be unique to a system, or shared with other systems.

Bibliographic record formats are used to describe the arrangement or structure of computer readable record of bibliographic items.

Types of Format

Formats can be of two types :

- Internal/Local format
- Exchange/Communication/Interchange format

Internal Local Format : Internal formats are so called because they are internal/local to a software system. They can be changed specifically as per the needs of the local system and do not have to conform to any external standards. For the internal format (the identifiers used and their records structure), system designers can adopt any conventions that they wish. Rules for input are more restricted, being constrained by existing cataloguing codes and practices and need to be compatible with other systems or with a standard exchange format. Their main aim is economy and efficiency in processing, while the ability to convert, if necessary, from the local format to an exchange format is an extra advantage. This conversion can be done by computer programme. An agency may, therefore, adopt its own internal processing format, but at the same time retain system compatibility with a national or international exchange format. Internal formats can be structured in infinite varieties or ways which depend on the software used.

Exchange/Interchange /Communication Format : Exchange formats are also known as interchange/communication formats. Exchange formats are used for exchange of records between systems. The systems should be sufficiently flexible to cope with the needs of many different software system. Ideally, they should facilitate the exchange of data which are to be used in wide range of different bibliographic application, from the production of traditional catalogue cards to records in databases which are used for On-line access/Internet access.

A major problem for designers of exchange format is the lack of international agreement on standards for constructing bibliographic: records. Although ISBD is available, but it is not accepted by many organizations.

Exchange Formats: Structure and Content

Bibliographic data formats adopted for exchange of data consist of three basic components :

1. **A defined physical structure :** Rules for the arrangement (on a computer storage medium) of data to be exchanged. This may

be linked to a container or carrier into which data may be placed. The carrier remains constant although the data change from record to record.

2. **Content designators :** Codes to identify the different data elements in the record (e.g., author, title, scale of map, starting date of journal, etc.).

3. **Rules :** Content of the record governed by rules for the formulation of the different data elements, very closely tied up with 2 above. The data elements separately identified by the codes in the exchange format have to be defined, not only in terms of content but also in form, if the records are to be suitable for use by another agency.

Structure : Records in automated systems may be of fixed length or variable length. Fixed length records in a file must each contain the same fields and any given field must always be of the same length from one record to another. If a field is repeatable, it must be repeated the same number of times in each record. Variable-length records may be variable because they do not contain the same number of fields (a given field may not occur in every record) or because a given field is not always of the same length. Bibliographic records do not fit naturally into the fixed-length pattern.

An example of a database whose records can be treated as fixed length is a mailing list for officials within organizations. In each record there can be fields for each of name, job title, province, state, postal code. Few of any of these data elements will always be of the same length, but most of them will have a similar length. Each data element is allocated a number of characters and any space not used will be filled with blank spaces. The system designer has to, allocate to each data element a suitable number of characters which will not be too small to accommodate the majority of records, but not too large also, to waste space by having records full of spaces. Most records in a mailing list will include all the fields mentioned above and there will not be too many fields in a mailing list database which are completely filled with spaces. In bibliographic records, the situation is different.

— Many fields occur only from time to time, for example cover title, ISSN, edition. The edition, appears in bibliographic records only when the document contain specific edition statement or when it is known to be other than a first edition.

— Many fields occur for a variable number of time in each record. For example: A document may have one author or it may have any number of joint authors. The same document may be a member of more than one series. A record may be assigned more than one subject descriptor.

— A data element may vary in length between records. This is true in most systems which do not code their data but record them in ordinary language.

Content Designator : Content designators are used to denote the identity of each data field (instead of identifying data fields by position) within a record. It may be grouped together at the beginning of the record with 'pointers' to the data they identify. The storage of the computer file invariably uses the method of indexing the location of the files at the beginning of the file. The computer calculates from the given starting character position of each file the likely position of that file on the tape/disk, moves the same very quickly to a position just before the start of that file at which point the tape / disk moves more slowly in order to locate the data. This index is known as a 'Directory'.

Standards For Record Format

Standardization of the records format in manually prepared bibliographic lists started to be a matter of international concern from the 1960s. The International Conference on Cataloguing Principles (ICCP) held in Paris 1961 set up the standard for the headings of author and title records in catalogues and bibliographies. The conference was sponsored by IFLA with the intention of evolving a set of basic principles to serve as guidelines in the design of catalogue codes all over the world. However, differences in headings continue to exist in various catalogues and bibliographies and they stood in the way of interchange of information.

The International Meeting of Cataloguing Experts (IMCE) convened by IFLA in Copenhagen in 1969 was another event of significance in the direction of bibliographic standards. The first standard developed in 1974 was meant for the description of monographs. It was followed by a series of specialised ISBDs for various forms of documents and the final integrated general format for all sorts of documents, called General International Standard Bibliographic Description, ISBD(G) was developed. ISBD (G) lists within its frame all bibliographic elements, which are required to describe and identify all types of materials, which are likely to appear in library collection. It assigns an order to these elements and prescribes a distinct punctuation system to differentiate them from each other. It also serves as the basis for specialised ISBDs.

Development of ISBD may be termed as the greatest achievement contributing to the standardization of bibliographic records for the following reasons :

1. It facilitates records from various sources to be interchangeable.
2. It assists in the interpretation of records across language barriers.
3. It assists in the conversion of bibliographic records to machine-readable form.

The maximum amount of description held within the ISBD frame will be adequate to meet the requirements of a wide range of bibliographic activities. All the elements are not meant for a single agency but all of them are useful to one or other agency. ISBD helps standardization of .cataloguing rules as well as the format of manual and machine readable bibliographic records.

I. MACHINE-READABLE RECORD FORMAT or MARC

A central organisation catalogues the documents under the MARC service and records bibliographical information of these documents on magnetic tapes and sends the copies of these tapes to other libraries. The libraries can use these tapes on computer for preparing printed catalogue cards or book form from their collection or entries. Use of MARC service is growing by the day in the world. Many libraries are now preparing their catalogues on magnetic tapes, such as the National Aeronautics and Space Administration.

Historical Background : Efforts were made to automate the services and internal procedures by Library of Congress in the year 1958. A committee was formed under the presidency of Gilvant W. King for this purpose. The aim of this committee was to explore the possibilities of automation of the services of Library of Congress.

This committee recommended automation of activities related to-cataloguing, process of searching-indexing and reacquisition of documents etc. in its report in 1963. As a result, MARC project was started in 1964 for automation of cataloguing procedures. Financial support was given to this project by the Council of Library Sources.

MARC Experimental Project (1966-68) : Library of Congress invited the libraries of its country to participate in this experimental project in 1966 and 16 of these libraries were selected in it. Different kinds of libraries were included in it, such as the Government, Public, University, Specialised and School libraries etc.

A conference of these libraries was called in February 1966 to discuss and understand following points:

- Trend, objective, lists, work and expectations from this programme.
- MARC Format.
- Material that would be sent every week to the participating libraries.
- Content of the proposals made by the participating libraries.
- This function will be performed by the Library of Congress.

Description on magnetic tapes was started by the Library of Congress in September, 1964. However, bibliographic information of books in English language were only included in this.

Initially the decision was made to end the experimental project in September 1966, however it was later extended to June 1968. This included and four new libraries were also included in this.

50,000 MARC documents were distributed during this project. The final report of this project was distributed in 1968, which contained the description of the experiences of Library of Congress and the participating libraries.

MARC-II project was started four months before the MARC-I project was over, after evaluation of its achievements.

MARC-II : The format MARC-II was a considerably improved one in the light of experiences and opinions of important libraries and a specific survey was carried out for studying the requirements of the users. MARC II format developed in 1968 was the result of Anglo-American cooperation. The new format was intended to be hospitable to all kinds of library materials; sufficiently flexible for a variety of applications in addition to catalogue production; and usable in a range of different computer systems. Despite Anglo-American cooperation there were two versions of MARC, i.e., LC MARC II and BNB MARC II.

(1) USMARC Format : There are three USMARC communication formats :

US MARC format for bibliographic data (UFBD)

US MARC format for authority data (UFAD)

US MARC format for holdings and locations (UFHL)

All the three US MARC formats are implementations of ANSI Z39.2, American National Standard for Bibliographic Information Interchange on magnetic tape which conforms with the ISO 2709.

Structure of US MARC : The physical structure of all US MARC formats (Fig. 1) are similar to the structure of the UK MARC record, although there are some differences in terminology and in the definition of fields:

Leader	Directory	Variable Control fields	Variable Data fields

Fig. 1. US MARC Structure

The Leader provides general information about the record. The Directory is the guide to the contents of the record and the other two contain data itself.

(i) Leader : This part of the record consists of data elements to process the record. It is a fixed field consisting of a total of 24 characters with positions counted from 0-23.

Character position

0-4	Logical record length
5	Record status
6	Type of record
7	bibliographic level 8-9 Blank
10-11	Indicator count & subfield code count
12-17	Base address
17-19	Implementation defined positions
20-22	Entry map
23	Undefined & set to '0'

They are used to indicate nine types of data such as length, status, type and bibliographical level of the record and blank characters, subfield code, base address, etc. Length indicates the total number of characters used in the record, status tells whether it is new, changed or deleted record, type tells whether it is printed or not, and bibliographical level states whether it is an analytic, monograph, serial or a collection and so on.

Leader—a sample

000439	n	a	m	bb	2	2	00133	bbbbbbb

(ii) Record Directory : The directory begins in character position 24. It is an index to the location of various fields, both control and variable length, within the record. The number of fields in the directory will be equal to the number of fields in the record. As the number of variable length fields can vary, the length of records directory can also vary. It is at the same time, a series of fixed fields which contain the field lag, length of the field and starting character position of each of the major types of data in the variable fields. A field terminator is used to mark the end. Directory enables the location of those parts of the record which are required in the processing of information. It is automatically generated by the computer programme.

The nature and function of Directory are identical to UK MARC with the following exceptions:

(i) US MARC records have less restriction on length of fields, with maximum 9999 characters;

(ii) US MARC contains no subrecord directory entries as analytical records are not handled *via* the directory;

(iii) Character positions are counted from zero.

Directory — sample

0001001300000	0084100013	0050001600054

082001300070100003500083245000890018260004800207300001900285

650003200274

(iii) Variable Fields : Following the directory are the variable fields, comprising of control field and data field. The control field precede data fields as in UK MARC and have neither indicators nor subfield codes. Control fields defined or reserved in US MARC are:

001 Control number

002 Subrecord map of directory

003 Subrecord relationship

004 Related record directory

005 Date and time of latest transaction

006 Fixed length data elements

007 Physical description fixed field

008 Fixed length data elements: Coded information useful for retrieval and manipulation of data.

009 For Local use

Data fields in US MARC follow the variable control field. Their definition depends on the format: bibliographic, authority or holdings/ locations.

Indicators (Two digits)	First subfield code	Subfield data	Second and subsequent subfield code	Subfield data	Field terminator

Fig 2. Structure of data field in US MARC

(iv) Variable Data Fields : Variable data fields are made up of single as well as groups of data elements. Each variable data field consists of indicators, subfield codes, and data elements and field terminator. Also a tag is assigned to each variable data field and that tag is stored in the directory. For example, 100 is the tag for main entry-personal name, 110 for main entry -corporate name, and 130 for uniform title heading, etc. Indicator is a code supplying additional information about the field and it is located at the beginning of the field.

Variable data fields—sample

1() $alowenfels, b alter $b 1897 -$eed. F Ib $a PetsbO

(2) UK MARC Format

British National Bibliography had shown active interest in the possibilities of MARC form 1966. Cooperative efforts with ASLIB and OSTI within the country and with LC abroad enabled it to develop a MARC format in 1968. This format had been further improved upon in the light of the objectives and needs of British libraries. It had given special emphasis to the need a distributed bibliographic record. There were no considerable changes in the format untill first edition of UK MARC Manual appeared in 1975. But later, the advent of BLAISE and the increased use of non-book materials in the educational field and publication of AACR-2 made it necessary to incorporate many corresponding changes in the format.

UK MARC is a single, unitary format designed to accommodate all types of material with some material specific fields. UK MARC format specifications are set out in UK MARC manual, second edition, 1980-87.

Structure of UK MARC : The physical structure of UK MARC is based on ISO 2709 and BS 4748 (Fig 3).

Record label	Directory	Control fields	Variable data fields

Fig. 3. UKMARC record structure

(a) Record Label : Record label is fixed field of 24 characters containing coded information about the record.

Character Position	*Information given*
0-4	Record length i.e. total number of characters including all data and content designation.
5	Record status i.e. new, changed, deleted, confirmed CIP, revised CIP.
6-9	Implementation codes used to indicate type of material and class of record.
10	Indicator count, always '2' as two indicators are used for each data field.
11	Subfield mark count, showing the number of symbols used to identify subfields, always '2'.
12-16	Base address of data, giving the total number of characters of the record label and the directory, including the end-of-directory field terminator.
17-19	Encoding level indicates the degree of completeness of the record i.e. Code Full level Blank.
20	Length of 'Length of Data Field' in each entry.
21	Length of 'Starting character position' in each entry.

22	Length of 'implementation' defined part in each entry.
23	For future use.

The other format is UNI-MARC.

(3) UNI MARC : An executive group for developing the Universal Machine Readable Catalogue was formed by IPLA. Its objective was to facilitate international exchange of the bibliographic information produced in machine readable form by the international bibliographic institutions, so that the Universal Bibliographical Central Programme of RPLA could be developed. The first edition of UNI MARC Manual was published in 1977 and its second edition was published in 1980, by cataloguing and information technology committee of the RPLA.

Content designators for a variety of materials got standardised in this Books, Periodicals, maps, globes, music, scores, sound recordings, motion pictures, video- recordings, pictures, drawings, sculptures, artifacts, computer files and other related forms of materials have been covered by this standard. Non-roman script is also accommodated.

UNI MARC uses a special block structure in the place of areas. Data in national formats may be carried in different position but UNI MARC can identify these data functionally and establish clearly designated areas for them as the blocks.

UNI MARC Structure

0 — INTRODUCTION BLOCK

001 Record identifier field

010 International Standard Book Number (ISBN)

011 International Standard Serial Number (ISSN)

020 National Bibliography Number

021 Legal Default Number

022 Government Publication Number

040 Block

1 — INFORMATION BLOCK

100 General Proceeding Dates

101 Language of the work

Detailed Record Structure of UKMARC

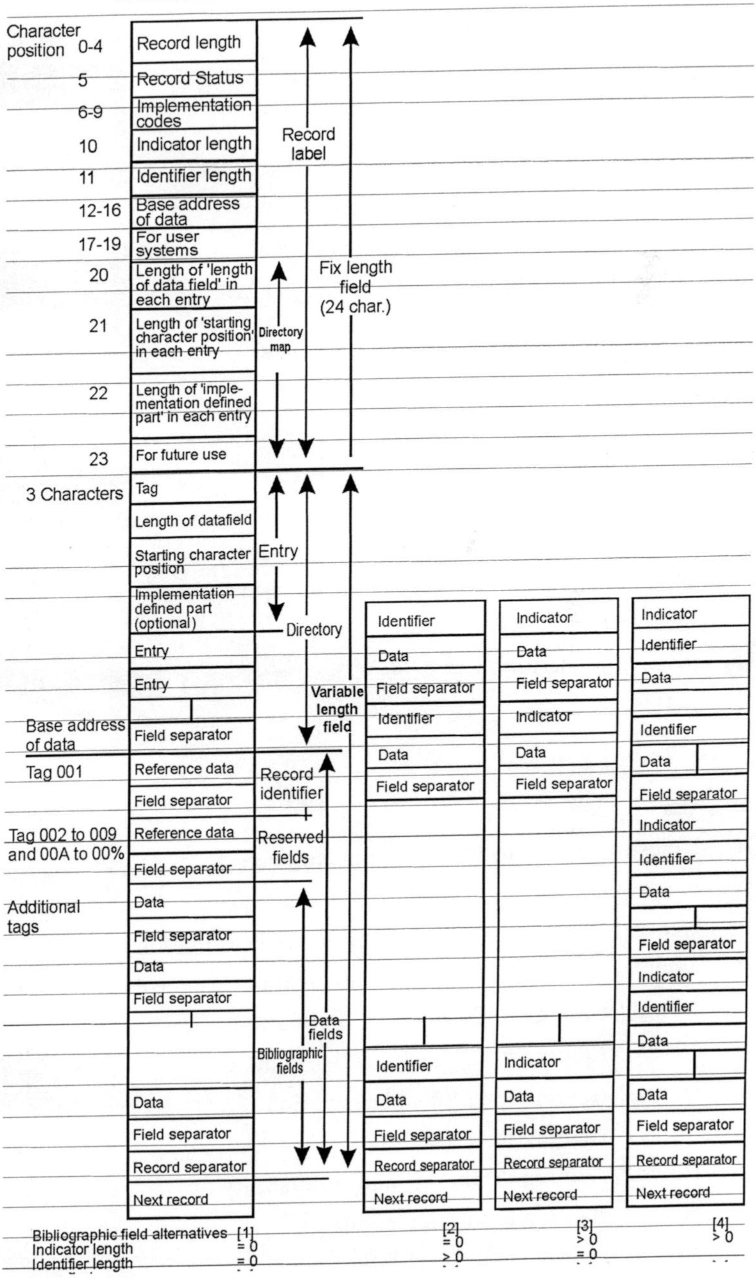

102 Country of production or publication
105 Coded Data Field : Books
106 Coded Data Field : Books-Physical Attributes
110 Coded Data Field : Serials
111 Coded Data Field : Serial-Physical Attributes
120 Coded Data Field : Cartography materials
122 Coded Data Field : Cartographic materials situation Data (s)
123 Coded Data Field :

2 — DESCRIPTIVE INFORMATION BLOCK

200 Title and Statement of Responsibility
204 General Material Designation
205 Edition Statement
206 Material Specific Area : Cartographic Materials Mathematical Data
207 Material Specific Area : Serials-Numbering
210 Publication, Distribution Etc.
215 Physical Description
225 Series.

3 — NOTES BLOCK

300 General Note
301 Notes Pertaining to Identification Numbers
302 Notes Pertaining to Coded Information
303 General Notes Pertaining to Descriptive Information
304 Notes Pertaining to Title and Statement of Responsibility
305 Notes Pertaining to Edition and Bibliographic History
306 Notes Pertaining to Publication Distributor etc.
307 Notes Pertaining to Physical Description
308 Notes Pertaining to Series
310 Notes Pertaining to Binding and Availability
311 Notes Pertaining to Linking Fields
312 Notes Pertaining to Related Titles

313 Notes Pertaining to Subject Access

314 Notes Pertaining to Intellectual Responsibility

315 Notes Pertaining to Material or types of Publication Specific Information

320 Bibliography Note

321 Availability of Indexes and Abstracts Note

324 Facsimile Note

326 Frequency Statement Note (Serials)

327 Contents Note

328 Dissertation (Thesis) Note

330 Summary or Abstract

4 — LINKING ENTRY BLOCK

410 Series

411 Subseries

421 Supplement

422 Parent of Supplement

423 Issued with

430 Continuous

431 Continues in Part

434 Absorbed

435 Absorbed in Part

436 Formed by Merger of

440 Continued by

441 Continued in Part by

442 Superceded by

443 Superceded in Part by

444 Absorbed by

445 Absorbed in Part by

446 Split

447 Merged with XXX to form

448 Changed back to

451 Other Edition in Same Medium

452 Edition in a Different Medium
453 Translated as
454 Translation of
461 Set Level
462 Subset Level
463 Piece Level
464 Piece — Analytic Level
468 Other Related Works

5 — RELATED TITLE BLOCK

500 Uniform Title
501 Collective Uniform Title
503 Uniform Conventional Heading
510 Parallel Title Proper
512 Cover Title
513 Added Title n Page Title
514 Caption Title
514 Running Title
516 Spine Title
517 Other Variant Title
520 Format Title (Serials)
530 Key-Title (Serials)
531 Abbreviated Title (Serials)
532 Expanded title (Serials)
540 Additional Title Supplied by Catalogue
541 Translated Title Supplied by Cataloguer

6 — SUBJECT ANALYSIS BLOCK

600 Personal Name Used as Subject
601 Corporate Name Used as Subject
602 Family Name Used as Subject
603 Title Used as Subject
606 Topical Name Used as Subject

607 Geographical Name Used as Subject

660 Geographic Area Code (GAC)

661 Chronological Coverage Code (CCC)

670 PRECIS

675 Universal Decimal Classification (UDC)

676 Dewey Decimal Classification (DDC)

680 Library of Congress Classification

7 — INTELLECTUAL RESPONSIBILITY BLOCK

700 Personal Name — Primary Intellectual Responsibility

701 Personal Name — Alternative Intellectual Responsibility

702 Personal Name — Secondary Intellectual Responsibility

710 Corporate Body Name — Primary Intellectual Responsibility

711 Corporate Body Name — Alternative Intellectual Responsibility

712 Corporate Body Name — Secondary Intellectual Responsibility

720 Family Name — Primary Intellectual Responsibility

721 Family Name — Alternative Intellectual Responsibility

722 Family Name — Secondary Intellectual Responsibility

8 — INTERNATIONAL USE BLOCK

II. COMMON COMMUNICATION FORMAT (CCF)

The first edition of CCF — the Common Communication Format was published in 1984 and the second edition in 1988. Bibliographic agencies around the world developed national and local formats based on the CCF. The first CCF user's group meeting was held at Geneva in 1989 and users recommended some minor changes or incorporation in the later editions.

UNESCO has brought out 'Implementation Notes' for users of the CCF, which explains how various features of the CCF may be implemented within the constraints of local computer software and provides further information on the use of the bibliographic data elements.

Scope and Use of CCF : Following are the scope and use of CCF:

— To permit the exchange of records between groups of information agencies, including libraries, abstracting and indexing services, referral systems and other kinds of information agencies.

— To permit the use of a single set of computer programs to manipulate records received from various informations agencies regardless of their internal record-creation practices.

— To serve as the basis of format for an agency's own bibliographic or factual database, by providing a list of useful data elements.

To assist the development of individual systems, UNESCO has published 'Implementation Notes' for users of the Common Communication\Formats (CCF).

Structure of CCF : The record structure of the CCF constitutes a specific implementation of the international standard ISO 2709. Each CCF record consists of four major parts:

— Record label

— Directory

— Datafields

— Record separator

Record Label : Each CCF record begins with a fixed-length label of 24 characters, the contents are as given below :

Character Position	*Content*
0-4	Record length. The length of the record includes the label, directory, data fields and record separator.
5	Record status, using the following code: a = New Record b = Replace record c = Deleting Record
6	Blank, this character position is not used.
7	Bibliographical level of the target item i.e. s = Serial a = Component part e = Made-up collection

8	Blank, this character position is not used.
9	Blank this character position is not used
10	'2' The subfield identifier length. This shows the number of indicator characters in each subfield identifier.
11	'2' The subfield identifier length. This shows the number of indicator characters in each subfield identifier.
12-16	Base address of data. The location within the record at which the first data field begins, relative to the first characters used as the subfield identifier.
17-19	Blank, these character positions are not used.
20	'4' The 'length of datafield' in the directory.
21	'5' The 'length of starting Character Content
22	'2' The length of implementation defined section of each entry in the directory. One is used for Segment identifier & other is used for Occurrence identifier.
23	Blank. This character position is not used.

Directory : The directory is a table containing a variable number of fourteen character entries; a field separator character terminates the table. Each directory entry corresponds to an occurrence of a data field in the record and is divided in five parts:

TAG 3 character	LENGTH OF DATA FIELD 4 character	STARTING CHARACTER POSITION 5 character	SEGMENT IDENTIFIER 1 character	OCCURRENCE IDENTIFIER 1 character

As an example of a directory entry in given here:

300003300028910

In this example, the tag encoded in the first three digits is '300', signifying that the datafield identified here is a Name of Person. The next four digits are '0033' showing that the datafield is of 33 characters in length. '000289' shows that the datafield begins two-hundred eighty-nine characters after the base address of the data. The digit ' 1' shows that this datafield belongs to the second segment of the record; datafield belonging to the primary segment will carry the format of Catalogue Entries segment identifier '0'. The final digit. '0', indicates that this is first occurrence of a datafield tagged 300 in segment 1.

Datafields : A datafield consists of:

— Indicator

— One or more subfields each of which is preceded by a subfield identifier.

— A datafield separator

A datafield, which has a single subfield will be organized as follows:

INDICATORS 2 characters	SUBFIELD IDENTIFIER 2 characters	SUBFIELD Variable	FIELD SEPARATOR 1 character

A datafield, which has a single subfield will be organised as follows:

INDICATOR 2 characters	FIRST SUBFIELD IDENTIFIER 2 character	FIRST SUBFIELD variable	SECOND SUBFIELD IDENTIFIER 2 characters	SECOND SUBFIELD variable	FIELD SEPARATOR 1 character

Here is an example of a single datafield

11@A Stephenson@BM.S@ D1953-@E673■

The tag for this datafield, which is '300', appears in the entry which represents this filed in the directory, not in the datafield itself. The first character appearing in the datafield, '1', is the first indicator which means that this person has primary responsibility for the contents of the item described in this segment of the record. The second digit, '1', indicates that the form of the name which appears here comes from the authority file of the agency creating the record. The form of the name on the item may be different from the form given here. Subfield A preceded by its subfield identifier '@ A', provides a significant element of the name of the person, in this case the family name. This is the data element by which the contents of this datafield will be ordered in a sequential index. Subfield B gives the remainder of the personal name. Subfield D gives a birth date, apparently taken from the authority file of the creating agency. Subfield E gives a three-digit code, '673' taken from a list of codes of the CCF. This code indicates that the person identified in this datafield is the person who directed the research reported in the work. The datafield is terminated by a unique character, the field separator, which for convenience is shown here as '■'. The actual character, which has no printed representation assigned to it, is character 1/14 of ISO 646.

The diagrammatic representation of the CCF record structure is shown on next page.

The first edition of CCF was published in 1984 and the second edition in 1988. The revision work has been based on the experiences of bibliographic agencies of several countries, which were interested in the implementation of CCF. In 1990 another publication, Implementation Notes for Users of Common Communication Format (CCF), was issued as a guide. This is to be used with the source document, i.e. CCF, ed 2. One more guide is also under preparation to help the AACR-2 users who are interested in CCF implementation.

The objective of CCF was staled as to provide a detailed and structured method for recording a number of mandatory and optional data elements in a computer readable bibliographic record for exchange purpose between two and more computerised systems. It is also useful to a single bibliographic agency engaged in structuring its own format simultaneously to keeping compatibility with the CCF. Non-computerized systems also can use CCF data elements because, it simplifies computerization at a later stage.

CCF is not meant for record of an institution for internal storage and processing purposes. Processing formats vary from institution to institution and also within the same institution. It is specially designed for retrieval and output within an institution.

By using an exchange formal like CCF an information system converts the data in its processing format into the common format for export and each system is designed to enable the conversion of data from the common format for import into its processing format. Thus, each system has to design only one conversion between its format and the common exchange format and back again. The economy lies in the elimination of the designing of computer programs for conversions between each and every pair of systems.

Diagramatic Representation of the CCF record structure

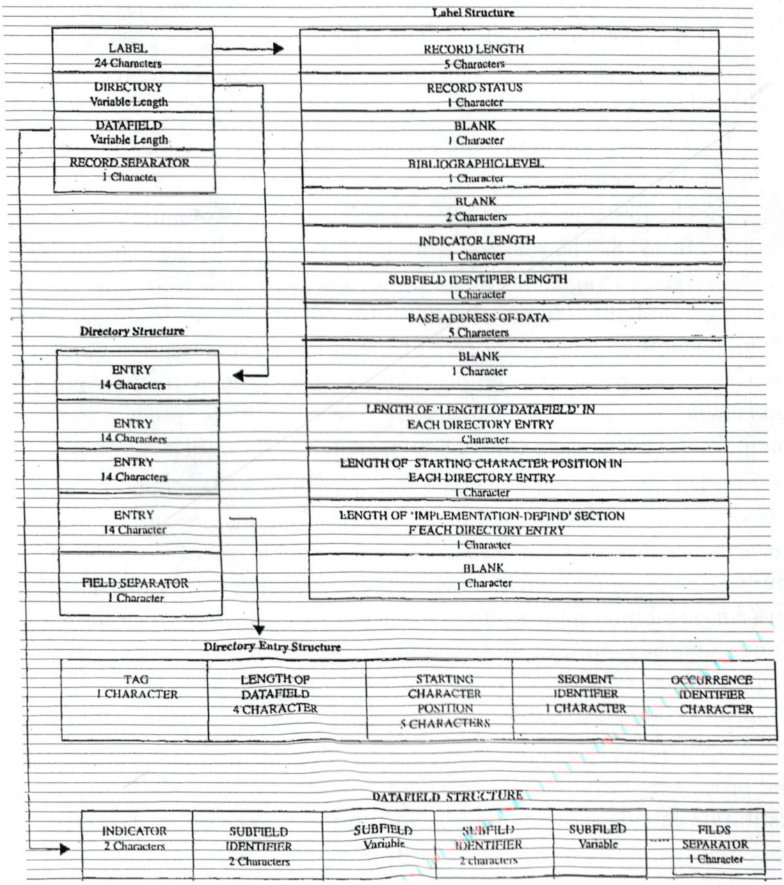

Q. : Write briefly about the followings:

– AACR–2, Recent developments

– Cataloguing Networks

– Cataloguing in Internet and Digital Environment

– OPAC

Ans. 1. AACR-2 – Recent Developments

Attempts to devise a common cataloguing code for the UK and US began early in 20th century, and resulted in the Anglo-American Cataloguing rules of 1908. Work on the revision of this code began in the 1930s but the UK members of the Committee had to withdraw on the outbreak of the World War II in 1949. The American Library Association (ALA) continued the work and produced a new code ALA rules, in 1949. Problems inherent to this code led to an International Conference, the International Conference on Cataloguing Principles (ICCP) held in Paris in 1961, which asserted the importance of drawing up a code of rules based on sound theoretical principles rather than on adhoc solutions to article problems. This led to the production of the Anglo-American Cataloguing Rules in 1967 in two different versions: the British text and the American text.

Despite these tremendous developments one major problem still remained. If one wants to have the international exchange of bibliographic information, then it is necessary for international standards to exist that world ensure that the bibliographic records produced by different agencies in different paces are compatible. One of the areas that needed urgent attention for standardization was the area of description of items. In 1969, IFLA sponsored an international meting of cataloguing experts at Copenhagen which led, in 1971, to the publication of the International Standard Bibliographic Description (ISBD). This was further developed for various non-book materials, leading to the publication in 1977 of a generalized version of ISBD, called ISBD (G). ISBD sat down rules on a number of matters including the specific parts of an entry, the various data elements to form an entry, preferred sources of information, and so on. Much of this was incorporated in the unified edition (the British and the American texts no longer existed) of AACR, called AACR-2 published in 1978. Major revisions of AACR took place over the years and a new edition, called AACR2R, appeared in 1988, and further minor amendments were made in 1993.

From the above discussion, it is clear there is now a very large measure of international agreement on the content of catalogue entries, and AACR-2 (with all the revisions) has become the de facto international code for cataloguing. In recent times technological innovations and advances in IT have called for major revolutions in cataloguing. With technological developments, newer media for storage and publication of information appeared ranging from microforms (microfilms, microfiche. etc.) to magnetic (floppy discs, tapes, etc.) and optical media (CD-ROM families). Consquently, the catalogue code had to incorporate new rules to handle these new media.

One of the most significant developments has been emergence of the Online Public Access Catalogue (OPAC) which is basically the gateway to a library's collection. This is an interlace through which users can search a library's catalogue, and can also perform a number of other operations, such as borrower record checking, reservation of items, online renewal, and so on. Although OPACs made their first appearance in the mid- 1970s, it was only at the beginning of the next decade that libraries in significant numbers began to switch from card to automated catalogues. Library Management Software Packages usually come with an OPAC module which can be used as it is. Though libraries prefer to tailor the standard OPAC module to suit their specific needs. The library can identify and design specific menus for staff and users, dialogues on specific fields, such, as author, title, subject, ISBN, etc., with right truncation facilities, and keyword searching with Boolean search facilities. With the recent advent of graphical user interfaces, it has become possible to include a range of information retrieval facilities menus or as options on bottoms, or check boxes.

The other developments include various online cataloguing networks and services, sometimes called, *Bibliographic Utilities*. These networks, or bibliographic utilities, such as OCLC (Online Computer Library Center), RLIN (Research Library Information Network), etc., provide cataloguing facilities to their member libraries. These are basically central cataloguing facilities where by member libraries can download the catalogue entries of specific materials. The largest of these is the OCLC. OCLC's *World Cat* (the OCLC Online Union Catalog) offer access to catalogue resources that no other single institutions possesses.

The most recent, and probably the most prominent, development of the era has been the Internet which has drastically changed the various aspects of our lives. Internet, and one of its most prominent services, the World Wide Web (WWW), has become the most widely used source of information for all concerned, and due to its exponential growth it has been extremely important to catalogue and there by exert some kind of bibliographic control on the information available on the Internet.

2. Cataloguing Networks

One of the major objectives of forming cataloguing networks is to perform the cataloguing operations centrally by one library/

organization while other participating members can use the catalogue. They are also called bibliographic utilities as they provide bibliographic utility services such as catalogues of materials to the members. Library of Congress, in Washington, D.C. (USA), since 1901, has made printed cards available containing cataloguing data, classification numbers (Library of Congress as well as Dewey Decimal Classification number) and subject headings. Mechanization was introduced as early as in 1970s to meet the growing demands for this service among libraries. Currently cards are printed from MARC records on demand and the Library of Congress (LC) also operates an 'alert service'. A participating library establishes a profile consisting of the subject areas that are of interest. Then, when LC enters a bibliographic record that matches this profile into its MARC database, a catalogue card is automatically produced and is sent to the library.

The United Kingdom was half a century behind the United States in providing a centralized service similar to that of LC. Though the British National Bibliography (BNB) started in 1950, a printed card service, called BNB cards, began in 1956. These BNB cards could be obtained by libraries for producing their own catalogue records. A MARC distribution service began in UK in 1969 and a large number of U K libraries and other institutions use BLMARC records for local cataloguing and housekeeping operations.

The United States led the world in setting up cataloguing networks and bibliographic utilities such as OCLC (Online Computer Library Center) RLIN (Research Libraries Information Network) and WLN (Western Library Network). Among these OCLC is the pioneer and is the most highly used bibliographic utility service.

OCLC is a nonprofit computer service and research organization whose network and services link more than 27,000 libraries in 64 countries and territories. OCLC services help the libraries to locate, acquire, catalogue, access, and lend library materials. OCLC, the world's largest library information network, offers the following services that help libraries further access to information and reduce information costs:

— WorldCat (the OCLC Online Union Catalog): The world's largest and most comprehensive bibliographic database. Libraries use the WorldCat"' database and OCLC's computerized telecommunications network to process materials and share information. WorldCat offers libraries and then users resources that no single library could provide:

- 38 million records in eight bibliographic formats representing 400 languages with holdings information,
- Growth by approximately 2 million bibliographic records each year; and
- Easy searching from First Search, FPIC, and other services.

— The OCLC system: Extensive online cataloging, interlibrary loan, union list, and selection services.

— OCLC First Search ® service: Online reference service that provides flexible searching and subject access to over 70 databases for end users.

— OCLC First Search Electronic Collections Online service: Provides remote access to large collections of journals through the Web. Now also available through the First Search Web interface.

— OCLC Access Services: Telecommunications and stand alone systems that facilitate on-line and off-line cataloging, resource sharing, reference, and selection services.

Now a question comes how can a library benefit from a networked facility. This can be better understood by taking the example of the services offered by the largest cataloguing network or bibliographic quality service in the world, viz., the OCLC. OCLC offers a range of cataloging services that help in increase productivity and reduce cost from batch services to CD-ROM, and one can transfer records quickly, efficiently, and cost-effectively to card catalog or local system. The OCLC Cataloging service is the largest and busiest online cataloging system in the world. It handles over one billion transactions a year and supports a range of services that help libraries in increase productivity and reduce costs. And with OCLC cataloguing, only one library needs to originally catalogue an item. OCLC offers a range of cataloguing options to meet your library's needs. One can:

— have bibliographic records automatically delivered at the time the vendors ship books using the OCLC PromptCat service,

— catalog online, where the hit rate is more than 95 percent for English materials,

— input your own original records.

— export records from OCLC and edit them on local system;
— tapeload cataloguing that is done outside OCLC's cataloguing systems;
— have OCLC convert older cataloguing to machine-readable form;
— move records to an off-line environment to edit and export and then batch edits and holdings back with OCLC;
— cataloguing Micro Enhancer software;
— have OCLC staff catalogue current materials, foreign language materials, or backlogs;
— seamlessly link selectors, acquisitions department, book vendors, and your local system to an online, ready for filing; and
— order custom-printed cataloguing cards according to specifications Cards arrive at node library — ready for filing.

Cataloguing with WorldCat gives an incomparable knowledge resource. One can:

— use high-quality records to improve search results; catalogue all materials;
— reduce staff time for copy cataloguing with OCLC *PromptCat* service; and
— custom order machine-readable tapes or catalogue cards.

The OCLC Catalogue service is an interactive online system that provides access to WorldCat (the OCLC Online Union Catalogue) and facilitates shared cataloguing. OCLC Cataloguing increases productivity and reduce cataloguing costs. Participating libraries retrieve and use bibliographic records contributed by other libraries and enter records for items not already cataloged. OCLC Cataloguing provides:

— global record sharing through *WorldCat;*
— keyword and browsable searching;
— full-screen record editing and cut, copy, and paste capabilities;
— a high hit rate—find over 95 percent of the English records you need; and
— access to name and subject authority records.

Electronic export capabilities to local systems in North America join OCLC through then OCLC- affiliated Regional Networks. Libraries outside North America receive OCLC services through OCLC Asia

Pacific Services, OCLC Europe, OCLC Latin America and the Caribbean, or via international. One of the major problem facing libraries in many countries, including those in India, relates to what is known as retrospective conversion or *Retrocon* in short. This relates to a basic question as to how libraries can convert their existing manual catalogues (card) to machine-readable catalogues. Thus, simply speaking, retrocon is a process that is used in libraries to convert existing manual catalogues to machine-readable catalogues. There are several options available and each one has its own merits and demerits. The simplest way is to manually convert (i.e., keying-in), each and every catalogue record which is impossible for a large library collection where several hundred thousand catalogue entries are available in card forms, because this will be very time-consuming and expensive process. One alternative way could be to decide a cut-off year for the retrocon process. Indeed, whichever method is used, each library has a cut-off date, beyond which catalogue records are not available in machine-readable forms; users looking for materials beyond certain date have to consult card catalogues. The cut-off year is decided by the library concerned on the basis of a study that determines beyond which year library materials are scarcely used.

Another option to *Retrocon* is to scan the card catalogues, provided they are available in printed/ neatly typed form and then to use a custom-built program to convert the scanned files to machine-readable catalogues. This method has new found useful in certain situations, and several companies nave taken this approach to do retroconversion job for libraries on a contract basis. The major difficulty of this process is that the success rate depends on the nature and quality of the scanning process. If the cards are not neatly printed or typed, then the quality of the scanned image and the corresponding ASCII file will be poor, resulting in number of errors in the catalogue entries. Hence, a significant amount of editorial time will be needed to ensure the quality of the machine- readable catalogue.

Yet another, and the most commonly followed method, is to use the services of bibliographic utilities like OCLC. As already mentioned earlier, one can avail the WorldCat service form OCLC for downloading catalogue data of all the materials held in a library. This process is much easy and does not need any local expertise. However, there are two major problems. First, this may prove to be expensive, particularly for libraries in India, because the price to be paid for such service is calculated in the US dollar and thus may be quite a big amount in local currency. The second problem may be that local materials and non-English language materials may not be available in OCLC's databases.

Each of the above options has its own merits and demerits. One option, that has been chosen by many, is to set up a centralized cataloguing agency, mostly at the national library level, that produces catalogue entries for all types of materials and makes available to other libraries in the country in machine-readable form. This approach helps off-set-the huge cost and other resource requirements of retroconversion.

3. Cataloguing in Internet and Digital Environment

Internet can simply be defined as a network of networks. It is an amalgamation of interrelated computer networks permitting electronic communication on a global scale. Internet has now changed the way we generate and use information. World Wide Web (WWW) is one of the most recent, and most widely used, service of the Internet that mimics a spider web of information, spread all over the world. The volume and variety of information available on the Internet and WWW is increasing at a very rapid rate. While on the one hand the Internet has made it easy for us to have access to information available anywhere in the world from our own computer, it has made our life difficult too. Due to the rapid growth and lack of appropriate mechanism for organization and control of information, the Internet has become, what some people call, an anarchy. It is difficult to know what is available on the Internet at a given instance.

Libraries have exercised control over their collection, however huge it may be, through appropriate cataloguing of their resources. Now the question is, can similar measures be taken for Internet resources? In other words, how can the information resources available on the Internet be catalogued? This has become a new challenge for librarians. It can be conceived of an information retrieval tool that is characterized by its use of hypertext links to information sitting on various servers all over the world. Several attempts, have begun and a number of research projects are underway to resolve various issues of cataloguing materials available on the Internet and the World Wide Web.

Cataloguing of Internet resources can be done by using a set of tools called ROADS. The ROADS stands for Resource Organization and Discovery in Subject-Based Services. It is a set of software tools designed to help create information gateways on the Internet. At its simplest, an information gateway, can be just a simple list of links maintained by hand. The information gateway approach allows a subject based list of links to be created and maintained. ROADS allows Internet resources to be fully described, allowing the end user to judge their relevancy before trying to access them and it is properly organized. The organization and description of resources adds value to an information gateway. ROADS allows to create a database of resource descriptions or templates. This is done via World Wide Web forms that you have to fill-in. This form is a data entry form containing a number of fields, such as title field, keyword field, etc. ROADS contains tools which will automatically create classified listing of the resources and a search mechanism.

Digital library is another new concept that can be defined as a library having all the information available in digital form. The digital library system, unlike traditional library systems, reside in a building or at any particular location. It is distributed virtually all over the world, and user would - get information, as needed, on the screen of his computer. In addition to traditional text-based information, data accessible through the digital library system will include:

— non-text information, (such as photographs, drawings, illustrations, art, etc.);
— streams of numeric data (such as satellite information, chronological data, meteorological data, etc.);
— digitized sound and moving visual images;
— multidimensional representation of forms (e.g., holograms); and
— the capacity to integrate these data into new representations drawn from many different sources.

Given this wide variety of information sources and their rapidly growing volume, it is not unlikely that a user will easily get drowned in the ocean of digital information unless the information is properly organized. One way to organize the information in the digital library environment is to properly catalogue all the materials, and to provide easy and multiple access points to the user so that he can easily retrieve the required, and only the required information. Several large-scale digital library research projects have been undertaken all over the world to bring out appropriate solutions to cataloguing and other problems.

OCLC, the Library of Congress, the British Library, etc., are again taking a leading role in these research activities.

4. Online Public Access Catalogue (OPAC)

An online public access catalogue is a library catalogue accessed via a computer terminal for the benefit of library users. OPACs were introduced in the US in the late seventies and in the UK in early eighties. These have also been introduced in some of Indian Libraries. An OPAC provides the users online access to the library's catalogue allowing them to search and retrieve records from the online catalogue, and depending on the underlying library management software it also offers other facilities such as online reservation, borrower status checking, and so on. With the advent of the Internet, and more recently with the World Wide Web (WWW), most library OPACs can now be searched by remote users, anywhere in the world, who have an access to the Internet. In an OPAC what the users see is an interface containing a menu, say, that works on several databases, the primary one being the library catalogue database. A catalogue database can simply be perceived as the machine-readable version of the card catalogue in a library. An online library catalogue is composed of a number of bibliographic records. A bibliographic record can be defined as a collection of data elements (author, title, publisher, ISBN, etc.) organized in a logical way which represents a bibliographic item. Thus, for any OPAC, there is a catalogue database working behind the scene that contains a number of bibliographic records. Each bibliographic record represents a catalogue entry containing all the bibliographic elements such as author, title, publisher, place of publication, year of publication, ISBN, and so on.

Now the question is, how does the system tell the user whether the library has a book written by a given author, say by A.K. Dhiman, and then if it is available, how does the user get the details, i.e., how does the system retrieve it, and moreover, here does the cataloguing part come in this picture? In order to have an idea about the processes, involved, we can simply divide an OPAC into four major components: the user interface, the main master file of bibliographic records, the index, and the display/print format.

— *The user interface* allows a user to interact with the system. Typically it offers various search options, such as author search, title search, keyword search, subject search, and so on. Although this is controlled by the underlying library management software, some cataloguing knowledge has gone into its design. The various search keys, author, title, keyword, subject heading, etc., are the parameters used by the users for searching a library catalogue and these have also been included as search keys in the online catalogue.

— *The main catalogue database* file is something like the card catalogues, each card being converted into a bibliographic record. However, in order for the computer (actually the software) to understand and manipulate the various data elements that form a bibliographic record, some measures are taken at the design stage of the catalogue database. Like in any database structure, a catalogue record is composed of a number of fields, and subfields, each field (or subfield) representing a data element (name of an author, title of a book, and so on).

It is important to note, how many fields (and subfields) should we create for a bibliographic database and how can it be standardized so that any two databases in a country, or anywhere in the world, will have the same structure. Here, the skills of a cataloguer, the standards and AACR-2 play an important role. While designing the database, an important step is concerned with assigning the appropriate tags and attributes to each field and subfield. This is extremely important and needs high level of standardization because this does not only ensure standardization but this also helps computer (the library management software) to handle and manipulate the data appropriately. Here, comes the standards such as MARC and its various versions.

— *The index file,* called the inverted file, which may be conceived as a back-of-the-book index file containing all the index terms (here, authors name, title words or full titles, keywords, subject headings, and so on) and appropriate pointers pointing to appropriate record(s) in the catalogue database. Here again some cataloguing knowledge is required, such as which fields are to be indexed, how subject headings are to be assigned and indexed, whether any vocabulary control tool will be used at the indexing stage or not, and so on.

— *The display/print format* directly relates to cataloguing and to AACR-2. Catalogue records, in a catalogue database file, are not arranged in the same way as we see on the catalogue card cabinets. In fact, each bibliographic record contains raw data associated with various attributes, and when we want to view it on the screen, or want to print it. The underlying software picks up the data and presents it according to an AACR-2 entry. This job is performed by the display format which is designed in accordance with the rules for generating entries according to AACR-2.

Thus, the OPACs are searched and queries are satisfied.